505

Making the most of Beef & Veal

ROBERT CARRIER'S KITCHEN

Making the most of Beef & Veal

Marshall Cavendish   London Sydney & New York

Editor	Grizelda Wiles
Editorial Staff	Carey Denton
	Roz Fishel
	Carol Steiger
Designer	Ross George
Series Editor	Pepita Aris
Production Executive	Robert Paulley
Production Controller	Steve Roberts

Photography
Bryce Attwell: 10, 36
Paul Bussell: 22, 76, 117, 87, 90
Laurie Evans: 11, 44, 82, 85, 107
Robert Goulden: 68
Jon Hall: 9, 12, 22
James Jackson: 33, 38, 70, 88
Chris Knaggs: 47, 73, 78, 83
David Levin: 14, 67
Peter Myers: 26, 28, 29, 34, 37, 42, 45, 49, 75
Roger Phillips: 86
Paul Webster: 40, 89
Paul Williams: 16, 32, 41, 80
Graham Young: 72
Cover picture: **Jon Hall**

Weights and measures
Both metric and imperial measurements are given. As these are not exact equivalents, please work from one set of figures or the other. Use graded measuring spoons levelled across.

Time symbols
The time needed to prepare the dish is given on each recipe. The symbols are as follows:

 simple to prepare and cook

 straightforward but requires more skill or attention

 time-consuming to prepare or requires extra skill

 must be started 1 day or more ahead

On the cover: Old English roast beef with Yorkshire pudding, page 13

This edition published 1986
© Marshall Cavendish Limited 1985

Printed in Italy by
L.E.G.O. S.p.a. Vicenza

Typeset by Performance Typesetting, Milton Keynes

Published by Marshall Cavendish House
58 Old Compton Street
London W1V 5PA
ISBN 0 86307 264 X (series)
ISBN 0 86307 331 X (this volume)

Contents

For me, cooking is a way of life. I like to bring out the best in food, and am always developing new recipe ideas. In *Making the most of Beef & Veal* I should like to share some of these ideas with you. Beef can be prepared in so many delicious ways, ranging from the traditional Old English roast beef with Yorkshire pudding to an exotic stir-fry recipe from the Orient, in which the beef is marinated in oyster and soy sauce. Cooking methods include roasting, grilling, pan frying, casseroling and pot-roasting, and I show you how to use these methods confidently and successfully.

Once you discover how many ways there are of cooking beef, you'll never again feel the need to 'play safe' with plain grilled steak. Instead, serve your guests Lattice steak with anchovy sauce – it looks a picture, tastes wonderful, and isn't much more complicated than a simple grill. When you're feeling ambitious, try my recipe for *Boeuf en croûte* – you cook your roast encased in a parcel of pastry which keeps the meat moist and succulent. Nowadays, we all have to be budget conscious, so I've thought up lots of economy recipes. What about trying my Moussaka with yoghurt topping, my New England red flannel hash for the family, oxtail braised in ale or a warming steak and kidney pudding? If you're planning a dinner party based on a main course of beef, check my star menus first – they feature complete meals from starter to dessert.

Veal used to be thought of as a luxury, reserved only for very special occasions, but the growing popularity of French and Italian food has led to more and more people wanting to try this much-prized, delicately flavoured meat and I'll show you how to roast it to perfection with fresh herbs or with my special spicy spinach stuffing, as well as all the other methods of cooking. If you have never thought of grilling or pan-frying veal for a dinner party, try your hand at a spectacular Twin grill of veal and beef, layered with two different sauces – and see for yourself that it is every bit as delicious as a roasted joint. Classic dishes need not be complicated; follow my instructions and see how simple it is to prepare pan-fried Weiner schnitzel or my *nouvelle cuisine* dish, Watercress veal, in which escalopes are served with a delicious watercress and walnut sauce.

There are money-saving recipes as well – cheaper cuts can be used for a wonderful selection of dishes from Sweetbreads anisette to Veal, ham and egg pie or Farmer's hock. Also in this volume, you'll find the information you need about buying and storing beef and veal to get the very best from them.

Happy cooking and bon appétit!

Robert Carrier

Beef

ROASTING BEEF

Roasting is the simplest of cooking methods, but you do need expensive cuts of beef, so it is important to roast to perfection, with the meat brown and appetizing outside, succulent and juicy within.

The inescapable truth is that only prime cuts of beef will give you a top-quality roast. Indeed, I would go so far as to say that what you cannot grill, you cannot roast. There is one exception to this, topside, which will roast tolerably well, especially if you keep it rare. But if you are in any doubt about the suitability of a cut for open-roasting, pot-roast it instead. This long, slow method of cooking, which involves simmering the meat in liquid for a long time, will do wonders for a tougher cut of beef.

Choosing beef for roasting
Beware of beef that is either pale or unnaturally red, beef that looks too lean and too compact in texture, and so-called 'tenderized' beef. Look instead for a joint which the butcher has tenderized by hanging: the meat will be a rich, succulent dark red, firm and moist to the touch and flecked with fat. If it comes from a young animal there will be only a hint of gristle, if any, between the meat and the layer of fat. The fat should always be a pleasant creamy white, not yellow.

Small chunks of beef do not make good roasts: they shrink away to almost nothing during cooking, and it is very difficult to control the degree of rareness. At least two ribs, or 1 kg /$2\frac{1}{4}$ lb boned meat, is the minimum you should go for. Otherwise, pot-roasting is, again, the answer.

Cuts of beef for roasting
Fillet, rib roast, sirloin and topside, taken from a good-quality, well-hung carcass, will all provide reliable roasts. Fillet is the most expensive of these cuts of beef; rib roast slightly less expensive, followed by sirloin. Topside is the cheapest, though many people prefer it to the more expensive fillet.
Fillet makes an elegant dish for a dinner party, either roasted plainly, or first spread with a delectable mixture of chopped mushrooms and herbs, then carefully wrapped up in a sheet of buttery puff pastry before going in the oven. And really, if you consider that 100–150 g /4–5 oz (uncooked weight) beef fillet makes an ample portion for one, compared with 175–225 g /6–8 oz rolled sirloin or topside, it is not prohibitively expensive for the extra-special occasion, even at today's prices.
Rib roast or fore rib is a fine cut, ideal for roasting. Allow at least 375 g /12 oz (uncooked weight) meat and bone per person, plus an extra 225 g /8oz.
Sirloin is a majestic joint. It is taken from the ribs, and includes a section of the fillet. It is cooked in the same way as rib roast and is very tender, with an excellent flavour. Allow 225–375 g /8–12 oz (uncooked weight) meat and bone per person.
Rolled sirloin: sometimes the fillet and bones are removed from the sirloin and the meat is rolled. Allow 175–225 g /6–8 oz (uncooked weight) per person.
Topside is a lean joint, usually sold boned and rolled. It makes a satisfactory roast if it is kept rare, but is generally lacking in flavour and not as tender as sirloin. Allow 175–225 g /6–8 oz (uncooked weight) boned rolled topside per person.

Storing beef for roasting
Remove any wrappings from the joint, lay it on a plate and cover it loosely with greaseproof paper or aluminium foil. It can then be stored on a low shelf of the refrigerator for a maximum of four days.

Do not forget to allow the meat to return to room temperature before roasting it. (If it has come straight out of the butcher's cold room and you intend to cook it the same day, you would be wise not to put it in the refrigerator at all.) Wipe the joint with a clean, damp cloth. It is a good idea to rub coarsely ground black pepper, and perhaps a mixture of lightly browned flour, dry mustard and sometimes herbs, into the meat as soon as it is taken out of the refrigerator, then leave it at room temperature for 2–3 hours so that it can lose its chill and absorb flavours at the same time. The meat should not be sprinkled with salt at this stage, as the salt will draw the juices out of the meat.

Moisturizing the meat
Joints which do not come naturally equipped with an outer coating of fat to keep them moist as they roast must have fat added to them before roasting.
Barding: before roasting, a thick strip of suet or fat salt pork is rolled around the entire length of the joint and tied on firmly in several places with string. Thin slices of fatty bacon can also be used.
Larding: before roasting, long, thin strips of fat salt pork are pulled through the meat with a special larding needle. These melt during roasting, basting the meat.
Rubbing with fat: butter, oil or dripping is rubbed over the meat before roasting. Avoid basting the meat too frequently. Lean meat will need to be basted about every 20 minutes. Fillet is especially lean and will need basting once or more during cooking. If the joint has a layer of fat on top, you should not have to baste at all: the fat will do it for you as it melts.

Roasting beef
If possible, you should roast a fillet or rolled joint by standing it on a rack in the roasting tin so that it cooks over dry heat instead of being allowed to swim in its own fat and juices. If the joint has bones, it is not necessary to stand it on a rack – the bones will support the joint and keep it upright in the roasting tin, well clear of the fat and juices in the bottom of the tin.

Using a meat thermometer: insert a the mometer into the centre of the meat befo cooking, taking care not to touch the bon Centre temperatures of the meat should rea 60C /140F for rare, 70C /160F for mediu and 80C /180F for well done.
Fillet is the only cut of beef for which recommend a high oven temperatu throughout the cooking time. This is ensure that the whole cooking process carried out as quickly as possible, for th longer this tender joint remains in the ove the greater is the danger of its drying out.

Fillet has very little fat of its own. It mu be larded, barded, or given a quick turn in pan of hot dripping or butter. This gives it light coating of fat and seals in the me juices.

The natural shape of a whole fillet nicely rounded at one end, tapering away the other – presents a slight problem in tha unless certain precautions are taken, by th time the thick end is ready, the thinner en will have cooked to an inedible frazzle. Th answer is to fold about 15 cm /6in (for

whole fillet) of thin end back on itself and to tie the two layers together tightly with string in several places, so that the meat is the same diameter throughout its length.

Weigh the fillet and calculate the cooking time (see chart on page 108). Sear it well, then transfer the fillet on a rack over a roasting tin, add 45–60 ml /3–4 tbls warm water or red wine to the tin and roast in an oven preheated to 220C /425F /gas 7.

Rib roast and sirloin: weigh the meat and calculate the cooking time (see chart on page 108) according to how you like your meat. Spread the joint all over with 50 g /2 oz dripping or butter, then lay it, flat side up, in a roasting tin. Sear the meat in an oven preheated to 220C /425F /gas 7 for 15–20 minutes, until its surface is richly browned and sealed with a crust. Then reduce the oven temperature to 170C /325F /gas 3, add 60 ml /4 tbls warm water or red wine to the roasting tin and roast for the calculated cooking time. Note that the cooking time per kg /lb for a larger joint is slightly less than a smaller one.

Rolled sirloin: weigh the boned joint and calculate the cooking time (see chart on page 108). Melt 50 g /2 oz dripping or butter in a frying-pan and sear the joint on all sides. Place the seared sirloin, fat side up, on a rack over a roasting tin, and roast for 15–20 minutes in an oven preheated to 220C /425F /gas 7. Then lower the oven temperature to 170C /325F /gas 3, add 60 ml /4 tbls warm water or red wine to the roasting tin and roast for the calculated cooking time.

Topside has no natural layer of fat to protect it, so you must bard it before roasting if the butcher has not already done so. Weigh the meat and calculate the cooking time (see chart on page 108), remembering that the topside should only be roasted to rare. Melt 50 g /2 oz dripping or butter in a frying-pan and sear the barded joint on all sides. Proceed as for rolled sirloin.

Roast beef to eat cold should be cooked until rare. Do not carve off any slices or pierce the joint with a fork, but allow it to become cold before cutting. This way it retains all the juices. Carve very thinly.

Serving roast beef

When the joint is cooked to your liking, season it to taste with salt and additional freshly ground black pepper. Transfer the joint to a very hot platter, large enough to allow the carver to operate properly. Unless it is fillet (which should be served immediately), leave it to stand in a warm place for 15–20 minutes. Keep it at the front of the turned-off oven with the door open, in the warming compartment of your oven or on top of the stove. This allows the meat juices to 'settle' (to coagulate slightly), making it easier to carve the beef neatly and thinly. Meanwhile, pour most of the fat from the roasting tin into a heatproof cup or jug. (This dripping can be used in another recipe.) Use the juices and sediment that remain in the tin, with some red wine, stock or water, and any juices that seep from the meat as it settles, to make your gravy. Don't forget to make sure your sauce-boat and plates are very hot, too.

A succulent joint of roast beef

Barding and larding beef

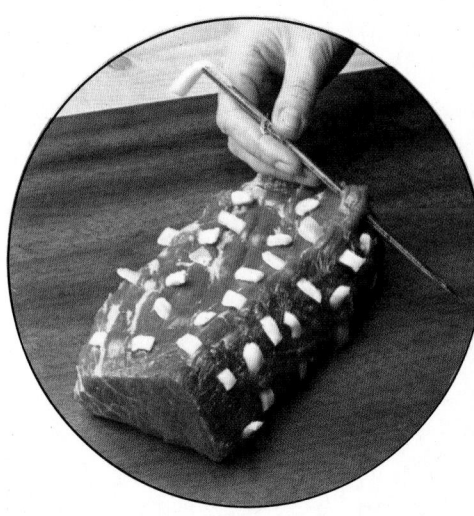

To bard, beat out a thick strip of suet or fat salt pork to the required size. Wrap it around the meat and tie it in several places with string. Bacon slices can also be used.

To lard, cut fat salt pork into lardons – thin strips 5 cm /2 in long. Clamp a strip into a larding needle. Thread the lardon through 15 mm /½ in of the meat, across the grain.

Thread several lardons across the meat to make a row, then make a new row behind the first but not level with it. Cover the fillet to achieve a chequer-board effect.

Roast fillet of beef

Cook roast fillet of beef as a special occasion dinner party dish.

bringing to room temperature, then ½–1 hour plus settling

Serves 6–8
1.1–1.4 kg /2½–3 lb fillet of beef, trimmed
salt and freshly ground black pepper
40 g /1½ oz melted butter or dripping
30 ml /2 tbls freshly chopped rosemary
1 bay leaf, crumbled
For the garnish
25 g /1 oz butter
450 g /1 lb mushrooms, thinly sliced
10 ml /2 tsp lemon juice
sprigs of watercress

1 About 2 hours before you intend to roast the beef, remove it from the refrigerator. Season it generously with pepper, tuck the narrow end under to make the fillet an even thickness and tie neatly with string.
2 Heat the oven to 220C /425F /gas 7. Brush the fillet with melted butter or dripping and season again with freshly ground black pepper.
3 Sear the meat on all sides in a shallow roasting tin, then place it on a rack in the tin and sprinkle with the rosemary and bay leaf. Add 60 ml /4 tbls warm water and roast for 18–22 minutes per kg /8–10 minutes per lb for very rare to rare; 30–36 minutes per kg / 14–16 minutes per lb for medium rare to medium.
4 Meanwhile, make the garnish: melt the butter in a frying-pan. Sauté the sliced mushrooms briefly, then stir in the lemon juice and keep warm.
5 Season the fillet with salt and serve, garnished with the sautéed mushrooms and sprigs of watercress.

Roast fillet of beef

Roast fore rib of beef

🕐 bringing to room temperature, then 1½–2¾ hours plus settling

Serves 6–8

2.3 kg /5lb fore rib of beef, on the bone
freshly ground black pepper
45 ml /3 tbls Dijon mustard
15 ml /1 tbls dried oregano
30 ml /2 tbls flour
300 ml /10 fl oz beef stock, home-made or
*   from a cube*
salt

To serve

roast potatoes
individual Yorkshire puddings (page 13)

1   Remove the fore rib of beef from the refrigerator at least 2 hours before you plan to roast it. Weigh the meat and calculate the cooking time, allowing 35 minutes per kg / 16 minutes per lb for rare, 45 minutes per kg /20 minutes per lb for medium, and 65 minutes per kg /30 minutes per lb for well done, plus 15 minutes. Season it generously with freshly ground black pepper and leave it to come to room temperature.

2   Heat the oven to 220C /425F /gas 7. In a small bowl, mix together the Dijon mustard and dried oregano.

3   Place the joint in a roasting tin and roast for 15–20 minutes, then reduce the oven temperature to 170C /325F /gas 3 and continue to roast for the calculated cooking time, basting and turning as necessary.

About 30 minutes before the meat is done, spread the mustard mixture over the fat.

4   Remove the beef from the oven, transfer to a heated platter and leave to settle for 15–20 minutes.

5   Meanwhile, remove excess fat from the roasting tin, leaving about 30 ml / 2 tbls. Add the flour and stir well over a low heat for 3–4 minutes. Gradually add the stock, stirring, and bring to the boil. Season with salt and freshly ground black pepper and simmer for 3 minutes.

6   Pour the gravy into a heated sauce-boat. Serve the beef with roast potatoes and individual Yorkshire puddings, with the gravy handed round separately.

Roast fore rib of beef

Old English roast beef with Yorkshire pudding

Roast sirloin, accompanied by Yorkshire pudding, makes a splendid dinner party dish.

bringing to room temperature,
then 2–2½ hours

Serves 5–6
2.3 kg /5 lb sirloin on the bone
30 ml /2 tbls flour
15 ml /1 tbls dry mustard
salt and coarsely ground black pepper
50 g /2 oz dripping or butter
Yorkshire pudding batter (see recipe right)
60 ml /4 tbls warm red wine or water

Remove the meat from the refrigerator at least 2 hours before you intend to roast it. Weigh the meat and calculate the cooking time, allowing 35 minutes per kg /16 minutes per lb for rare, 45 minutes per kg / 20 minutes per lb for medium, plus 15 minutes.
2 Heat the grill to low. Place the flour in a cake tin and grill until the flour is lightly browned stirring often. Mix the browned flour with the mustard and plenty of coarsely ground black pepper. Wipe the beef clean, spread it with the dripping or butter and sprinkle with the flour mixture. Leave to stand at room temperature until it has lost its chill.
3 Prepare the Yorkshire pudding batter following the recipe right, then put it aside to rest. Plan to put it in the oven 30 minutes before the end of the calculated cooking time for the beef. Heat the oven to 220C /425F /gas 7.
4 Place the beef on a rack over a roasting tin and roast for 15–20 minutes. Lower the oven temperature to 170C /325F /gas 3, add the warm wine or water to the tin and roast for the calculated cooking time, basting occasionally.
5 About 30 minutes before the end of the cooking time of the beef, increase the oven temperature to 220C /425 /gas 7, lift the rack with the joint and pour the Yorkshire pudding batter into the roasting tin underneath. Replace the beef and bake for 30 minutes. Do not open the oven door during this period, or the pudding will sink. Sprinkle the beef with salt and serve on a heated serving platter with the Yorkshire pudding cut into squares.

• This method does not allow time for the beef to settle before carving, as the oven door must not be opened (in order to remove the beef) while the pudding is cooking. If you prefer to let your beef settle, remove it from the oven when the calculated cooking time is completed, then increase the oven temperature to 220C /425F /gas 7 and make individual Yorkshire puddings; see right.

Old English roast beef with Yorkshire pudding

Yorkshire pudding

Put these individual puddings into the oven when you remove the beef. They will cook to perfection while the beef settles and you make gravy. Serve the Yorkshire puddings as soon as they are cooked, as they do not take kindly to being kept waiting.

1½ hours,
including standing

Makes 9
100 g /4 oz flour
a pinch of salt
2 medium-sized eggs
150 ml /5 fl oz milk
45 ml /3 tbls beef dripping from the roasting tin

1 Prepare the batter 1 hour before the beef is cooked. Sift the flour and salt into a bowl and make a well in the centre. Break the eggs into the well and add 30 ml /2 tbls of the milk. Using a wooden spoon, gradually draw the flour into the eggs and milk, work to a smooth paste. Gradually add the remaining milk, beating vigorously. Leave the batter to rest until the beef is ready.
2 When the beef is cooked, remove it from the oven and alter the oven temperature to 220C /425F /gas 7. Transfer the beef to a heated serving platter and leave to stand in a warm place for 15–20 minutes to settle.
3 Place 5 ml /1 tsp of the beef dripping from the roasting tin in each of 9 × 7.5–9 cm /3–3½ in tins. Place the tins on a baking sheet and put in the oven for 2–3 minutes, until the fat is smoking.
4 Remove the hot tins from the oven, quickly pour 30 ml /2 tbls of the batter into each tin, then return the tray of tins to the top shelf of the oven and bake for 15 minutes, or until the puddings are puffed up, crisp and golden brown. Do not open the oven door during this time, or they will sink. Serve immediately.

• Alternatively, the batter can be baked in 1 large tin. Heat 30 ml /2 tbls dripping in a 20 × 25 cm /8 × 10 in tin and cook the pudding at 220C /425F /gas 7 for 20–30 minutes, until puffed up, crisp and golden brown. Serve the pudding cut into squares.

Gravy

How many people make really good gravy? Use my recipe, and you'll always have a smooth, delicious tasting gravy.

10 minutes

Makes about 300 ml /10 fl oz
30 ml /2 tbls beef dripping from the roasting tin
30 ml /2 tbls flour
275 ml /10 fl oz beef stock, home-made or from a cube
60 ml /4 tbls red or white wine
salt and freshly ground black pepper

1 Pour all but 30 ml /2 tbls of the fat in the roasting tin into a heatproof cup or jug. Reserve this dripping for another recipe.
2 Place the roasting tin over a low heat and stir the flour into the remaining fat. Cook, stirring, until light brown. Gradually add the beef stock and meat juices to the tin and bring to the boil, stirring and scraping the bottom and sides of the tin with a spoon to incorporate all the crusty bits.
3 Add the red or white wine to the tin, season to taste with salt and freshly ground black pepper and simmer for 3 minutes, stirring occasionally until the gravy has thickened.
4 Pour the gravy into a heated sauce-boat and serve immediately.

Roast rolled topside of beef

Choose rolled topside of beef when you need a relatively economical joint for a family dinner, with careful cooking it will taste as good as the more expensive cuts.

bringing to room temperature,
then 1 – 1¼ hours roasting plus settling

Serves 6
1.1–1.4 kg /2½–3 lb topside of beef, boned and rolled
25 g /1 oz dripping
45 ml /3 tbls flour
22.5 ml /1½ tbls dry mustard
freshly ground black pepper
25 g /1 oz butter
90–120 ml /6–8 tbls red wine
salt
gravy (see recipe left)

1 At least 2 hours before you intend to roast the beef, remove it from the refrigerator and wipe it clean with a damp cloth. Weigh the meat and calculate the cooking time allowing 33 minutes per kg /15 minutes per lb, plus 15 minutes. Heat the dripping in a frying-pan and quickly sear the meat on all sides. Remove it from the pan and leave it to cool.
2 Heat the grill to low. Place the flour in a shallow cake tin and grill, stirring often, until it is lightly browned. Mix the browned flour with the mustard and plenty of freshly ground black pepper. Spread the meat with the butter, then pat the flour mixture over it and leave the meat to stand until it has lost its chill. Heat the oven to 220C /425F / gas 7.
3 Place the beef on a rack over a roasting tin. Add the red wine to the roasting tin. Roast in the oven for 15–20 minutes, then lower the oven temperature to 170C /325F / gas 3 and roast for the calculated cooking time, basting occasionally. Add a little more red wine or some water to the roasting tin if necessary.
4 When the beef is cooked, remove it from the oven and place it on a heated serving platter. Leave it to stand in a warm place for 15–20 minutes to settle.
5 Sprinkle the beef with salt to taste and serve immediately, with gravy.

Boeuf en croûte

Fillet of beef, surrounded by herbed mushrooms and wrapped in flaky puff pastry, makes an elegant and impressive dish that's not at all difficult to do.

bringing to room temperature, then about 1¼ hours plus cooling

Serves 6
1 kg /2¼ lb fillet of beef,
*   trimmed*
freshly ground black pepper
25 g /1 oz butter
225 g /8 oz made-weight puff pastry,
*   defrosted if frozen*
100 g /4 oz mushrooms,
*   thinly sliced*
5 ml /1 tsp mixed dried herbs
5 ml /1 tsp freshly chopped parsley
salt
beaten egg, to glaze
sprigs of watercress, to garnish

1   Remove the fillet of beef from the refrigerator about 2 hours before you intend to roast it. Wipe it clean, tuck the narrow end under to make a neat shape, tie it with string and sprinkle with pepper.

2   Heat the butter in a frying-pan and fry the meat quickly to brown it on all sides, then reduce the heat and fry for 15 minutes longer, turning occasionally. Remove the meat from the pan and leave in a cool place until completely cold.

3   Fry the mushrooms in the butter remaining in the pan for 2 minutes. Add the mixed dried herbs and parsley and cook until the liquid is completely reduced. Remove from the heat, add salt to taste and leave until completely cold.

4   Roll out the pastry to a rectangle approximately 10 cm /4 in larger all round than the beef. Spread half the mushroom mixture over the centre of the pastry.

5   Remove the string from the beef and place the meat on the mushrooms. Brush the

Boeuf en croûte

pastry edges with beaten egg. Wrap over the long sides and press the seam to seal, then lift up the short sides to completely encase the meat and pinch the seams together. Place on a dampened baking sheet with the seams underneath.

6   Roll out any trimmings and cut them into decorative shapes, such as leaves and tassels. Brush 1 side of each shape with beaten egg and stick them, egg side down, on the pastry parcel. Place the parcel in the refrigerator and leave to rest for 2 hours.

7   Heat the oven to 200C /400F /gas 6. Brush the pastry with the beaten egg and bake in the centre of the oven for 25–30 minutes, until the pastry is well risen and browned. Place on a heated serving platter, garnish with watercress and serve.

No-roast roast beef

Lovers of perfectly rare beef, pink and juicy from end to end, with just the outer surface richly crusted, should try this no-roast method when next cooking a large joint. The method involves cooking the beef at a very high temperature for a short while, then turning off the oven and allowing the beef to cook from the heat of the oven. It is only suitable for large pieces of meat.

3 hours standing, then about 2½ hours

Serves 6 or more
2.5 kg /5½ lb rib roast or sirloin on the bone
freshly ground black pepper
50 g /2 oz dripping or butter
salt
gravy (see page 13)

1   Remove the joint of beef from the refrigerator and wipe it clean with a damp cloth. Weigh the meat and calculate the initial cooking time, allowing 11 minutes per kg /5 minutes per lb. Sprinkle it generously with freshly ground black pepper and rub this into the surface of the meat. Leave the meat to stand at room temperature for about 3 hours, until it has lost its chill. Heat the oven to 250C /500F /gas 10.

2   Spread the joint with the dripping or butter and lay it on a rack over a roasting tin.

3   Place the meat in the oven and cook for the calculated initial cooking time. Then switch off the heat and leave the joint to cook for a further 2 hours. Do not open the oven door at all during this period.

4   When the 2 hours is up, open the oven door and, without removing the tin from the oven, touch the beef with your finger. If it feels hot, serve it right away. The meat might feel lukewarm (some ovens do not retain their heat as well as others; electric ovens are often rather better than gas in this respect). If so, set the oven at 250C /500F / gas 10, close the door and leave the meat for about 10 minutes. This will heat the meat without cooking it any more.

5   Sprinkle the beef with salt and additional pepper if necessary. Serve it on a heated serving platter, accompanied by gravy.

Carving a sirloin on the bone

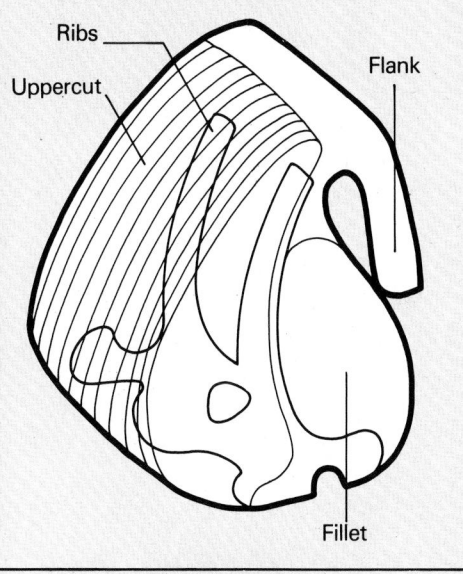

Ribs
Uppercut
Flank
Fillet

Stand the joint upright on its backbone. Cut through the flank and remove it. Carve it into thin slices and overlap on a plate.

Run the knife round the fillet, to free it from the bones. Remove, carve thinly and arrange on the serving plate.

Run the carving knife down against the rib bone and then turn and cut across the backbone to loosen the uppercut.

Place the uppercut, fat side up, on the carving board. Carve the meat into thin slices and arrange on the serving plate.

The portions here are from the flank, fillet and uppercut. Serve each guest with meat from two parts of the joint.

Carving a rib roast

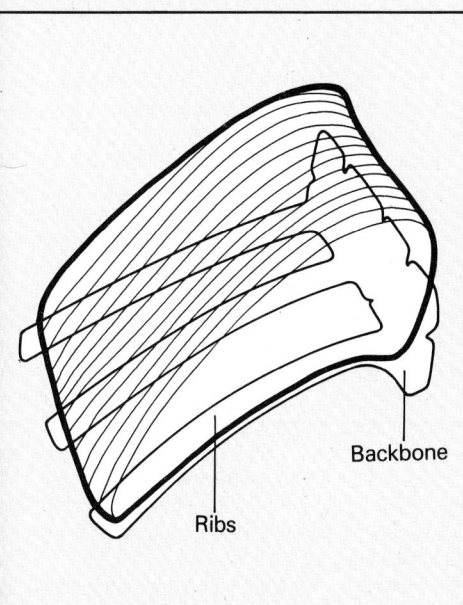

Backbone
Ribs

Rest the joint on the rib bones, with the fat side up and the backbone to your right. Run the knife down the backbone, then along the ribs to loosen the meat from the bones.

Remove the meat from the bones and place it, fat side up, on the carving board. Carve the meat into thin slices and arrange on the serving plate.

GRILLING BEEF

Grilling is one of those techniques that all cooks think they know how to do. It is simple, but you must follow a few basic rules for perfect results every time.

There is no magic secret to grilling, only one cardinal rule: grilling demands your undivided attention from start to finish. Never attempt to combine it with other activities because only seconds separate a rare steak from a medium one, medium from well-done and well-done from disaster.

The cuts of beef suitable for grilling are not by any means cheap, so it is worth a little time and effort to cook them perfectly and also to take a bit of trouble over accompanying sauces. Many of the sauces I suggest to accompany these simple grills are classics in their own way. They may take a little time and the ingredients may also be quite expensive, but the results of a rich, smooth bearnaise sauce for example, will be well worth the effort. The sauces I suggest with the recipes that follow are very versatile, they can easily be mixed and matched with different cuts of steak. Nevertheless they are dishes which you will probably want to save for a special occasion.

What beef to grill

Steaks of all shapes and sizes are perfect for grilling. When you buy a piece of steak the meat should not be too pink. A deeper, more blood-coloured red indicates that the meat has been well-hung and should be tender. The meat should be shot through with tiny flecks of fat and the fat around it should be firm. Many people think that creamy coloured fat is an indication of top-quality beef. In fact, the colour of the fat depends on what the cattle have been fed on and is no indication of the quality.

Obviously the kind of steak you buy depends on what you prefer. Fillet steak is always tender, for example, but some people think it lacks flavour – they prefer the stronger taste of rump or sirloin. Your choice may also depend on price, so I have detailed the types of steak you may wish to grill, starting with the most expensive.

Fillet: the fillet is a long narrow muscle that runs along the backbone of the animal. It is thicker at one end, tapering away to nothing at the other end and is cut across the grain into steaks. As it is very lean, the steak cut from it is often barded with extra fat before cooking.

To bard the fillet buy a thin sheet of pork fat that is large enough to wrap around the whole piece of meat. Tie it in position at intervals with string. When the piece of fillet is cut into steaks each one will have a collar of fat.

Meat intended for grilling is never larded. Running a larding needle through the meat has much the same effect as poking it with a fork to turn it over: all the juices are released and the meat dries out.

The fillet is divided into several cuts.

Chateaubriand: this is a large, thick cut from the thickest end of the fillet. This bit of the fillet weighs from 350–900 g /12 oz–2 lb and serves from 2–5 people. Either cook completely under the grill, or grill partially and finish off in the oven. To serve, carve the Chateaubriand into 15 mm /½ in slices, slicing downwards at a slight angle. Serve it with a Chateaubriand sauce (see recipe).

Fillet steak: is cut from the middle of the fillet. Each steak weighs about 125 g /4 oz and is about 25 mm /1 in thick.

Tournedos: this is a small, round cut from the thin end of the fillet, but it makes up in thickness what it lacks in diameter. It should be about 4 cm /1½ in thick and weigh about 175 g /6 oz. A tournedos is usually barded before cutting.

Medallion or filet mignon: this is an even smaller cut from the tail of the fillet. It weighs about 50–75 g /2–3 oz, and is about 25 mm /1 in thick.

Sirloin steak: this is cut about 20–40 mm / ¾–1½ in thick from the top of the sirloin. This cut, often known as an entrecôte, is cut from between the wing ribs. A sirloin steak is not as fine-textured or tender as fillet but it is less coarse than rump.

T-bone: this is a complete slice through the sirloin including the bone and the fillet. It is a very large steak usually weighing about 450 g /1 lb and it is about 20 mm /¾ in thick. It serves one generously.

Porterhouse steak: this again is a large steak but unlike the T-bone it usually serves 2. It weighs 350–450 g /¾–1 lb and is about 4 cm /1½ in thick. It is cut from the wing rib of the sirloin without the bone.

Rump: this is tougher than fillet or sirloin but many people prefer it because, arguably, it has the best flavour. It is cut from just behind the sirloin and is usually 20 mm /¾ in thick with a thick side band of fat.

Storing steak

Beef is usually hung for 10–20 days before being cut up for sale. During this ageing process the fibres are broken down to produce a more tender and flavoursome meat. After buying, steak can be kept in the refrigerator for 3–5 days. Put it on a plate and cover it loosely with a fresh sheet of greaseproof paper or foil. Bring it out of the refrigerator 2–3 hours before cooking to allow it to come to room temperature.

How to grill

Heating the grill: successful grilling depends first and foremost on the intensity of the heat and how you control it. So that the steak is seared, sealing in all the precious juices, you must heat the grill as high as possible. Make sure that is is heated to maximum before you start grilling.

As a quick test, a slice of fresh bread 7.5 cm /3 in from the grill will brown to toast on one side in 30–40 seconds.

The instructions with some cookers

South American beefsteak

recommend you leave the grill pan in place while heating the grill – but don't leave the grid in it. The grid should be cold when the meat is placed on it or it will start to cook from both sides making a nonsense of your careful timing.

There is often very little juice from grilled steak and it is inclined to burn in the bottom of the grill pan. I like to line the bottom of the pan with foil to avoid this and save on washing up.

Preparing the steak

If your steak has a border of fat, trim it down a little but don't cut it all away. A little edge of fat tastes delicious crisply grilled. Slash the fat at regular intervals before you cook the steak, otherwise it will contract at a different rate from the rest of the steak and cause the meat to buckle up. Finally give the steak a good whack with a meat bat.

Seasoning: some cooks maintain that salting the meat before it is grilled draws out the juices and prevents it from browning

roperly. I can find little evidence to support his theory. I suspect this is a hangover from he days when only coarse-grained salt was vailable. To be on the safe side, season the neat with freshly ground black pepper when ou take it out of the refrigerator, but leave alting until just before you grill it.

Try seasoning with a light sprinkling of erbs at the same time as you pepper the teak. The provençal blend of thyme, avory, basil, parsley, bay leaf and fennel ives an exciting flavour.

Moistening the steak: just before grilling he steak brush it with a half and half nixture of melted butted and olive oil. This elps to keep it moist and makes it brown venly and well.

Positioning the grid: the thinner the meat he closer to the heat the grid should be. 7.5 m /3 in is a good average distance and a ormal steak can be cooked right through at his distance. For a thicker steak sear it at his distance and then lower the position of he grid. A distance of 12.5 cm /5 in from he heat is about right – this will give the teak a chance to cook right through to the niddle before the outside begins to burn.

Cooking time: once you have decided the degree of rareness that you like then just follow my chart of cooking times (overleaf).
Blue (au bleu): the steak is charred brown on the outside but just hot in the centre – in other words it is very rare. Filet mignon is not suitable for serving blue.
Rare: the red juices inside still flow freely
Medium: the juices are set but the centre of the meat is still pink.
Well-done: the last traces of pink have just turned to beige leaving the meat moist and juicy, not dry.

Individual or supersize?

An idea that I am becoming increasingly fond of is to have supersize steak. This is one large slice of steak, usually rump, that weighs about 1 kg /2 lb and is enough to serve 4 comfortably. It is no more extravagant than individual steaks for the same number of people and it makes a superb presentation at the table.

A single, large steak is easier to cope with under a household grill than individual steaks and, with a well-heated grill and meticulous timing, you can pin-point the degree of rareness with great accuracy. It is an ideal dish to serve at a small dinner party with good friends.

Even if they do not all like their meat cooked to the same degree all is not lost. You will find that a large piece of meat like this carries on cooking on the serving platter for several minutes after leaving the grill. If one of your guests prefers meat more well-done than the others, carve that portion last. It should be a degree more cooked.

Garnishes

Unless a particular recipe should instruct otherwise grilled steaks should be served dry. Hand an accompanying sauce around separately in a sauce-boat. Another point to remember if you serve your steak very rare, make sure you choose a sauce that will mingle well with the juices. Some ideas are Bearnaise sauce (*page 20*), Bordelaise sauce (*page 22*), Châteaubriand sauce (*page 23*) or Sauce fines herbes (*page 20*).

A ball or pat of savoury chilled butter to top a freshly grilled steak (see the recipe for Maître d'hôtel, *page 23*) is always a popular garnish.

Timings for grilling beef

Cut and Weight	Thickness	Distance of grid from heat	Cooking time each side		Result
Fillet steak 125 g /4 oz	3 cm /1¼ in	7.5 cm /3 in	2	minutes	blue
			3		rare
			3½		medium
			4–4½		well-done
Tournedos 175 g /6 oz	4 cm /1½ in	7.5 cm /3 in	3	minutes	blue
			4½		rare
			6		medium
			7–8		well-done
Chateaubriand (serves 2–3) 450 g /1 lb	3–4 cm /1¼–1½ in	12.5 cm /5 in	7	minutes	blue
			9		rare
			10–11		medium
			12–13		well-done
Sirloin or rump 225 g /8 oz	20 mm /¾ in	7.5 cm /3 in	1	minute	blue
			2		rare
			3		medium
			4–5		well-done
Porterhouse sirloin or rump 450 g /1 lb	4 cm /1½ in	7.5 cm /3 in	★2	minutes	blue
			★3		rare
			★4		medium
			★5		well-done
T-bone 450 g /1 lb	20 mm /¾ in	7.5 cm /3 in	3	minutes	blue
			4		rare
			6		medium
			8–9		well-done
Filet mignon 50–75 g /2–3 oz	25 mm /1 in	7.5 cm /3 in	2	minutes	rare
			2½		medium
			3		well-done
Super rump 900 g /2 lb	5 cm /2 in	12.5 cm /5 in	6	minutes	blue
			7		rare
			8		medium
			10–12		well-done

★ 3 minutes each side at high heat, then reduce heat to low and cook as times in chart.

Medallions with anchovy and walnut sauce

Once this delightful sauce is glazed under the grill, it won't wait for anyone. So don't begin the final cooking until your guests are ready and waiting at the table. Walnut oil is expensive, but worth it! Serve the medallions with new potatoes or french beans.

bringing to room temperature, 35–40 minutes

Serves 6
12 medallions, 25 mm /1 in thick, weighing about 50–75 g /2–3 oz
freshly ground black pepper
salt
melted butter
olive oil
watercress, to garnish
For the anchovy and walnut sauce
4 anchovy fillets
24 shelled walnut halves
2 large egg yolks
175 ml /6 fl oz walnut oil
freshly ground black pepper

1 Wipe the steaks with absorbent paper and beat once or twice on each side with a meat bat. Season well with black pepper and leave to come to room temperature.
2 To make the sauce, pound the anchovy fillets and 12 of the walnut halves to a paste, using a pestle and mortar. Stir in the egg yolks, then whisk in the walnut oil drop by drop – as for mayonnaise – until the sauce emulsifies and thickens. Chop the remaining walnuts finely and stir them into the sauce. Season with freshly ground black pepper to taste and set aside while you cook the medallions.
3 Heat the grill to high.
4 Just before cooking, season the steaks with salt and brush with melted butter and olive oil. Brush the grill grid with oil and place the steaks on it. Grill 7.5 cm /3in from the heat, 2 minutes each side for rare, 2½ minutes each side for medium and 3 minutes each side for well done.
5 Transfer the steaks to a heated flameproof serving platter and spoon a little of the anchovy and walnut sauce onto each one. Place under the grill for about 30 seconds, watching constantly, until the sauce glazes over. Garnish with watercress and serve immediately.

Beef fingers with red pepper and ginger

Beef fingers with red pepper and ginger

2 hours marinating, then 2–4 minutes

Serves 4
450 g /1 lb fillet of beef
90 ml /6 tbls sesame seed oil
1 red pepper, seeded and chopped
1 fresh ginger root, peeled and cut into strip
salt and freshly ground black pepper
olive oil
15 ml /1 tbls finely chopped chives
plainly boiled rice, to serve
stir-fried vegetables, to serve

1 Cut the fillet into fingers, 7.5 × 2 cm /. × ¾ in.
2 In a bowl, mix together the sesame see

il, the chopped red pepper and the ginger oot. Season with salt and freshly ground lack pepper.

Put the beef fingers into the marinade, urn to coat well, cover the bowl and leave to narinade for about 2 hours.

Heat the grill to high. Brush the grill rid with olive oil.

Remove the beef fingers from the narinade with a slotted spoon, place them on the grill grid and grill 7.5 cm /3 in from he heat, for a total of 2 minutes for well-lone, turning them once.

Meanwhile, pour the marinade into a mall saucepan and heat through for 2 ninutes.

Divide the cooked beef fingers between ndividual heated serving plates. Spoon a ittle of the cooked marinade over each erving and garnish with finely chopped :hives. Serve immediately, with plainly oiled rice and stir-fried vegetables.

South American beefsteak

Crisp green beans combine well with these succulent steaks.

bringing to room temperature, then 10–15 minutes

Serves 4
4 sirloin steaks, 20 mm /¾ in thick, weighing about 225 g /8 oz each
salt and freshly ground black pepper
10 ml /2 tsp dry mustard
10 ml/2 tsp soft brown sugar
10 ml /2 tsp grated onion
50 g /2 oz softened butter
melted butter
olive oil
green beans, to serve

1 Wipe the steaks with absorbent paper and trim off any excess fat. Slash the remaining fat at intervals with a sharp knife. Beat once or twice on each side with a meat bat. Season the steaks with black pepper and leave to come to room temperature.
2 Heat the grill to high. In a small bowl, combine the dry mustard with the soft brown sugar, grated onion and softened butter and salt and freshly ground black pepper to taste. Work together to make a smooth paste.
3 Just before cooking, season the steaks with salt and brush generously with melted butter and olive oil. Brush the grill grid with oil, place the steaks on the grid and grill 7.5 cm /3 in from the heat, 2 minutes each side for rare, 3 minutes each side for medium and 4–5 minutes each side for well-done.
4 When the steaks are cooked, transfer to a heated serving platter and spread a quarter of the mustard paste over each. The paste will melt with the heat of the steaks. Serve with green beans, sautéed in butter.

Rump steak with cream sauce

These tasty steaks are delicious served with a crisp watercress and endive salad.

bringing to room temperature, then 15–25 minutes

Serves 4
4 rump steaks, 20 mm /¾ in thick, weighing 225 g /8 oz each
freshly ground black pepper
melted butter
2 shallots, finely chopped
15 ml /1 tbls paprika
150 ml /5 fl oz thick cream
15 ml /1 tbls finely chopped tarragon
salt
olive oil

1 Wipe the steaks with absorbent paper and beat once or twice with a meat bat. Trim excess fat and slash remaining fat. Season generously with pepper and leave to come to room temperature.
2 Heat the grill to high.
3 Meanwhile, make the sauce. Melt 15 g /½ oz butter in a small saucepan, add the finely chopped shallots and paprika and cook, stirring occasionally, for 5 minutes, or until the shallot softens. Stir in the thick cream and simmer for 5 minutes, until the sauce reduces and thickens. Strain the sauce into a heated bowl and stir in the finely chopped tarragon. Correct the seasoning and keep hot over a pan of simmering water.
4 Just before cooking, season the steaks with salt and brush with some more melted butter and oil. Brush the grid with oil, place the steaks on the grid and grill 7.5 cm /3 in from the heat, 2 minutes each side for rare, 3 minutes each side for medium or 4–5 minutes each side for well done.
5 Arrange the cooked steaks on a heated serving dish and serve the sauce separately, in a heated sauce-boat.

Grilled steak with sauce fines herbes

🍴 bringing to room temperature, then 50 minutes - 1 hour

Serves 4
1.1 kg /2½ lb rump steak, 5 cm /2 in thick
salt and freshly ground black pepper
25–50 g /1–2 oz softened butter
For 275 ml /10 fl oz short-cut sauce espagnole
40 g /1½ oz fat salt pork, finely diced
22.5 ml /1½ tbls butter
1 Spanish onion, coarsely chopped
1 large carrot, coarsely chopped
1 celery stalk, coarsely chopped
1 bay leaf
1.5 ml /¼ tsp dried thyme
30 ml /2 tbls flour
7.5 ml /1½ tsp tomato purée
300 ml /10 fl oz beef stock, home-made or
   from a cube
45–60 ml /3–4 tbls dry white wine
30 ml /2 tbls Quick meat glaze (see page 23)
For the sauce fines herbes
3 sprigs of parsley
3 sprigs of tarragon
3 sprigs of chervil
90 ml /6 tbls dry white wine
40 g /1½ oz butter
1 shallot, finely chopped
juice of 1 lemon

1　Season the steak with pepper and leave to come to room temperature.
2　Make the short-cut sauce espagnole. Sauté the fat salt pork in the butter until transparent. Add the chopped vegetables, bay leaf and dried thyme; continue to sauté briskly until browned.
3　Add the flour, lower the heat and sauté, stirring, for 2–3 minutes, until golden.
4　Dilute the tomato purée with a little of the beef stock and stir into the pan. Slowly stir in the remaining stock and the wine. Bring to the boil, stirring constantly.
5　Stir in the meat glaze, then simmer for about 20 minutes with the lid half-on, stirring occasionally.
6　Press the sauce through a fine sieve, season to taste with pepper and reserve.
7　Make the sauce fines herbes. Remove the leaves from the herbs and reserve. Chop the stems and simmer them gently for 5 minutes with the white wine. Discard the stems. Heat the grill to high.
8　In another saucepan, melt 25 g /1 oz butter and add the finely chopped shallot and the strained liquid. Simmer until reduced by half. Add the short-cut sauce espagnole and simmer for 10 minutes.
9　Season the steak with salt on both sides and brush with the softened butter. Brush the grill with oil, place the steak on the grid and grill 12.5 cm /5 in from the heat, 7 minutes each side for rare, 8 minutes each

Grilled steak with sauce fines herbes

side for medium, 10–12 minutes each side for well done.
10　Carve the steak into slices, arrange on a heated serving dish and keep warm.
11　Bring the sauce back to boiling point, then remove from the heat. Add the lemon juice and swirl in the remaining butter. Add the reserved herb leaves. Pour over the grilled slices and serve immediately.

Entrecôtes Bearnaise

🍴 bringing to room temperature, then 35–40 minutes

Serves 4
2 × 450 g /1 lb sirloin steaks, each 4 cm /1½
   in thick
salt and freshly ground black pepper
50 g /2 oz softened butter
olive oil
For the bearnaise sauce
4–6 sprigs of fresh tarragon, chopped
4–6 sprigs chervil, chopped
15 ml /1 tbls chopped shallot
2 black peppercorns, crushed
30 ml /2 tbls tarragon vinegar
150 ml /5 fl oz dry white wine
3 egg yolks
225 g /8 oz unsalted butter, diced into
   10 mm /½ in cubes
salt
lemon juice
cayenne pepper

1　Slash the fat around the steaks. Season with pepper and spread with softened butter. Leave to come to room temperature.
2　Make the bearnaise sauce. Place half the tarragon and chervil in a saucepan with the shallot, peppercorns, tarragon vinegar and white wine. Boil until the liquid has reduced to 30 ml /2 tbls, then reserve.
3　Beat the egg yolks with 15 ml /1 tbls cold water, then place in the top pan of a double boiler, or a bowl set over a saucepan. Strain in the reduced liquid. Using a wire whisk, stir briskly over hot but not simmering water until light and fluffy.
4　Whisk in a piece of butter. When it has melted and been incorporated, add another. Continue in this way until the mixture begins to thicken, then add a few pieces at a time. Whisk thoroughly all the time, stirring from the bottom of the pan until the butter has melted. Heat the grill to high.
5　Season the sauce to taste with salt, lemon juice and cayenne pepper. Strain through a fine sieve to give it a good gloss and stir in the remaining chopped herbs. Keep the sauce over warm (not hot) water until ready to serve.
6　Brush the grid of the grill pan with a little olive oil and season the steaks on the grid and grill 7.5 cm /3 in from the heat for 3 minutes each side, then reduce the heat and cook for 3 minutes each side for rare, 4 minutes for medium and 5 minutes for well-done. Baste frequently with the pan juices.
7　Slice the steaks on a slanting diagonal and transfer to a heated serving platter. Serve with the bearnaise sauce.

Lattice steaks with anchovy butter

bringing to room temperature, then 20–25

Serves 4
× 225 g /8oz rump steaks, 20 mm /¾ in thick
freshly ground black pepper
olive oil
salt
melted butter
bouquets of parsley, to garnish
For the garnish
50 g /2 oz canned anchovy fillets
about 12 black olives
For the anchovy butter
50 g /2 oz softened butter
10 ml /2 tsp anchovy essence

Wipe the steaks with absorbent paper and trim off any excess fat. Slash the remaining fat at intervals with a sharp knife to prevent the steaks curling under the grill. Season generously with freshly ground black pepper and leave to come to room temperature.

Meanwhile, prepare the garnish. Drain the anchovy fillets and cut them into fine strips with a small sharp knife. Halve and stone the black olives. Reserve.

Make the anchovy butter. In a small bowl, using a fork, cream together the softened butter and the anchovy essence.

Heat the grill to high. Brush the grid with olive oil.

Just before cooking, season the steaks with salt. Brush them lightly with melted butter and olive oil.

Place the prepared steaks on the grid and grill 7.5 cm /3in from the heat, 2 minutes each side for rare, 3 minutes each side for medium, 4–5 minutes each side for well done.

Transfer the steaks to a heated serving dish and quickly spread with the anchovy butter. Arrange a fine lattice of anchovy strips over each steak and place a halved olive in the centre of each square. Serve, garnished with bouquets of parsley.

Rump steak with hot sauce

bringing to room temperature, then 12–16 minutes

Serves 4–6
5 cm /2 in thick rump steak, weighing about 1 kg /2¼ lb
salt and freshly ground black pepper
olive oil
For the hot sauce
150 ml /5 fl oz tomato ketchup
120 ml /8 tbls olive oil
30 ml /2 tbls Worcestershire sauce
1.5–2.5 ml /¼–½ tsp Tabasco sauce
15–30 ml /1–2 tbls lemon juice
celery salt
freshly ground black pepper

1 Wipe the steak with absorbent paper and trim off any excess fat. Slash the remaining fat at intervals with a sharp knife to prevent the steak curling under the grill. Season to taste with freshly ground black pepper and leave to come to room temperature.
2 Make the hot sauce. Combine the sauce ingredients in a small saucepan, seasoning to taste with celery salt and freshly ground black pepper. Simmer over a gentle heat for a few minutes, until the flavours are well blended. Do not allow the sauce to boil, or it will separate.
3 Heat the grill to high. Brush the grid with olive oil and place the steaks on the grid and grill 7.5 cm /3 in from the heat for 3 minutes each side. Reduce the heat and cook for 3 minutes each side for rare, 4 minutes for medium and 5 minutes for well-done. Baste frequently with the pan juices. Reheat the sauce towards the end of the cooking time.
4 Transfer the cooked steak to a warm serving dish and season to taste with salt and freshly ground black pepper. Cut the steak into long, thin slices and serve accompanied by the hot sauce.

Chinese beef with oyster and soy marinade

4 hours marinating, bringing to room temperature, then 10–15 minutes

Chinese beef with oyster and soy marinade

Serves 4
700 g /1½ lb sirloin steak
thin slices of preserved ginger (optional)
2 spring onions, thinly sliced
2–4 whole spring onions, to garnish
For the marinade
45 ml /3 tbls oyster sauce
2.5 ml /½ tsp chilli sauce (hot pepper sauce)
30 ml /2 tbls soy sauce
45 ml /3 tbls peanut oil
45 ml /3 tbls dry white wine

1 Cut the beef into 25 mm /1 in cubes and place in a large bowl. Combine the marinade ingredients and pour over the meat. Leave to marinate in the refrigerator overnight, or for at least 4 hours.
2 Bring the meat to room temperature. Remove the grill grid and line the pan with foil then heat the grill to high.
3 Drain the meat and reserve the marinade. Thread the meat onto 4 long skewers, with 2 thin slices of preserved ginger - if using - between every 2–3 cubes of meat.
4 Brush the meat with marinade, balance the skewers on the rim of the pan and grill about 10 cm /4 in away from the heat, turning the skewers and basting with the marinade.
5 When cooked to your taste, about 8–10 minutes, sprinkle the brochettes with the thinly sliced spring onion and serve garnished with the whole spring onions.

Entrecôte a la bordelaise

Bordelaise sauce is a classic sauce from the Bordeaux region of France, flavoured with claret, beef marrow and shallots.

bringing to room temperature, making the sauce, then 4–10 minutes

Serves 4
4 × 225 g/8 oz sirloin steaks, 20 mm/¾ in thick
freshly ground black pepper
salt
melted butter, for brushing
olive oil, for brushing
fresh parsley, to garnish
For the sauce bordelaise
2 shallots, finely chopped
1 garlic clove, finely chopped
225 ml/8 fl oz claret
1 bay leaf
150 ml/5 fl oz short-cut sauce espagnole (page 20)
salt
30 ml/2 tbls finely sliced beef marrow
5 ml/1 tsp finely chopped parsley
5 ml/1 tsp lemon juice
freshly ground black pepper

1   Wipe the steaks with absorbent paper and trim off any excess fat. Slash the remaining fat at intervals with a small sharp knife to prevent the steaks curling under the grill. Beat once or twice on each side with a meat bat. Season with freshly ground black pepper and leave to come to room temperature.
2   Prepare the sauce bordelaise. In a small saucepan, simmer the finely chopped shallots and garlic with the claret and bay leaf until the wine had reduced to half its original quantity.
3   Add the sauce espagnole and simmer for 20 minutes. Strain the sauce through a fine sieve and return it to the saucepan. Skim the surface of the sauce with strips of absorbent paper.
4   Heat the grill to high.
5   Bring a small saucepan of salted water to the boil and poach the finely sliced beef marrow for 5 minutes. Drain and mix with a little of the finely chopped parsley. Put on one side.
6   Add the remaining parsley and the lemon juice to the sauce and season to taste with salt and freshly ground black pepper. Keep warm over a low heat while you prepare the steaks.
7   Just before cooking the steaks, season with salt and brush generously with melted butter and olive oil. Brush the grill grid with oil. Place the steaks on the grid and grill 7.5 cm/3 in away from the heat, 2 minutes each side for rare, 3 minutes each side for medium and 4–5 minutes each side for well-done.
8   Place the steaks on a heated serving platter. Sprinkle the marrow mixture on top and serve the sauce separately in a heated sauce-boat. Serve immediately, garnished with fresh parsley.

Chateaubriand with roast potatoes sprinkled with herbs.
In front, Tournedos with maître d'hôtel butter

Porterhouse steak with pizzaiola sauce

bringing to room temperature, making sauce, then 12–16 minutes

Serves 2
1 porterhouse steak, 4 cm/1½ in thick, weighing 450 g/1 lb
salt and freshly ground black pepper
melted butter
olive oil
For the pizzaiola sauce
15 ml/1 tbls olive oil
1 garlic clove, sliced
225 g/8 oz canned tomatoes, coarsely chopped
15 ml/1 tbls finely chopped parsley
1.5 ml/¼ tsp dried oregano
salt and freshly ground black pepper
7.5–15 ml/½–1 tbls Worcestershire sauce

1   Wipe the steak with absorbent paper and beat it once or twice on each side with a meat bat. Season with pepper and leave to come to room temperature.
2   Make the pizzaiola sauce. Heat the olive oil in a small saucepan, add the sliced garlic and cook over low heat until the garlic is transparent. Add the coarsely chopped tomatoes and their juice, the finely chopped parsley and dried oregano. Season to taste with salt and freshly ground black pepper. Simmer the sauce for 15–20 minutes, until slightly reduced. Stir in the Worcestershire sauce, season and keep warm.
3   Heat the grill to high. Just before cooking, season the steak with salt and brush with melted butter and olive oil. Brush the grill grid with oil and place the steak on it. Grill 7.5 cm/3 in from the heat for 3 minutes each side then reduce the heat to low and cook 3 minutes each side for rare, 4 minutes each side for medium or 5 minutes each side for well-done.
4   Serve immediately with the sauce handed round separately.

5 Season the steak with salt and brush it generously with melted butter and olive oil. Brush the grill grid with oil and place the steak on it. Grill 12.5 cm /5 in from the heat, 9 minutes each side for rare, 10–11 minutes each side for medium or 12–13 minutes each side for well-done.

6 Put the cooked steak on a carving board and carve it downwards at a slight angle, into 6 even slices. Transfer the meat to a heated serving dish and serve, with the chateaubriand sauce handed round separately.

● An alternative method of cooking this steak is to seal in the juices under the grill, 7.5 cm /3 in from the heat for 3 minutes each side, then transfer to an oven heated to 160C /300F /gas 2 and cook 15 minutes for rare, 20 minutes for medium or 25 minutes for well-done.

Tournedos with maître d'hôtel butter

Succulent tournedos with pats of maître d'hôtel butter are one of the quickest of grills: simple to prepare, but attractively presented and delicious to eat.

bringing to room temperature, then 9–16 minutes

Serves 6
6 tournedos steaks, each 4 cm /1½ in thick
salt
freshly ground black pepper
melted butter
olive oil
flat-leaved parsley, to garnish
For the maître d'hôtel butter
75 g /3 oz butter, softened
25 ml /1½ tbls finely chopped parsley
25 ml /1½ tbls lemon juice
salt
freshly ground black pepper

1 Wipe the steaks with absorbent paper and beat them once or twice on each side with a meat bat. Season them generously with freshly ground black pepper and leave to come to room temperature.
2 Cream together the softened butter with the parsley. Season with the lemon juice and salt and freshly ground black pepper to taste. Roll the butter into a sausage shape in greaseproof paper and chill in the refrigerator.
4 Heat the grill to high.
5 Season the steaks with salt and brush them generously with melted butter and olive oil. Brush the grill grid with olive oil and place the steaks on it. Grill 7.5 cm /3 in from the heat, 4½ minutes each side for rare, 6 minutes each side for medium or 7–8 minutes each side for well done.
6 When the steaks are cooked, arrange them on a heated serving platter. Remove the maître d' hôtel butter from the refrigerator, unwrap and cut into 6 slices. Top each steak with a pat of maître d' hôtel butter. Garnish with the flat-leaved parsley and serve at once.

Chateaubriand

This method of preparing beef fillet was invented by Montmirail, chef to Vicomte Chateaubriand.

bringing to room temperature, making sauce, then 18–26 minutes

Serves 2
Chateaubriand steak 4 cm /1½ in thick,
weighing 450 g /1 lb
freshly ground black pepper
salt
melted butter
olive oil
For 45 ml /3 tbls quick meat glaze
425 g /15 oz good quality canned consommé
For the Chateaubriand sauce
45 ml /3 tbls chicken stock, home-made or
from a cube
100 g /4 oz cold, unsalted butter, diced
15 ml /1 tbls finely chopped parsley
7.5–15 ml /½–1 tbls lemon juice
salt and freshly ground black pepper
pinch of cayenne pepper

1 Wipe the steak with absorbent paper and beat it once or twice on each side with a meat bat. Season the steak generously with freshly ground black pepper and leave to come to room temperature.
2 To make the quick meat glaze: boil the consommé rapidly for about 20 minutes until it is reduced to just 45 ml /3 tbls, and is a syrupy glaze. Use 15 ml /1 tbls of this and store the rest in a small jar in the refrigerator, or freeze in an ice cube tray.
3 Combine the quick meat glaze and the chicken stock in a saucepan and stir together until well blended. Bring to the boil and boil fast until reduced to 15 ml /1 tbls. Heat the grill to high.
4 Reduce the heat under the sauce and whisk in the diced butter a piece at a time, until the sauce thickens and emulsifies. The sauce should start to emulsify before the butter melts; if the sauce is too hot and melts the butter too quickly, remove the pan from the heat while you whisk. When all the butter is incorporated season to taste with lemon juice, salt, freshly ground black pepper and cayenne pepper. Put the sauce in a bowl over warm water until ready to serve.

PAN FRYING BEEF

Pan frying is one of the simplest and tastiest ways of preparing a meal. With a tender cut of meat, the right pan and the minimum of effort, you have the makings of a truly gourmet evening.

When you are choosing beef for pan frying, buy the same top-quality steaks as you would for grilling (*see page 16*). Ask the butcher to cut them all the same thickness as this makes timing the cooking easier. Fillet steaks should be 3 cm /1¼ in thick, while the eye of the fillet can be cut slightly thicker into tournedos, which are then wrapped in pork fat and are ideal for frying. Rump and sirloin steaks should be at least 20 mm /¾ in thick. T-bone steaks can also be fried. Check the chart opposite before purchasing steaks for frying.

If the cut has a bone in it, ask the butcher to trim off any protruding corners, so that the meat will lie as flat as possible in the frying-pan when cooking.

If using minced beef, for best results mince the meat yourself or ask the butcher to do it specially for you. If buying ready-minced, ask for the high-quality type.

Preparing beef for frying

After you take the meat out of the refrigerator, most cuts should be well trimmed to remove any fat. Then wipe them dry with absorbent paper, season them well with freshly ground black pepper and leave them to come to room temperature. Just before cooking, season them again with salt and more black pepper.

Choosing a frying-pan

An all-purpose frying-pan should be heavy, with a handle that does not conduct heat and will not melt if inadvertently left over a gas flame. The pan should have a flat bottom so that it stands steadily and conducts heat evenly. It is also useful to have a frying-pan with a lid – or one that will take a lid from one of your saucepans.

Given a choice between an old-fashioned iron pan and a modern, coated one, I would go for the former every time. Black iron is the professionals' choice, though you will need to season the pan by washing, drying and heating it, brushing it all over inside with oil and leaving it to stand overnight. Then wipe off any excess oil and rub the pan clean with salt. The oil will prevent rust getting a grip on it. From then on the pan should never be washed but simply wiped clean with kitchen paper and then stored in a dry place.

Fats for frying

Butter gives the best flavour when pan frying but as it burns at a low temperature it will quickly turn black and bitter if the heat is high and/or prolonged. To remedy this, add some oil – about 30 ml /2 tbls every 25 g /1 oz butter. Oil will not burn until it reaches a very high temperature, it will give the butter some protection. Alternatively, use clarified butter.

Pan frying beef

It is easiest to fry beef if all the pieces in the pan are the same thickness. Size is less important, as it is the thickness that governs the cooking time. The meat must brown quickly on the outside to seal the surface. This is called searing and it retains all the juices inside the steak, making it succulent.

Do not overcrowd the pan. Putting in too many steaks at once lowers the temperature of the fat and makes it difficult for the steam to escape. The meat will then simmer in its own juices instead of frying. If necessary use two frying-pans, or fry in batches.

Heat the butter and oil until the butter melts and starts to sizzle, then put the meat in the pan. Make sure that the bottom surface is flat against the pan and well into the hot fat. Fry over high heat for minutes, then turn the meat and cook the other side over high heat for a further minutes. This initial cooking sears the surface and gives it a good, brown look.

Steak chasseur

Lower the heat to moderate. Continue to cook the beef, uncovered. Use tongs or two wooden spoons to turn it occasionally. If you were to use a fork, the juices would be lost through the fork holes. Continue cooking until the meat is done to your taste: the maximum time is 20 minutes. Use the chart as a guide.

Never discard the precious mixture of fat and juices remaining in the frying-pan. Either pour them over the fried meat as they are, or deglaze the pan with a splash of wine or stock and pour this over the meat. A small knob of butter stirred in at the last moment will make the juices rich and glossy.

Minute steak (a thin slice from the top part of the sirloin) and flash-fry steak (pre-tenderized, thin steak) are good pan fried but they only require one minute on each side to cook completely.

Stir-frying beef

This method of cooking is both quick and easy because all stir-fried food is cut into small, uniform pieces before being cooked rapidly in the minimum of oil – just enough to prevent sticking. As more of the food's surface is exposed to heat, it cooks quickly without losing its texture, flavour or vitamin content.

The best utensil to use for stir-frying is a Chinese *wok*, a wide, curved-bottomed pan traditionally used in China for stir-frying. The advantage of cooking with a wok is that its shape concentrates the heat in the centre of the base of the pan and food can be pushed towards or away from the heat as necessary.

However, you can achieve the same results with a large, heavy-bottomed frying-pan by placing it over the small gas ring of a gas cooker so that the heat is concentrated in the middle. Traditionally, wooden chop-sticks are used for stirring the ingredients during cooking, although a pair of forks works equally well.

To quick-fry beef, cut fillet, rump or skirt steak into pieces 5 cm /2 in square and then slice each square against the grain into thin strips 3 mm /⅛ in thick. Marinate the strips for at least half an hour in a mixture of cornflour blended with water, soy sauce and sake (Chinese rice wine) or dry sherry. The benefits of marinating are that it helps keep in the juices of the meat and also adds flavour.

Dry frying beef

Dry frying is an alternative to grilling, producing much the same charred surface as that on a grilled or barbecued steak. As the method uses almost no fat, it is very good for slimmers. You can successfully dry fry any cut of meat that can be grilled, but the method is not suitable for coated food. Use a heavy frying-pan, and very little fat. Alternatively buy a specially ridged iron pan which will give your steaks an attractive diamond-patterned finish.

To dry fry steaks, heat a heavy, well-seasoned pan to the stage where a drop of water shaken onto the surface sizzles and bounces on contact. Then wipe the pan quickly all over with a piece of fat cut from the meat and impaled on a long fork, or with

Timings for pan frying beef

Cut	Weight	Thickness	Frying time each side*		Result
Fillet	125 – 175 g /4–6 oz	3 cm /1¼ in	3	minutes	blue
			4	minutes	rare
			7–8	minutes	medium
			9½–10	minutes	well-done
Tournedos	125 – 175 g /4–6 oz	5 cm /2 in	3–4	minutes	blue
			5½–6	minutes	rare
			7	minutes	medium
			8½	minutes	well-done
Chateaubriand (serves 2)	500 g /16 oz	4.5 cm /1¾ in	2½	minutes	blue
			3½	minutes	rare
			4–4½	minutes	medium
			6–6½	minutes	well-done
Sirloin	150–175 g /5–6 oz	20 mm /¾in	2	minutes	blue
			2½	minutes	rare
			3–3½	minutes	medium
			5–5½	minutes	well-done
Thick sirloin (serves 2)	325–350 g /11–12 oz	4 cm /1½ in	2½	minutes	blue
			3½	minutes	rare
			4–4½	minutes	medium
			6–6½	minutes	well-done
Rump	200–250 g /7–8 oz	20 mm /¾ in	2	minutes	blue
			2½	minutes	rare
			3½–4	minutes	medium
			4½–5	minutes	well-done
Thick rump (serves 2)	400–500 g /14–16 oz	3–4 cm /1¼–1½ in	3	minutes	blue
			4	minutes	rare
			7–8	minutes	medium
			9½–10	minutes	well-done
T-Bone	500 g /16 oz (weight including bone)	3 cm /1¼ in	2½–3	minutes	blue
			3½–4	minutes	rare
			7–8	minutes	medium
			9½–10	minutes	well-done

* Including initial 2 minutes at high heat on each side

a thick wad of absorbent paper dipped in oil. The grease should start smoking lightly almost immediately. Add your steak and sear it on both sides, then reduce the heat to medium and continue to cook until the meat is done to your taste. If you are using a ridged pan, rotate the steaks at different angles across the ridges to make an attractive pattern on the surface of the meat. Do this on both sides.

An important tip, don't use fat skimmed from stock or jellied roasting juices for dry frying. It is impossible to get rid of all the moisture and, if left, this is liable to spit once it heats up. Keep these fats for the steady browning of meat intended for a pot-roast or casserole, or use them as flavourings for stews and soups.

Steak chasseur

Sauce *chasseur* is another French classic. It consists of mushrooms sautéed with onions and then flavoured with white wine.

1 hour marinating, then 20 minutes

Serves 4
4 × 150–175 g /5–6 oz sirloin steaks
60 ml /4 tbls olive oil
½ garlic clove
salt and freshly ground black pepper
50 g /2 oz butter
350 g /12 oz mushrooms, sliced
1 medium-sized onion, finely chopped
150 ml /5 fl oz canned consommé
65 ml /2½ fl oz dry white wine mixed with 15 ml /1 tbls tomato purée and 5 ml /1 tsp cornflour

1 Rub the steaks with 30 ml /2 tbls oil and the garlic. Season with pepper, leave 1 hour.
2 Melt half the butter with 15 ml /1 tbls oil in a frying-pan over medium heat. Fry the steaks according to taste (see chart above).
3 Melt the remaining butter in a separate pan and add the rest of the oil. Sauté the mushrooms for 5 minutes. Add the onion, cook 1 minute.
4 Remove the steaks from the pan, season and keep warm. Add the consommé to the pan, boil to reduce by half. Add the wine mixture and boil for 1 minute. Stir in the mushrooms and onions. Return the steaks to the pan and heat through.

*an-fried sirloin steaks with herbs, with
rilled tomatoes and French fries*

Pan-fried sirloin
teaks with herbs

bringing to room temperature,
then 10–20 minutes

erves 4
sirloin steaks, 150–175 g /5–6 oz each
eshly ground black pepper
lt
5 g /1 oz butter
0 ml /2 tbls olive oil
0 ml /4 tbls hot beef stock, home-made or
  from a cube
ice of ½ lemon
5 ml /1 tbls finely chopped fresh parsley
5 ml /1 tbls finely chopped fresh chervil
hervil sprigs, to garnish

Season the steaks with freshly ground
lack pepper and then leave them to come to
oom temperature – then season them once
gain.
Heat the butter and oil in a heavy-based
rying-pan. When the butter is sizzling, put
he steaks into the pan and fry over high
eat for 2 minutes on each side. If you like
our steaks blue, they will now be ready. If
ot, lower the heat to medium and cook for
further 1½–3½ minutes each side. Transfer
he steaks to a heated serving dish.
Add the hot beef stock and the lemon
uice to the juices in the pan, stir and heat
hrough, then pour over the steaks. Sprinkle
ith the finely chopped fresh parsley and
hervil, garnish with chervil sprigs and
erve.

ournedos au
hâteau

bringing to room temperature,
then 40 minutes

erves 4
tournedos steaks, each 5 cm /2 in thick
5 ml /1 tbls green peppercorns, chopped
00 g /4 oz butter, softened
small onion, finely chopped
0 g /2 oz mushrooms, finely chopped
lt
reshly ground black pepper
5 ml /1 tbls thick cream
slices of bread, cut into rounds
0 ml /2 tbls oil

Mix the peppercorns into 50 g /2 oz of
he butter until evenly distributed. Shape
he butter into a roll between a piece of
reaseproof paper and chill in the
efrigerator until ready for use.
Heat 25 g /1 oz of the butter in a sauce-
an over low heat and cook the chopped
nion until pale and soft. Add the
nushrooms to the onions, mix well and
eason with salt and pepper. Add the cream,
tir to make a thick purée and keep warm.
Melt the rest of the butter in a frying-

pan over medium heat and fry the bread
until golden and crisp on both sides to make
croûtons. Keep warm.
4 Heat the oil in the frying-pan over
medium heat and when hot fry the steaks,
5½–6 minutes per side for rare, 7 minutes
per side for medium (see chart, *page 25*).
5 Place the croûtons on a heated serving
dish, cover each with one quarter of the
mushroom purée and put the steaks on top.
Place a generous pat of peppercorn butter on
top of each steak and serve.

Stir-fried beef with
broccoli

This Chinese-style dish can be served as
part of a Chinese meal, or try it as a
main course, served with soft noodles.

20 minutes, 30 minutes
marinating, then about 30 minutes

Serves 4
450 g /1 lb rump or skirt steak
225 g /8 oz broccoli
90 ml /6 tbls peanut oil
5 ml /1 tsp salt
4 garlic cloves, finely chopped
3 spring onions, cut into 25 mm /1 in
  sections, white and green parts reserved
  separately
15 ml /1 tbls Shaohsing wine or medium-dry
  sherry
For the marinade
1.5 ml /¼ tsp sugar
1.5 ml /¼ tsp salt
7.5 ml /1½ tsp thin soy sauce
7.5 ml /1½ tsp thick soy sauce
about 1.5 ml /¼ tsp freshly ground black
  pepper
10 ml /2 tsp Shaohsing wine or medium-dry
  sherry
7.5 ml /1½ tsp potato or tapioca flour
For the sauce
10 ml /2 tsp thick soy sauce
15–22.5 ml /1–1½ tbls oyster sauce
5 ml /1 tsp potato or tapiaco flour

1 Cut the beef across the grain into
rectangular slices about 4 cm × 25 mm /1½
× 1 in and 5 mm /¼ in thick. Put them into a
large, deep bowl.
2 Add all the marinade ingredients to the
meat. Then add 15 ml /1 tbls of water and
stir vigorously with chopsticks or a fork to
coat the beef thoroughly.
3 Refrigerate for 30 minutes, stirring the
ingredients once during this time.
4 Meanwhile, peel and discard the hard
outer layer of the broccoli stems. Then cut
the broccoli into large, bite-sized pieces.
5 Mix the sauce ingredients with 90 ml /6
tbls water and reserve.
6 Bring plenty of water to the boil in a
saucepan. Add 15 ml /1 tbls of the oil and
the salt. Add the broccoli, return to the boil,
then continue to boil for about 3 minutes.
Drain, then cool under cold water and drain.
7 Heat the remaining oil in a wok or a
large, heavy-bottomed frying-pan over high
heat until a wisp of smoke rises. Add the
garlic and white parts of the spring onions

and stir several times with a wok scoop or
metal spatula. Add the beef and flip and toss
for 1–1½ minutes.
8 Pour in the wine or sherry and continue
to stir. When the sizzling subsides and the
beef is still underdone, transfer it to a warm
plate, draining well.
9 Add the green part of the spring onion
and the broccoli and stir until they are hot,
lowering the heat if necessary. Push the
broccoli around the sides of your wok or
frying-pan and pour the sauce into the
centre, stirring well once. As soon as the
sauce bubbles, return the beef to the wok or
frying-pan and stir everything together until
it is piping hot. Transfer the stir-fried beef
with broccoli to a warm serving plate and
serve immediately.

Pan-fried steaks in
beer

1 hour marinating,
then 25 minutes

Serves 4
2 thick sirloin steaks, 325–350 g /11–12 oz
  each
30 ml /2 tbls olive oil
1 garlic clove, finely chopped
salt
freshly ground black pepper
50 g /2 oz butter
For the sauce
350 g /12 oz small, white button
  mushrooms, sliced
40 g /1½ oz butter
15 ml /1 tbls lemon juice
15 ml /1 tbls flour
150 ml /5 fl oz lager
5–10 ml /1–2 tsp soy sauce

1 Cut the steaks in half and brush them
with the olive oil. Then sprinkle them with
half the finely chopped garlic, the salt and
the freshly ground black pepper to taste.
Allow the steaks to absorb these flavours for
1 hour.
2 To prepare the sauce, sauté the sliced
button mushrooms in 40 g /1½ oz butter and
the lemon juice for about 5 minutes, or until
tender. Add the flour and stir for 1 minute
until well blended; then pour in the lager
and bring the mixture to the boil.
3 Boil the sauce for 1 minute. Add the soy
sauce, and the remaining chopped garlic,
and season to taste with more freshly ground
black pepper. Keep warm.
4 Melt the 50 g /2 oz butter in a frying-pan
and fry the steaks on each side 2½ minutes
for blue, 3½ minutes for rare, 4–4½ minutes
for medium and 6–6½ minutes for well-done.
5 Either place the steaks on a heated
serving dish or leave them in the frying-pan
and then cut the meat diagonally into 25
mm /1 in wide strips. Pour the bubbling
mushroom and beer sauce over the meat and
serve as soon as possible.

● It is important to use small, white button
mushrooms rather than the larger, open
caps as these tend to discolour the sauce too
much with their dark juices.

Serves 4
500 g /1 lb rump steak
45 ml /3 tbls flour
salt
75 g /3 oz butter
100 g /4 oz onion, finely chopped
75 g /3 oz white button mushrooms, thinly
* sliced*
15 ml /1 tbls tomato purée
275 ml /10 fl oz beef stock, home-made or
* from a cube*
150 ml /5 fl oz soured cream
15 ml /1 tbls dry sherry
freshly ground black pepper
boiled rice, to serve

1   Pound the meat out thinly and cut diagonally across the grain into neat strip about 5 mm × 5 cm /¼ × 2 in, discardin any fat.

2   Combine 15 ml /1 tbls flour with 2.5 m /½ tsp salt in a polythene bag. Add the mea close the bag and shake until the strips a coated with the flour. Turn them out an shake off any excess flour.

3   Melt half the butter in a large, dee frying-pan or sauté pan. When very hot, ad the beef and brown rapidly on all sides – th strips should remain juicy and pink on th inside. Remove the beef from the pan an keep it hot.

4   In the same fat, sauté the onion unt soft and golden. Add 15 g /½ oz butter an the mushrooms, and continue to sauté, sti ring, for about 3–4 minutes, until tende Remove the onions and mushrooms from th pan and keep hot with the beef strips.

5   Add the remaining butter to the pa and, when melted, stir in the remainin flour. Cook over a low heat for about minutes, stirring.

6   Add the tomato purée and beef stock t the pan and bring to the boil slowly, stirrin until the sauce is smooth. Then continue t simmer for about 2–3 minutes, stirrin occasionally, until the sauce is thick.

7   Fold in the meat strips, onions an mushrooms. Stir in most of the soure cream and the sherry. Adjust the seasonin adding freshly ground black pepper an more salt if necessary. Reheat briefly, but d not allow to boil, garnish with the remainin soured cream and serve with boiled rice.

Stir-fried beef with corn

🥢 bringing to room temperature, then 20 minutes

Serves 4–6
500 g /1 lb rump steak, thinly sliced
15 ml /1 tbls dry sherry
15 ml /1 tbls soy sauce
7.5 ml /1½ tsp cornflour
15 ml /1 tbls peanut oil
1 small onion, quartered
125 g /4 oz mange-tout
5 ml /1 tsp salt
400 g /14 oz canned miniature corn cobs,
* rinsed and drained*
400 g /14 oz canned straw mushrooms,
* drained*
10 ml /2 tsp sugar
plain boiled noodles, to serve (optional)

1   In a bowl, blend the sherry and soy sauce into the cornflour. Add the beef and then

Stir-fried beef with corn

turn it so that is is thoroughly coated.

2   Heat the oil in a wok or frying-pan. Fry the onion for 2 minutes over a high heat. Remove the beef from the cornflour mixture with a slotted spoon, reserving the liquid. Add the beef to the wok or frying-pan and stir-fry until lightly browned. Add the mange-tout and the salt and stir-fry for another 30 seconds.

3   Add the miniature corn cobs and the straw mushrooms and stir-fry for 1 minute. Add the sugar to the pan and blend.

4   Blend the remaining cornflour liquid with 10 ml /2 tsp cold water and stir it into the pan. Cook for another minute until thickened. Serve as part of a Chinese meal, or pile the stir-fried beef and vegetables onto plain, boiled noodles.

Beef stroganoff

🍴🍴 bringing to room temperature, then 50 minutes

Dry-fried tournedos with mushrooms

🍴 bringing to room temperature, then 20–30 minutes

Serves 4
4 tournedos steaks, 125–175 g /4–6 oz each
salt and freshly ground black pepper
olive oil
butter
150 g /5 oz button mushrooms, finely
* chopped*
2 small shallots, finely chopped
300 ml /10 fl oz dry white wine
5 ml /1 tsp dried chervil
a pinch of dried tarragon
½ beef stock cube, crumbled
10 ml /2 tsp finely chopped fresh parsley

Season the tournedos with freshly ground black pepper and leave them to come to room temperature. Just before cooking, season them again with salt and freshly ground black pepper.

Heat a heavy-based frying-pan until a drop of water shaken onto the surface sizzles and bounces on contact. Wipe the pan quickly with a wad of absorbent paper dipped in olive oil.

Put the tournedos in the pan; dry fry over high heat for 2 minutes on each side. Then reduce the heat to medium and fry for a further 1½–4½ minutes each side, until done to your taste (see chart *page 25*). After about 3 minutes, pour off the pan juices and reserve. Transfer the steaks to a heated serving dish and keep warm.

Melt 25 g /1 oz butter in the same pan and fry the finely chopped mushrooms and shallots for 2–3 minutes. Add the dry white wine, dried chervil and tarragon and crumbled beef stock cube, together with the reserved pan juices. Continue to cook over moderate heat so that the mushrooms and shallots have softened by the time the liquid has reduced by about half.

Stir a further small nut of butter into the pan, together with the finely chopped parsley. Season with salt and freshly ground black pepper to taste, and add any juices that may have collected around the tournedos. When the butter has melted, pour the sauce over the tournedos and serve.

Bitoks à la russe

bringing to room temperature,
then 45 minutes

Serves 4
500 g /1 lb lean minced beef
100 g /4 oz fresh white breadcrumbs
45–60 ml /3–4 tbls milk
100 g /4 oz butter, softened
large pinch of paprika
salt and freshly ground black pepper
30 ml /2 tbls flour
1 egg
30 ml /2 tbls olive oil
1 large Spanish onion, finely chopped
For the sauce
60 ml /4 tbls beef stock, home-made or from
a cube
45 ml /3 tbls soured cream
15 g /½ oz butter

Soak half the breadcrumbs in the milk for 5 minutes. Drain and squeeze out any excess milk.

In a large bowl combine the soaked breadcrumbs with the minced beef, 50 g /2 oz of the butter and the paprika. Season with salt and freshly ground black pepper and blend with a wooden spoon. Divide the mixture into 4 balls.

Put the flour in a shallow dish and season with salt and freshly ground black pepper. Beat the egg lightly in a shallow dish and put the remaining breadcrumbs in another shallow dish.

Flatten the meat balls into patties. Toss in the flour, shaking off any excess. Dip in the egg and toss in the breadcrumbs, firmly patting the coating on the meat patties.
5   In a large frying-pan heat 15 ml /1 tbls olive oil with 25 g /1 oz butter and sauté the patties slowly for 5–7 minutes on each side, or until golden brown and just cooked through. Transfer to a heated serving platter and keep warm.
6   Meanwhile, in a small frying-pan heat the remaining butter and oil and sauté the finely chopped onion until soft and a deep golden colour. Remove with a slotted spoon and keep warm.
7   To make the sauce, drain off any excess fat from the pan in which the patties were cooked and pour in the beef stock. Bring to the boil, scraping the sides and bottom of the pan with a wooden spoon to dislodge any crusty bits. Stir in the soured cream and reheat without boiling, then remove from the heat. Finally, beat in the butter, a small piece at a time.
8   Garnish each patty with onion, pour the cream sauce over and serve.

Peppered steaks

This is a favourite way of cooking steak together with a small amount of rich, creamy sauce.

bringing to room temperature,
then 30 minutes

Serves 4
*4 fillet steaks, each about 175 g /6 oz and
cut about 4 cm /1½ in thick*
15 ml /1 tbls black peppercorns
15 ml /1 tbls olive oil
25 g /1 oz butter
30 ml /2 tbls brandy
150 ml /5 fl oz dry white wine
30 ml /2 tbls thick cream
parsley sprigs, to garnish
chicory, to garnish

1   Crush the peppercorns coarsely in a mortar or grind them in a coffee grinder until just broken up.
2   Coat the steaks with the crushed pepper.
3   Heat the oil and butter in a frying-pan. When it is sizzling, add the steaks. Fry them on each side for 4 minutes for rare, 7–8 minutes for medium, 9½–10 minutes for well-done. Transfer the steaks to a heated serving platter and keep warm.
4   Pour the brandy into the frying-pan and set it alight. When the flames subside, add the white wine. Cook for about 1 minute to heat the wine, then stir in the cream. Stir for a few seconds over the heat but do not let it boil.
5   Remove the sauce from the heat and pour over the peppered steaks. Garnish with the parsley sprigs and chicory.

Peppered steaks

CASSEROLING & POT-ROASTING BEEF

Beef casseroles, pot-roasts and braises offer excellent opportunities for the cook to create individual masterpieces, and these methods can make less expensive cuts meltingly tender, flavoursome and aromatic.

Casseroling, pot-roasting and braising are wonderfully easy ways to make even the least desirable cuts of meat taste delicious.

Essentially similar, these three methods all involve lengthy, slow cooking in a covered pot, either on top of the stove or in the oven. In casseroles – or stews – the meat is cut into evenly-sized pieces, while in pot-roasting and braising the meat is left whole, then sliced to serve. Braising recipes usually require slightly more liquid than those for pot-roasting, in which the moisture from the meat provides most of the liquid for cooking.

Choosing the meat
Use these methods to cook any cuts of beef that you wouldn't risk roasting – the long, slow cooking will tenderize the toughest of meats. It goes without saying that most roasting and grilling cuts will make superb casseroles, but there are a few exceptions. Paradoxically, some prime cuts, such as fillet or sirloin, do not take kindly to the long slow cooking you need to blend the flavours and produce a rich sauce, and they may disintegrate in the process. The best cuts of beef to casserole are chuck and blade. The top part of the shin and flank are also very tasty but need much longer cooking. I generally find that if I ask for 'braising steak' rather than specifically for chuck or blade, the meat requires longer cooking to make it tender.

For pot-roasting and braising, look for topside or top rump; ask the butcher to trim the fat well before rolling it. These joints are best boned and rolled and tied securely with string before cooking to hold them in shape.

The cooking pot
Give some thoughts to the pot you are going to use. For casseroles, pot-roasts and braises cooked on top of the stove you can use a flameproof casserole or a heavy-based saucepan; for cooking in the oven the casserole need only be ovenproof. It should have a heavy base and tightly fitting lid, so that no steam can escape. Do not choose one that is too large or the liquid will be dissipated over the surface of the pan and will boil away.

If you do not have a flameproof casserole, brown the meat in a frying-pan and transfer it to an ordinary ovenproof casserole for the final cooking. But be sure to boil the cooking liquid in the frying-pan, scraping the bottom and sides of the pan thoroughly.

Preparing the meat
For casseroles, cut boneless beef into 25 mm–4 cm /1–1½ in cubes. It pays to take your time over this, making the cubes all the same size as far as possible so that they will cook evenly. Cut out any gristle and fat as you go along.

Bring the meat to room temperature, and make sure it is thoroughly dry. If necessary

dry it on absorbent paper. If the meat is wet it will steam in the pan and not brown properly when you fry it. If the recipe tells you to dust the meat with flour, do so only at the last moment – the flour seems to draw out moisture and make the meat damp and tacky if left for too long.

The flavour of the meat can be improved by marinating it for a few hours or overnight with wine, oil and herbs, which may then also be used in the cooking. After marinating, drain the meat well and pat it dry with absorbent paper before flouring it and proceeding with the recipe.

Browning the meat
The flavour and colour of any casserole, are greatly improved if the meat and vegetables are first browned in fat. You have a wide choice of fats. Fresh beef dripping is suitable: if the joint is a fatty one, trim off some of the fat and render it down in a frying-pan. Discard the crisp remains of skin and use the liquid fat to brown the meat. Bacon fat is also tasty. Oil gives a good even browning with no obtrusive flavour. Butter used on its own will burn but a mixture of butter and olive oil, my favourite fat, gives the best of both worlds – a buttery flavour with little danger of burning.

Heat the fat in a flameproof casserole or heavy frying-pan. When the butter has foamed and then subsided add the joint or, for casseroles, a small batch of meat cubes and brown thoroughly on all sides. Don't overcrowd the pan, or the steam released by the meat will not be able to escape, and before you know where you are the meat will be simmering in its own juices. Once it does this, nothing will make it brown.

Control the heat under the pan carefully so that the meat browns steadily and thoroughly. If the pan becomes too hot the meat will burn and give the casserole a bitter taste.

When the meat is browned, remove it from the casserole and add any flavouring vegetables and brown these, stirring them occasionally so that they colour evenly. If the recipe tells you to soften onions without colouring them, do so with the heat turned right down.

Flavouring vegetables can also be added to a pot-roast or braise; these are usually browned in the same fat, although they can also be added raw. Remove the meat from the pan while you brown the vegetables to avoid overcrowding.

Traditionally the vegetables for a braise are made into a *mirepoix* – all evenly diced to the same size and browned well in the dripping. The vegetables then form a bed on which the meat rests while it is cooking. Other flavourings such as diced fat salt pork, streaky bacon and herbs can be included according to taste.

Cold-start cooking
For the cheaper, less tender cuts of meat, t[he] cold-start method of casseroling, po[t-] roasting and braising may be preferabl[e] Any initial browning of the meat will on[ly] further toughen it by causing the muscles [to] contract. Put the uncooked meat an[d] vegetables in a casserole and cover wit[h] water or stock, bring slowly to the boil an[d] cook at a very low simmer until the meat [is] tender. This can be done on the top of t[he] cooker or in the oven. The sauce from th[is] method of cooking is usually serve[d] unthickened: see recipe for Beef braised wit[h] carrots.

Adding liquid to the casserole
If your casserole is cooked under a tight[ly] fitting lid very little liquid will be lost due [to] evaporation. If anything it will be increase[d] by the juices released by the meat itself.

The long, gentle cooking will develo[p]

vours, blending them and transforming the liquid into a rich sauce. However, the quality and flavour of the sauce will inevitably be closely related to the quality of the liquid that you put into it at the start. Use a good rich, brown stock and, if wine is included, don't assume that you can cook with something you could not drink.

The sediment and morsels that remain in the pan after browning your meat and vegetables hold the very essence of their flavours, so make sure that these are blended into your casserole. Remove the browned meat and vegetables from the pan, add a little liquid from the recipe and scrape the bottom and sides clean with a wooden spoon. Add the remaining liquid and return the pan to the heat. Bring to the boil and let it reduce a little before returning the meat and vegetables to the pan. If the recipe contains little liquid, deglaze the pan with 45–60 ml / 3–4 tbls water and pour over the meat.

Cooking a casserole

More casseroles are ruined by excessive heat than by anything else. Throughout its cooking time, it should be kept to a faint, barely perceptible simmer.

When cooking on top of the stove, an asbestos or wire heat diffuser will certainly help but you must still watch it like a hawk. Oven cooking is more convenient. A setting of 150C /300F /gas 2 or 170C /325F /gas 3 is usually about right but oven thermostats vary, so still check the casserole and turn the oven temperature down if it is bubbling too hard.

To finish a casserole

When your casserole is cooked, your sauce may need thickening. If this is to involve simmering or boiling remove the meat first, and skim the sauce of any surface fat.

The simplest method of thickening is by reduction. This method can always be used provided the casserole has not been too highly seasoned and already has some thickening – such as a dusting of flour before the meat was sautéed. Boil the sauce briskly, stirring constantly to stimulate evaporation.

Another classic thickening agent is *beurre manié*. This is made by combining equal volumes of butter and flour in a small bowl and mashing them to a smooth paste. Take up tiny pieces of this paste on your spoon and stir them into the simmering sauce. Because of its high butter content the paste will have no difficulty in dissolving without giving the flour a chance to form lumps. Bring the sauce to the boil and simmer for 3–4 minutes to ensure the flour is cooked. Once you have finished your sauce, all that remains to be done is to correct the seasoning, return the meat to the sauce and make sure it is thoroughly hot again.

Beef Marseilles

Beef Marseilles is a deliciously tasty beef casserole, made with typically Mediterranean ingredients such as black olives, orange zest and red wine.

45 minutes,
then 2¾ hours cooking

Serves 6
1.4 kg /3 lb braising or stewing steak, cut
   into 5 cm /2 in cubes
30 ml /2 tbls olive oil
salt and freshly ground black pepper
2 medium-sized onions, sliced
2 garlic cloves, crushed
600 ml /1 pt red wine
2 large strips orange zest
bouquet garni
bay leaf
175 g /6 oz black olives, stoned
100 g /4 oz mushrooms, quartered
15 ml /1 tbls flour
25 g /1 oz butter
15 ml /1 tbls freshly chopped parsley
flat leaved parsley, to garnish
For the croûtons
25 g /1 oz butter
1 slice of white bread, crusts removed, cut
   into 4 triangles

1 Heat the oven to 170C /325 F /gas 3. Heat the olive oil in a frying-pan and fry the meat in the oil in batches until browned on all sides. With a slotted spoon, transfer the meat to an ovenproof casserole and season with salt and pepper to taste.
2 Sauté the onions in the oil remaining in the frying-pan until golden. Add the garlic and cook for a further minute. Add the onions and garlic to the casserole, then add the red wine, orange zest, bouquet garni and bay leaf.
3 Cover the casserole and cook in the oven for 2½ hours. Remove the orange zest, bouquet garni and bay leaf from the casserole, then stir in the olives and mushrooms. Blend the flour and butter together to make a *beurre manié* and stir into the casserole. Return the casserole to the oven for 15 minutes.
4 Make the croûtons: melt the butter in a frying-pan over a medium heat and fry the triangles of bread until golden on both sides.
5 Serve the casserole sprinkled with chopped parsley, accompanied by the croûtons and garnished with flat leaved parsley.

Beef Marseilles

Yankee pot-roast

Portuguese pot-roast

overnight marinating,
then 3¼–3¾hours

Serves 6–8
1.6–1.8 kg /3½–4 lb topside or silverside of beef, rolled
425 ml /15 fl oz red wine
juice of ½ lemon
60 ml /4 tbls olive oil
2 garlic cloves, finely chopped
5 ml /1 tsp paprika
2 bay leaves
2 cloves
12 black peppercorns
salt and freshly ground black pepper
1 beef stock cube, crumbled
30 ml /2 tbls tomato purée
beurre manié made by mashing together 15 g /½ oz butter and 15 ml /1 tbls flour

1 In a large bowl, combine the red wine, lemon juice and 30 ml /2 tbls olive oil and flavour with the garlic, paprika, bay leaves, cloves and black peppercorns. Add the beef and turn to coat. Cover and leave in the refrigerator to marinate overnight.
2 Remove the meat from the refrigerator and bring to room temperature in the marinade. Drain and pat dry with absorbent paper, reserving the marinade.
3 Heat the oven to 150C /300F /gas 2. Season the meat with salt and freshly ground black pepper. Heat the remaining olive oil in a large, flameproof casserole and brown the meat on all sides.
4 Remove the meat and add the reserved marinade, together with the crumbled stock cube and tomato purée; bring to the boil, add the meat, cover and cook in the oven for 2½–3 hours or until tender.
5 Transfer the meat to a heated dish and remove the string. Keep warm and boil sauce for 5 minutes until reduced by a third.
6 Strain the reduced sauce into a saucepan, bring to the boil and gradually whisk in the *beurre manié*. Boil for another 3–4 minutes, stirring, until thick. Season to taste.
7 To serve, slice the beef thinly and lay the slices on a heated serving dish. Spoon a little sauce over the sliced meat and pour the remaining sauce into a warmed sauce-boat.

Italian braised beef

Potato croquettes and boiled haricot beans make good accompaniments to this dish known as *stracotto di manzo* in Italian.

30 minutes,
then about 3 hours cooking

Serves 6
1.5 kg /3¼ lb top rump
45 ml /3 tbls olive oil
25 g /1 oz ham or bacon fat, finely chopped
2 medium-sized carrots, finely chopped
1 celery stalk, finely chopped
1 garlic clove, finely chopped
300 ml /10 fl oz red wine
bay leaf
400 g /14 oz canned tomatoes
salt and freshly ground black pepper
freshly chopped parsley, to garnish

1 Heat the oven to 170C /325F /gas 3. T the joint into a compact shape.
2 Heat the olive oil in a deep flamepro casserole into which the joint will fit fair tightly. When the oil is hot, fry the me briskly, turning, to seal all surface Transfer to a plate.
3 Add the ham or bacon fat, onio carrots, celery and garlic to the pan and f over moderate heat, stirring frequently, f 5 minutes or until slightly coloured.
4 Add the wine, bay leaf and the tomato and their juice. Bring to the boil and allo to bubble for a minute or so. Season wi salt and pepper, return the meat to t casserole and cover tightly. (If necessar line the lid with foil to improve the seal.)
5 Transfer the casserole to the centre the oven and cook for 3 hours or until ve tender, turning the meat halfway throug the cooking time.
6 Remove the meat from the casserol slice thickly and arrange on a warm serving platter. Keep warm.
7 Remove the bay leaf from the cassero and purée the remaining vegetables ar juices in a blender or by pressing through sieve. Reheat, skim off any surplus fa check the seasoning and pour over the slice meat. Garnish with freshly chopped parsl and serve.

Yankee pot-roast

45 minutes,
then 2¾–3¼ hours cooking

Serves 6
1.4 kg /3 lb piece of boneless lean brisket or chuck steak
25 g /1 oz lard
30 ml /2 tbls olive oil
275 ml /10 fl oz beef stock, home-made or from a cube
400 g /14 oz canned tomatoes
4 large carrots, quartered
2 Spanish onions, quartered
1 large turnip, quartered
4 whole cloves
2 allspice berries or 1.5 ml /¼ tsp ground allspice
15 ml /1 tbls soy sauce
2 bay leaves
salt and freshly ground black pepper
freshly grated nutmeg
150 ml /5 fl oz red wine
sprig of parsley, to garnish
For the vegetable garnish
6 small carrots, cut into 5 cm /2 in pieces
2 button onions
3 small turnips, quartered
a little beef stock
4–6 small potatoes
For the beurre manié
25 g /1 oz butter
30 ml /2 tbls flour

1 Heat the lard and olive oil in flameproof casserole, add the meat an brown it on all sides over a high heat. Pou off the excess fat. Add the beef stock an canned tomatoes with their juice and brin to the boil. Skim, then reduce the heat. Ad the carrots, onions, turnips, cloves, allspice

y sauce, bay leaves and salt, black pepper
d freshly grated nutmeg to taste.

Cover the casserole tightly and cook over
very low heat for 2½–3 hours, or until the
:at is tender, turning the meat over once.

Meanwhile, put the red wine in a small
n and boil over a high heat until it is
duced to 60–90 ml /4–6 tbls.

Thirty minutes before serving time,
epare the vegetable garnish. Poach the
epared carrots, onions and turnips in a
tle beef stock, or stock and water, until
st tender. Boil the potatoes.

Using a slotted spoon, transfer the meat
a heated serving dish and garnish with the
eshly cooked vegetables.

Make the *beurre manié* by mashing
gether the butter and flour until smooth.
im the fat from the sauce in the casserole
th a slotted spoon, then strain the sauce
to a small saucepan. Cook over a high heat
til bubbling, then thicken by adding the
urre manié a little at a time.

Add the reduced wine and more salt,
eshly ground black pepper and freshly
ated nutmeg, if necessary. Spoon a little
uce over the meat and vegetables and
rnish with a sprig of parsley. Serve the
st of the sauce in a heated sauce-boat.

alian braised beef

Beef olives

🔪🔪 1 hour,
then 1¼–1½ hours

Serves 6
1 kg /2¼ lb topside of beef
salt and freshly ground black pepper
125 g /4 oz fresh white breadcrumbs
50 g /2 oz shredded suet
60 ml /4 tbls finely chopped fresh parsley
5 ml /1 tsp dried thyme or marjoram
5 ml /1 tsp finely grated lemon zest
freshly grated nutmeg
2 eggs, beaten
25 g /1 oz butter
30 ml /2 tbls olive oil
1 medium-sized onion, finely chopped
125 g /4 oz mushrooms, finely chopped
425 ml /15 fl oz beef stock, home-made or
from a cube
beurre manié made by mashing together
15 g /½ oz butter and 15 ml /1 tbls flour

1 Cut the beef into 6 thin slices and beat
each slice between cling film with a wooden
rolling pin to flatten and tenderize the meat.
Cut each piece in half across, to give 12
slices. Season the slices generously.
2 For the stuffing, mix the breadcrumbs

with the suet, chopped parsley, dried thyme
or marjoram, grated lemon zest, and
nutmeg, salt and black pepper to taste. Add
the beaten eggs and mix well.
3 Spread each slice of meat with stuffing.
Tuck the long edges in slightly to neaten,
and roll the slice up from a short edge. Tie
securely with fine string.
4 Heat half of the butter and olive oil in a
large, flameproof casserole. Sauté the finely
chopped onion for 5–7 minutes. Add the
mushrooms and sauté for a further 3–4
minutes. Remove and keep warm.
5 Heat the remaining butter and olive oil
in the casserole. Put in as many beef olives
as will fit in 1 layer and cook, turning frequently, until browned. Remove and brown
the rest of the beef olives.
6 Return all the beef olives to the casserole
with the sautéed onion and mushrooms.
Pour over the beef stock, bring to the boil,
then reduce the heat, cover and simmer
gently for 1¼–1½ hours, until tender.
7 Remove the beef olives from the
casserole and cut off the strings. Arrange
them, side by side, in a heated serving dish.
Add the *beurre manié* to the liquid in the
casserole in tiny pieces, whisking vigorously.
Bring to the boil and simmer for 3 minutes,
until thickened. Correct the seasoning and
pour the sauce over the beef olives.

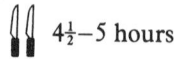

Boeuf à la bourguignonne

🔪🔪🔪 2½–3 hours

Serves 4

900 g /2 lb blade beef, cut into 25 mm /1 in
  cubes
45 ml /3 tbls olive oil
75 g /3 oz butter
225 g /8 oz green bacon, diced
60 ml /4 tbls flour
salt and freshly ground black pepper
60 ml /4 tbls cognac
2 medium-sized carrots, chopped
1 medium-sized leek, chopped
4 shallots, chopped
1 Spanish onion, chopped
1 garlic clove, finely chopped
1 calf's foot, split or 225 g /8 oz piece of fat
  salt pork
bouquet garni
300 ml /10 fl oz red burgundy
150 ml /5 fl oz beef stock, home-made or
  from a cube
15 ml /1 tbls sugar
18 button onions
juice of ½ lemon
175 g /6 oz button mushrooms, stalks
  removed
15 ml /1 tbls finely chopped fresh parsley

1   Heat the oven to 170C /325F /gas 3.
2   Heat 30 ml /2 tbls olive oil and 25 g /1
oz butter in a flameproof casserole and sauté

Boeuf à la bourguignonne

the bacon. Remove, with a slotted spoon.
3   Season the flour with salt and pepper
and use to coat the beef. Add the beef to the
casserole and sauté in batches until browned
on all sides. Return all the cooked beef to the
casserole.
4   Heat the cognac in a ladle, ignite and
pour over the meat. When the flames die
out, remove the meat from the casserole
again with a slotted spoon.
5   Add the chopped carrots, leek, shallots,
onion and finely chopped garlic to the fat
remaining in the casserole. Sauté over a high
heat for 15 minutes, stirring occasionally,
until the vegetables are browned all over.
6   Pour off any excess fat and add the calf's
foot or fat salt pork, bouquet garni, red wine
and beef stock. Season with salt and pepper
and bring to the boil. Return the beef and
bacon to the casserole, cover and cook in the
oven for 1½ hours.
7   Fifteen minutes before the beef is
cooked, heat 25 g /1 oz butter and 15 ml /1
tbls sugar in a frying-pan. Add the whole
button onions and sauté for 12–15 minutes,
shaking the pan frequently until the onions
are glazed and evenly cooked through.
8   In a separate pan heat the remaining
butter and oil with the lemon juice and sauté
the mushrooms caps for 5 minutes over a low
heat, stirring occasionally.
9   Remove the calf's foot or fat salt pork
and bouquet garni, correct the seasoning
and add the plazed onions and mushrooms.
Sprinkle with chopped parsley and serve
immediately.

Jamaican beef casserole

🔪🔪 4½–5 hours

Serves 4–6

1.1 kg /2½ lb braising steak, cut into 25 mm
  /1 in cubes
60 ml /4 tbls flour
salt and freshly ground black pepper
25 g /1 oz butter
30 ml /2 tbls olive oil
2 Spanish onion, thinly sliced
3 green chillies, seeded and finely chopped
1 garlic clove, chopped
5 ml /1 tsp ground ginger
400 g /14 oz canned tomatoes
2.5 ml /½ tsp dried thyme
1 green pepper, seeded and sliced

1   In a large bowl, season the flour with sa
and pepper. Add the meat and coa
thoroughly with the seasoned flour.
2   In a flameproof casserole heat the butt
and olive oil. When foaming subsides, ad
the beef and sauté in batches until golde
brown on all sides. Remove from the pa
with a slotted spoon.
3   Add the onion, chilli, garlic and ging
to the casserole. Fry, stirring occasionall
until the onions are soft but not brown.
4   Add the tomatoes with their juice an
the thyme. Season with salt. Bring to th
boil, stir, return the meat to the casserol
cover and simmer very gently for 3½ hours.

Add the sliced green pepper and cook the [cas]serole for a further 30–60 minutes, or [un]til the meat is very tender. Correct the [sea]soning, if necessary, and serve from the [cas]serole.

[B]eef Biriani

2 hours

[Se]rves 6–8
[45]0 g /1 lb good quality braising steak, cut
  into 4 cm /1½ in cubes
[2 c]ardamom pods
[2 l]arge black cardamom pods
[4 c]loves
[8 black peppercorns
[3 m]edium-sized onions
[5 c]m /2 in piece of fresh root ginger
[60 ml /4 tbls margarine
[2 b]ay leaves
[sa]lt
[5 m]l /1 tsp cinnamon
[45]0 g /1 lb basmati rice
[10–15 ml /2–3 tsp sugar
[2.]5 ml /½ tsp cumin seeds
[pin]ch of saffron strands
[30 ml /2 tbls boiling water
[1–]2 drops cochineal or red food colouring

[1] Crush 2 of the cardamom pods, the [bl]ack cardamom pods, 2 of the cloves and 5 [of] the peppercorns in a mortar and pestle. [Fi]nely grate 1 onion and half the ginger.
[2] Heat 15 ml /1 tbls of the margarine in a [la]rge pan over low heat and stir in the [cr]ushed spices, one of the bay leaves and the [gr]ated onion and ginger; continue stirring [fo]r 3 minutes.
[3] Add the meat to the pan, season with salt [an]d stir continuously until the meat juices [ha]ve evaporated. Add 600 ml /1 pt water to [th]e pan, raise the heat and simmer until the [m]eat is cooked, about 1 hour. Drain the [m]eat, reserving the liquid.
[4] Crush the remaining cardamom pods [an]d cloves with the cinnamon using a [m]ortar and pestle. Halve 1 onion lengthways [an]d slice the halves lengthways. Chop the [re]st of the onions and the ginger. Wash the [ri]ce and soak it in cold water for 10 minutes.
[5] Meanwhile, brown the onion slices in 30 [m]l /2 tbls of the margarine in a large sauce-[pa]n over medium heat for 10 minutes or [un]til crisp. Remove with a slotted spoon.
[6] Add the chopped onion, ginger, ground [sp]ices and remaining bay leaf to the fat [re]maining in the saucepan. Stir together and [co]ok over a medium heat until the onion is [li]ghtly golden, then add the strained rice. [St]ir for 3 minutes, then add the reserved [st]ock, the sugar and salt to taste. If [ne]cessary, add water to make the liquid [co]ver the rice by at least 4 cm/1½ in.
[7] Bring to the boil, cover the pan tightly, [re]duce the heat and simmer. When the rice [is] half-cooked, about 10 minutes, add the [re]served meat. Continue cooking, covered, [on] very low heat until all the liquid has been [ab]sorbed, about 20 minutes.
[8] Meanwhile heat the remaining [m]argarine in a small shallow pan over [m]edium heat until it sizzles. Add the cumin

seeds and the rest of the peppercorns, stir together then stir into the rice.
9   Soak the saffron strands in the boiling water for 1 minute and add the cochineal or food colouring to 15 ml /1 tbls water.
10   Pour the saffron with its water and the cochineal-coloured water over the rice in 2 separate areas of the pan with white rice in between. Carefully mix the coloured areas together with two forks for a mixture of pink, yellow and white. Scatter the browned onion slices over the rice mixture and serve.

Skillet stew

🍴 1 hour 30 minutes

Serves 4–6
450 g /1 lb minced beef
½ large onion, finely chopped
1 garlic clove, finely chopped
30 ml /2 tbls freshly grated
  Parmesan cheese
4 slices white bread, crusts removed
60 ml /4 tbls milk
2 medium-sized eggs, beaten
salt
freshly ground black pepper
60–90 ml /4–6 tbls olive oil
1 Spanish onion, sliced
1 green pepper, sliced
1 large carrot, sliced
1 celery stalk, sliced
150 ml /5 fl oz dry white wine

For the tomato sauce
15 ml /1 tbls olive oil
30 ml /2 tbls finely chopped onion
1 garlic clove, finely chopped
400 g /14 oz canned tomatoes
1.5 ml /¼ tsp dried basil
5 ml /1 tsp tomato purée
salt and freshly ground black pepper

1   Make the tomato sauce. Sauté the onion and garlic in the olive oil until the onion is soft. Add the tomatoes and their juice, basil and tomato purée, and season with salt and pepper. Simmer, uncovered, for 30 minutes, stirring and mashing with a wooden spoon. Purée, adjust the seasoning and reserve.
2   In a bowl, mix together the minced beef, chopped onion, garlic and Parmesan cheese.
3   Soak the bread slices in the milk, then squeeze dry and shred the bread into the beef mixture. Add the beaten eggs and mix well. Season generously.
4   Form the meat mixture into 24–36 balls. In a wide, flameproof casserole, heat the oil and sauté the meat balls in batches, adding more oil as needed and turning them until browned. Reserve the meat balls.
5   Away from the heat, stir 60 ml /4 tbls water into the juices in the pan. Return the pan to the heat and add the sliced vegetables. Simmer for 5–10 minutes, add the meat balls and heat through.
6   Pour in the tomato sauce and white wine and simmer for 30 minutes, and serve.

Skillet stew

Beef stew with parsley dumplings

Beef stew with parsley dumplings mak
a hearty, warming meal for the family.

 2½ hours

Serves 4–6
1.4kg /3 lb beef chuck or good quality
braising steak
45 ml /3 tbls seasoned flour
25 g /1 oz butter
30 ml /2 tbls olive oil
575 ml /1 pt beef stock, home-made or fro
a cube
salt
freshly ground black pepper
12 button onions
12 small carrots
60 ml /4 tbls beurre manié made by mashi
together 25 g /1 oz butter and 30 ml /
2 tbls flour
For the parsley dumplings
125 g /4 oz flour, sifted
10 ml /2 tsp baking powder
2.5 ml /½ tsp salt
25 g /1 oz butter
1 small egg, beaten
30 ml /2 tbls finely chopped fresh parsley
125 ml /4 fl oz milk

1   Cut the meat into 5 cm /2 piec
discarding most of the fat and all of t
gristle. Toss each piece in seasoned flour a
shake off the excess.
2   In a large heavy-based flamepro
casserole, heat the butter and olive oil. Sau
the meat on all sides until lightly browne
Blot the surface fat from the casserole wi
absorbent paper. Pour in the beef stock a
bring to the boil. Season, cover and simm
gently for 1¼ hours.
3   Add the button onions and carrots to t
casserole, cover, simmer for 30 minutes.
4   Meanwhile, prepare the parsley dum
lings. In a bowl combine the sifted flou
baking powder and the salt. Cut in t
butter and rub in until the mixtu
resembles breadcrumbs. In another bow
combine the beaten egg, chopped parsl
and milk. Add enough of this mixture to t
flour mixture to make a soft dough.
5   Drop tablespoons of the dumpling batt
into the stock round the meat a
vegetables. Cover the casserole and simm
very gently for 20 minutes or until t
dumplings are cooked.
6   To serve, spoon the meat and vegetabl
into a heated serving dish and arrange t
dumplings on top. Keep warm. Bring t
cooking liquid to a boil and whisk in t
beurre manié a little at a time. Cook, stir
ing, until the sauce has thickened. Pour t
sauce over the beef and parsley dumplin
and serve at once.

French beef stew

 3 hours

Boiled beef and carrots

This is a traditional English braised beef
recipe. You can use new or old carrots.

overnight soaking,
then 2 hours

Serves 4
1.1 kg /2½ lb salted brisket or silverside of
beef
6 cloves
10 black peppercorns
bouquet garni including
2 or 3 celery leaves
2 bay leaves
4 medium-sized onions, quartered
700 g /1½ lb carrots
For the dumplings
250 g /9 oz flour
5 ml /1 tsp baking powder
4 allspice berries, crushed
4 juniper berries, crushed
6 black peppercorns, crushed
pinch of salt
100 g /4 oz fresh beef suet or chilled beef
dripping, grated

Boiled beef and carrots

1   Soak the beef overnight.
2   Put the beef into a large saucepan with
fresh water to cover, and add the cloves,
peppercorns, bouquet garni, bay leaves and
onions.
3   Set the pan over a moderate heat and
bring the water to the boil. Skim, then cover
and simmer for 1 hour.
4   Meanwhile, make the dumplings. Sift
the flour and baking powder into a mixing
bowl and add the spices and salt. Mix in the
suet or dripping.
5   Make a well in the centre of the dry
ingredients, pour in 125 ml /4 fl oz cold
water, and mix to a stiff dough. Divide it
into 16 pieces and form into balls.
6   When the beef has cooked for 1 hour,
skim the liquid of any fat. Put the dumplings
into the saucepan with the beef and cook for
a further 10 minutes, then add the carrots.
Cook for a further 20 minutes, until the
carrots are tender.
7   To serve, take out the beef, carve it into
fairly thick slices and arrange them on a
large, heated serving dish surrounded by the
carrots, onions and dumplings. Pour a little
of the cooking liquid over the meat and serve
the rest separately in a sauce-boat.

rves 4–6

1–1.4 kg /2½–3 lb topside beef
ml /4 tbls seasoned flour
g /½ oz butter
ml /1 tbls olive oil
5 g /8 oz fat salt pork, diced
Spanish onions, finely chopped
arlic cloves, finely chopped
nerous pinch of dried thyme
ay leaves, crumbled
0 ml /7 fl oz red wine
0 ml /10 fl oz beef stock, home-made or
from cube
lt and freshly ground black pepper
button onions
button mushrooms about 150 g /5 oz

Cut the beef into 4 cm /1½ in cubes,
carding any fat and gristle. Toss the beef
bes in the seasoned flour.

Heat the butter and olive oil in a heavy-
sed flameproof casserole. When the
aming subsides, add the diced fat salt pork
d gently sauté until the fat runs. Add the
ef in batches and sauté until brown on all
les. Remove and keep warm.

Add the finely chopped onions and garlic
the casserole, and cook until soft and just
ginning to brown, stirring occasionally.
turn the beef to the casserole and add
yme and crumbled bay leaves.

Reserve 30 ml /2 tbls wine and boil the
st until reduced by half.

Pour the wine over the beef and add
ough beef stock to cover the meat. Season
th salt and freshly ground black pepper to
ste. Cover the casserole and simmer slowly
r 2 hours, or until the beef is tender and
uce is thick, stirring occasionally.

Meanwhile, put the button onions in a
ucepan of cold water and bring to the boil.
mmer for 5 minutes, or until the onions
e just tender. Drain and refresh.

About 30 minutes before the beef is
oked, add the button mushrooms and
ained onions.

Stir in the red wine and serve.

epper and anchovy
eef

 2½ hours

rves 4–6

kg /2¼ lb braising steak, trimmed and cut
into 4 cm /1½ in cubes
ml /2 tbls olive oil
large Spanish onion, finely chopped
ml /1½ tbls flour
0 ml /7 fl oz dry red wine
0 g /14 canned tomatoes
large garlic cloves, crushed
ml /1 tsp dried thyme
bay leaf
lt
eshly ground black pepper
small red pepper, cut into thin rings
0 g /4 oz mushrooms finely chopped
g /2½ oz anchovy-stuffed green olives,
halved

epper and anchovy beef

1 Heat the olive oil in a large flameproof
casserole. Sauté half the cubes of beef until
evenly browned. Transfer to a plate with a
slotted spoon and repeat with the remaining
cubes.
2 Add the chopped onion to the fat in the
pan and cook over a low heat for about 10
minutes, or until soft.
3 Return the beef to the pan. Sprinkle in
the flour, stirring well to coat. Add the wine,
canned tomatoes and their liquid, crushed
garlic, dried thyme and bay leaf. Season to
taste with salt and freshly ground pepper.
Stir well and bring to simmering point.
Cook, covered, over a low heat for 1¾ hours,
stirring occasionally.
4 Add the pepper rings, finely chopped
mushrooms and halved anchovy-stuffed
olives and cook for a further 30 minutes, or
until the pepper rings are tender.
5 Remove the bay leaf from the beef,
correct the seasoning and serve immediately.

Beef cooked in beer

This stew is an adaptation of the
traditional Belgian dish *Carbonnade à la
flamande.*

2½ hours

Serves 6

1–1.5 kg /2¼–3¼ lb chuck or braising steak
salt and freshly ground black pepper
125–150 g /4–5 oz good dripping or lard
50 g /2 oz flour
450 g /1 lb onions, chopped
250 g /9 oz unsmoked streaky bacon, diced
2 bottles strong lager
2 sprigs thyme or 2.5 ml /½ tsp dried thyme
1 bay leaf
15 ml /1 tbls light brown sugar
15 ml /1 tbls wine vinegar

1 Heat the oven to 240C /475F /gas 9. Cut
the beef into large bite-sized pieces and
season with salt and freshly ground black
pepper. Sauté the pieces in batches.
2 Transfer the meat with a slotted spoon
to a large casserole, sprinkle with the flour
and mix well. Transfer the casserole to the
oven and cook, uncovered, for 10 minutes.
3 Meanwhile, brown the chopped onions
in the fat remaining in the frying-pan over
medium-high heat. Add the browned onions,
and diced bacon to the beef mixture.
4 Pour the lager over the meat, adding
water to cover if necessary. Add the thyme,
bay leaf, sugar and vinegar, cover the
casserole and return it to the oven. Reduce
the heat to 170C /325F /gas 3 and cook for
about 2 hours or until the meat is tender.
Remove the bay leaf and thyme and serve.

BEEF SAUSAGES & OFFAL

Most countries feature sausages of one sort or another in their cuisines, and to the British they're almost a national institution. Offal, too, is a reliable favourite, from tasty steak and kidney pie to party-style tongue.

Homely sausages are a mainstay of many a family meal – not surprising since they're so economical and easy to cook. Offal, too, makes filling, warming dishes, as well as more unusual ones suitable for a dinner party.

Sausages

The meat content of beef sausages sold commercially in Britain may vary since they need contain only a minimum of 50% meat, the rest made up of binders, fillers and other ingredients. Generally, the more expensive the sausages, the higher the meat content.

Beef sausages are usually seasoned with black pepper, nutmeg, mace, cayenne pepper and ground ginger. You can also buy varieties that are flavoured with herbs.

A sausage isn't strictly a sausage unless the meat is contained in something, but so-called skinless ones are available, as are packets of sausage-meat. If you want to make your own sausages, the casings – either natural or synthetic – can be bought from butchers who make their own sausages.
Cooking: Sausages are usually fried or grilled, but sausages in skins can also be blanched or boiled, baked or barbecued.

Oxtail

Since the ox stores its reserve fat in its tail, it is in the winter that oxtail is at its best and meatiest. Occasionally you may see a whole, unskinned oxtail in a small butcher's shop, but it is more usual to find it already skinned and jointed into pieces.

Since there is quite a lot of fat and bone on an oxtail, buy 275 g /10 oz per person. The meat should be red and the fat white, and there should be no smell.
Preparing: trim off the excess fat, then soak in cold water for two hours to allow the blood to soak out. Drain the pieces and pat dry with absorbent paper.
Cooking: use the larger pieces for casseroles and stews, and the smaller end pieces for soup.

Kidney

Ox kidneys are the largest type available, with a dark colour and a strong flavour. They are usually bought by weight, sometimes ready prepared and diced. They must always be eaten very fresh, so look for plump, firm kidneys with a good brown colour, avoiding any that look dull or mottled or that smell unpleasant.
Preparing: if the kidney is in a piece, soak it in lightly salted water for 2 hours before using, then slice vertically in half, cut out the central core and cut the flesh into dice.
Cooking: long, slow, moist cooking is necessary to tenderize ox kidneys. They are used to flavour steak pies and puddings, casseroles and soups. Allow 125–175 g /4–6 oz per 450 g /1 lb beef.

Tongue

By far the most popular kind of tongue is one that has been wet-cured in pickling brine. This improves the flavour and gives the meat a pinkish colour. Fresh ox tongue has a less interesting flavour than pickled and tends to be grey in colour.

If you have a choice, select a tongue that is short and thick rather than long and thin. A smooth skin indicates that the tongue comes from a young animal. Allow 150–175 g /5–6 oz raw ox tongue per portion.
Preparing: the flavour of fresh ox tongue is improved by soaking overnight in cold, salt water.
Cooking: simmer slowly or braise.

Liver

Ox liver is larger, coarser and much stronger in flavour than other livers, but it is considerably cheaper. All liver should be eaten when very fresh (it is never hung like other meat), so avoid any that looks dull or dry, especially if it has a bluish tinge or smells unpleasant. It is normally sold by weight, sliced along the length of the lobe into 5–10 mm /¼–½ in slices. As it is very economical with virtually no waste, and is also very rich, you need allow only 100–125 g /3½–4 oz per portion, whatever the cooking method.
Preparing: wash the liver briefly under cold, running water and pat dry with absorbent paper. If the liver is in one piece, remove any outer skin, then slice along the length of the lobe into even slices of the required thickness. Cut out any large veins.
Cooking: liver contains very little natural fat and will easily become solid and unpalatable if it is overcooked. The most successful way of cooking ox liver is to soak it in milk or slightly salted water for 2 hours, then cook it very gently by casseroling or braising. Do not fry or grill.

Heart

As with all offal, heart should be as fresh as possible. It should be moist and firm, with a pleasant smell. One ox's heart, stuffed, will serve six to eight.
Preparing: wash the hearts thoroughly in cold, running water to remove any blood clots. Trim off all excess fat with a knife, then snip out the artery and vein stubs with long, pointed scissors. Soak the hearts in cold, salted water for one to eight hours, then place them in a saucepan and cover with fresh, cold water, bring to the boil and simmer for two minutes to blanch them. Drain and rinse under cold water.
Cooking: although heart can be roasted or thinly sliced and quickly sautéed in butter, it is better braised, casseroled or pot-roasted. The long, slow cooking ensures tenderness and enables the heart to absorb the flavours of the other ingredients. Heart may also be stuffed or used in kebabs.

Shrovetide sausage

🍴 1 hour 15 minutes

Serves 4
450 g /1 lb beef sausages, at room temperature
butter or dripping for greasing
40 g /1½ oz butter
3 medium-sized onions, thinly sliced into rings
sprigs of parsley, to garnish
For the pancakes
100 g /4 oz flour
1.5 ml /¼ tsp salt
2 medium-sized eggs
250 ml /8 fl oz milk
15ml /1 tbls melted butter or oil
a little oil for frying
For the relish
50 g /2 oz butter
1 medium-sized onion, chopped
400 g /14 oz canned tomatoes, drained
60 ml /4 tbls mild mango chutney (chop a\ large pieces of mango)
1.5 ml /¼ tsp dried marjoram
salt and freshly ground black pepper

Serves 4

*1 oxtail (or the larger pieces from 2 oxtails),
     skinned, jointed, trimmed and soaked*
salt and freshly ground black pepper
45 ml /3 tbls flour
50 g /2 oz butter
1 Spanish onion, finely chopped
1 medium-sized turnip, thinly sliced
2 medium-sized carrots, sliced lengthways
6 celery stalks, coarsely chopped
300 ml /10 fl oz brown ale
30 ml /2 tbls black treacle
1 blade of mace
5 ml /1 tsp allspice
1 garlic clove, crushed
2 bay leaves
5 ml /1 tsp dried thyme
5 ml /1 tsp lemon juice

1 Pat the oxtail joints dry with absorbent paper, then sprinkle generously with black pepper and roll in 30 ml /2tbls flour.
2 Melt the butter in a flameproof casserole, add the oxtail pieces and brown them over a moderate heat. Remove them from the pan, using a slotted spoon, and reserve.
3 Add all the vegetables to the casserole and sauté for 3–4 minutes. Remove with a slotted spoon and reserve. Stir in the remaining flour and cook, stirring, until it is lightly browned, then slowly pour in the ale, stirring constantly. Add the treacle and stir for 3–4 minutes, until the gravy thickens.
4 Return the oxtail pieces to the casserole, surround them with the vegetables and add a little salt, the mace, allspice, garlic, bay leaves and thyme. Just cover with water, then simmer very gently for 2½–3 hours, or until the meat is very loose on the bone.
5 Stir in the lemon juice, season to taste with salt and pepper and serve at once.

Farmers' sausages

 45 minutes

Makes about 20 sausages
1 kg /2 lb lean minced beef
10 ml /2 tsp salt
15 ml /1 tbls ground coriander
5 ml /1 tsp grated nutmeg
350 g /12 oz hard pork back fat, diced
2.5 ml /½ tsp ground cloves
2.5 ml /½ tsp black pepper
*½ small garlic clove, squeezed with a garlic
     press or very finely chopped*
dripping or lard for shallow frying

1 Mix together all the ingredients except the dripping or lard. Form the mixture into sausage shapes or patties, using about 50 g / 2 oz mixture for each one (or put it into sausage skins, using a sausage filler, and then form into links).
2 Heat the dripping or lard in a large frying-pan over medium-low heat and fry the sausage shapes or patties in several batches if necessary, for 10–15 minutes. Turn them occasionally and fry until cooked through and well browned.

First make the relish: melt the butter in saucepan, add the onion and fry until soft t not coloured. Add the tomatoes, chutney d marjoram, mashing the tomatoes with a oden spoon. Season to taste.

Simmer the relish gently for 20 minutes, until thick. Remove the pan from the at, sieve the relish into a bowl and let it l to tepid while you finish the dish.

Heat the oven to 180C /350F /gas 4. ease a baking tin large enough to hold the sages in a single layer. Moisten the sages with warm water, then place them the tin, side by side. Bake them for 20–25 nutes, turning once or twice, until they browned on all sides.

Meanwhile, make the pancakes: sift the ur and salt into a bowl and make a well in centre. Put the eggs and half the milk o the well and mix, gradually drawing in flour and beating briskly to form a ooth, thick batter. Beat in the remaining lk and then the butter or oil.

To cook the pancakes, grease the base of 18 cm /7in frying-pan with about 2.5 ml tsp oil and heat until the pan and oil are oroughly hot. Pour in about 30 ml /2 tbls the batter and immediately swirl around thinly coat the base of the pan.

6 Cook for about 1 minute, until the pancake has set and is lightly browned, then turn and cook the other side for a few seconds. Turn out onto an ovenproof plate.
7 Repeat with the remaining batter to make 8 pancakes, interleaving them with pieces of greaseproof paper or foil. Then wrap the stack loosely in foil and place in the bottom of the oven to keep warm.
8 Melt the 40 g /1½ oz butter in a frying-pan, add the sliced onions and fry over a low heat, stirring frequently, until they are lightly coloured.
9 Remove the sausages and pancakes from the oven. Drain the sausages on absorbent paper. Spread 15 ml /1 tbls relish over the centre of each pancake, place a sausage on top and wrap the pancake around the sausage. Place the wrapped sausages on a heated serving platter and top with the onion rings, garnish with sprigs of parsley and serve at once, with any remaining relish handed separately.

Braised oxtail in ale

 2 hours soaking,
 then 3 hours 15 minutes

Steak and kidney pudding

🔪🔪 4–5 hours

Serves 4
For the suet crust pastry
butter for greasing
175 g /6 oz self-raising flour
75 g /3 oz shredded suet
1.5 ml /¼ tsp salt
For the filling
450 g /1 lb chuck steak
175 g /6 oz ox kidney
25 ml /1½ tbls flour
salt and freshly ground black pepper
1 medium-sized onion, finely chopped
150 ml /5 fl oz beef stock, home-made or
*   from a cube*

1 Thoroughly butter the inside of an 850 ml /1½ pt pudding bowl and a piece of double-thickness greaseproof paper large enough to cover the top generously.
2 To make the suet crust, mix the flour, suet and salt together in a basin, then mix to a soft, elastic dough with about 90 ml /6 tbls of cold water.
3 Turn onto a lightly floured surface, knead the dough briefly, then roll into a circle about 5 cm /2 in larger all round than the bowl top.
4 Cut out one quarter of the dough and reserve for the lid. Line the bowl with the rest of the pastry, dampening and joining the cut edges in the bowl. The pastry should extend just above the bowl rim.
5 Cut the steak into 5 mm /¼ in thick slices, then into strips about 2.5 × 7.5 cm /1 × 3 in. Wash the kidney, remove the white central core and cut the kidney into small pieces.
6 Season the flour with salt and pepper and toss the steak and kidney pieces in it. Roll a piece of kidney inside each strip of meat and pack these into the lined bowl, sprinkling each layer with chopped onion. Add enough stock to come halfway up the bowl.
7 Turn the pastry edges down over the meat and brush with water. Roll the remaining pastry into a circle to fit exactly inside the top of the basin, and press the edges to seal.
8 Pleat the greaseproof paper down the centre – to allow the pudding to expand while cooking – and place over the top of the pudding. Cover this with a piece of pleated foil and tie in place with string.
9 Lower the bowl into a large saucepan containing enough fast-boiling water to reach halfway up the bowl. Cover tightly with the lid.
10 Steam steadily for 3½–4½ hours – the longer the better – topping up the pan with boiling water as necessary.
11 To serve, remove the bowl from the pan and stand it on a plate. Heat the remaining beef stock. Take off the foil and paper, make a hole in the centre of the crust and add the hot beef stock. Knot a clean table napkin around the bowl and serve.

Oxtail and vegetable soup

🔪🔪 making quick meat glaze,
2 hours soaking, then 4 hours

Serves 4–6
1 oxtail (or the small end pieces from 2
*   oxtails), skinned, jointed, trimmed and*
*   soaked*
15 ml /1 tbls flour
25 g /1 oz butter
15 ml /1 tbls olive oil
1 bacon knuckle
salt and freshly ground black pepper
2 medium-sized carrots, finely chopped
2 medium-sized onions, finely chopped
2 small turnips, finely chopped
5 celery stalks, finely chopped
2 bay leaves
3 sprigs of parsley
5 ml /1 tsp dried thyme
2.5 ml /½ tsp dried marjoram
2.5 ml /½ tsp dried tarragon
5 ml /1 tsp tomato purée
2.5 ml /½ tsp cayenne pepper
30 ml /2 tbls Quick meat glaze (see page 32)
30 ml /2 tbls port, Madeira, Marsala or
*   medium sherry*

1 Pat the oxtail joints dry with absorbent pepper and sprinkle them with flour. Melt the butter and oil in a large, heavy-based saucepan over a moderate heat, then add the

Steak and kidney pudding

oxtail pieces and brown them on all sides.
2 Add the knuckle, 5 ml /1 tsp salt, vegetables, herbs and black pepper. Cook covered, over a very low heat for 10 minutes, then pour in cold water to cover.
3 Bring to the boil over a high heat, skim off any scum that rises to the top, then lower the heat. Simmer very gently for 3½ hours.
4 Remove the bacon knuckle and discard. Take out the pieces of oxtail and bone them carefully. Return the meat directly to the pan.
5 Stir in the tomato purée, cayenne pepper and meat glaze and season to taste with salt and pepper. Stir in the port, Madeira, Marsala or sherry, stir and serve at once.

Belgrade bite-sized sausages

🔪🔪 45 minutes,
plus resting or chilling

Serves 6–8
900 g /2 lb boneless beef: back rib, skirt,
*   flank or neck, or a mixture of these*
200 g /7 oz fresh beef suet, or raw beef
*   marrow*
5 ml /1 tsp salt
2.5 ml /½ tsp freshly ground black pepper
15 ml /1 tbls finely chopped onion
suet or pork fat for greasing

Trim all connective tissue and membrane from the meat and the suet. Chop em very finely, first separately and then gether, with heavy, sharp knives, until a rfectly smooth meat pulp is produced; or rée them together in a food processor.

Knead together the beef purée with the t of the sausage ingredients. Fry a little of e mixture; taste and adjust the seasoning necessary. Rest for 30 minutes, or rigerate for up to 12 hours.

With dampened hands, shape the sage-meat into 60 walnut-sized balls. ll each meatball backwards and forwards til it is about 5 cm /2 in long. Straighten the ends by tapping them with your gertips. Refrigerate the sausages until you e ready to cook them.

Grease a grid with a piece of suet or pork . Heat the grill to high.

Grill the sausages, initially close to the at source, searing them at high heat for 1 nute on each side. Reduce the heat and ok for a further 8–10 minutes, until well loured but still succulent.

Sprinkle the chopped onions with salt, d serve the sausages immediately, garshed with the onions, pickled pimentos or erkins and the whole, grilled chillies.

ressed tongue with talian green sauce

se steps 1–5 in this recipe as the basic ethod to cook a pickled or fresh ngue. Improve the flavour of fresh ngue by soaking it overnight in salted ter to cover.

4¾ hours,
then overnight pressing

ressed tongue with Italian green sauce

1 Scrub the tongue with a stiff brush under cold, running water to clean it thoroughly. Trim away any visible gristle and fatty lumps from the root or underside. Put the tongue in a bowl of cold water and soak for 1 hour to remove excess salt.
2 Drain the tongue, fit it into a large cooking pot and cover with cold water. Bring to the boil over a low heat, skimming frequently as the liquid approaches boiling point, until the surface is clear of froth.
3 As soon as the liquid starts simmering, add the vegetables, bouquet garni, garlic, allspice and peppercorns. Keep the liquid at a gentle simmer for 2½ hours, or until the tip of the tongue is very tender when pierced with a fine skewer.
4 Lift the tongue out of the pot. (If pressing the tongue, strain and reserve the liquid.) Rinse the tongue under running, cold water until cool enough to handle.
5 Peel the skin off in strips. If necessary, pull out all the bones and trim any gristle from the base of the tongue with a sharp knife. If using this as the basic method for cooking pickled or fresh tongue, it is now ready for slicing and serving.
6 To press, curl the tongue into a deep,

round cake tin or soufflé dish just large enough to hold it (15 cm /6 in diameter is ideal). If you have to squeeze it in, so much the better.
7 Add enough of the cooking liquid to cover, place a plate or saucer on top and weight it down with a 1 kg /2 lb weight. Leave to cool, then chill in the refrigerator until the jelly is set, preferably overnight.
8 For the sauce, rinse the watercress well and remove the leaves.
9 Blanch the watercress leaves in boiling water for 1 minute. Drain, refresh under cold, running water and drain again.
10 Combine the watercress, parsley, onion, garlic and lemon juice in a blender or food processor. Reduce the contents to a purée, then pour in the olive oil slowly, 15 ml /1 tbls at a time, blending. Add the anchovy fillets and blend until smooth.
11 Scrape the sauce into a bowl with a spatula. Stir in the roughly chopped capers, season with salt, if necessary, and pepper.
12 To serve, turn out the tongue, slice and arrange in an overlapping row on a serving dish and garnish with watercress. Spoon some of the sauce down the centre and serve the remainder in a sauce-boat.

USING LEFTOVER BEEF

Whatever size joint of beef you buy, when it is cooked, there will always be one or two last pieces, which no amount of skillful carving will make presentable. Try some of these ideas for using up the leftovers.

In most cases leftover beef will be from a joint that has been roasted rare, so the meat will be moist and succulent. This is ideal for recipes which requires a little cooking rather than simple reheating. A pot-roasting joint, such as brisket, will be fattier, so when the beef has been chilled, remove the fat and use the meat in recipes which require chopped or coarsely minced beef.

Storing: remove the meat from the bone when cold – this will prevent the meat drying out. Wrap it in foil or cling film and keep in the refrigerator for up to 3 days. Chop or cut the meat at the last moment before you need to use it, otherwise the smaller pieces will dry out. It is always better to chop cooked meat rather than mincing it; minced cooked beef turns too easily into a paste-like mixture.

Never cook a dish that contains pre-cooked meat for a long time: it will make the meat hard and indigestible. To replace moisture and flavour lost during the first cooking, add stock or gravy and extra seasoning or flavourings. If the meat is to be fried or baked, protect it from the dry heat with a coating of egg and breadcrumbs, batter, a covering of mashed potato or pastry. Try some of the following ideas.

- Add an Italian or spicy curry sauce.
- Use small amounts of leftover beef to stuff vegetables such as aubergines, peppers, baked potatoes, tomatoes, cabbage and vine leaves. Add rice or breadcrumbs to make the meat go further.
- Strips of cold beef are useful for cold salads. Mix lightly cooked young vegetables with beef and toss in a dressing for a summer lunch.
- If you have several slices of cold roast beef over, try Roast Beef Redbridge (*page 45*).
- Add the beef to pancakes and fritters or mix it with vegetables and sauces, and serve Chinese-style.

Creamy beef sauté

 30 minutes

Serves 4
15 ml /1 tbls oil
25 g /1 oz butter
1 medium-sized onion, sliced
175 g /6 oz button mushrooms, sliced
100 g /4 oz green pepper, seeded and sliced
150 ml /5 fl oz white wine
300 g /10 oz rare cooked beef, cut into thin
   strips, 5 cm /2 in long
salt and freshly ground black pepper
150 ml /5 fl oz soured cream
15 ml /1 tbls creamed horseradish sauce
10 ml /2 tsp cornflour
chopped fresh parsley, to garnish

1 Heat the oil and butter together in a large frying-pan. Add the onion and sauté for 2 minutes. Add the mushrooms and green pepper and continue to cook for 2 minutes.
2 Pour over the white wine and stir in the beef. Simmer until the liquid has reduced by half, then season with salt and pepper to taste.
3 Stir in the soured cream and horseradish and heat through. Blend the cornflour with a little water, stir into the sauce and simmer for 1 minute. Serve hot, with chopped parsley sprinkled over.

- For added colour, use a mixture of green, red and yellow peppers.

Golden topped beef casseroles

Serve these appetizing individual casseroles with lightly cooked spring greens, beans or brocoli.

 1 hour 10 minutes

Serves 4
15 ml /1 tbls oil
1 medium-sized onion, chopped
1 garlic clove, crushed
2 carrots, thinly sliced
2 sticks celery, sliced
400 g /14 oz canned tomatoes
5 ml /1 tsp mixed herbs
salt and freshly ground black pepper
225 g /8 oz cooked beef, cut into 15 mm /¼
   in cubes
225 g /8 oz potatoes
225 g /8 oz parsnips
1 small cooking apple
50 g /2 oz butter

1 Heat the oven to 190C /375F /gas 5.
2 Heat the oil in a pan, add the onion and cook gently for 3 minutes. Add the garlic, carrots and celery and cook for a further 2 minutes.
3 Add the tomatoes with their juices, breaking them up with a wooden spoon. Add mixed herbs and season with salt and pepper to taste. Simmer for 10 minutes. Stir in the beef. Spoon the mixture into 4 individual 425 ml /15 fl oz casseroles or ovenproof dishes.
4 Roughly grate the potatoes, parsnips and apple and mix them together in a bowl. Melt the butter in a pan, add the grated vegetables and cook gently for 5 minutes. Season to taste with salt and freshly ground black pepper, then divide between the pies as toppings. Bake in the oven for 25–30 minutes until golden brown then serve.

Mini moussakas

 1 hour 40 minutes

Serves 4
2 large aubergines
salt
300 ml /10 fl oz milk
25 g /1 oz butter
30 ml /2 tbls flour
50 g /2 oz Gruyère cheese, freshly grated
freshly ground black pepper
37.5 ml /2½ tbls olive oil
2 large garlic cloves, finely chopped
4 large tomatoes, skinned, seeded and
   chopped
225 g /8 oz cooked beef, cut into strips

1 Halve the aubergines lengthways a remove the flesh from the centre, leaving 5 mm/¼ in thick shell. Chop the scooped c flesh and score the skins with a knife. P the skins and flesh in a colander, sprinkl with salt and leave to drain for 30 minutes
2 Meanwhile, in a saucepan, bring t milk to the boil. In another heavy-bas

ucepan, melt the butter and blend in the
ɔur, stirring constantly. Cook for 2–3
.inutes to make a pale roux. Gradually
ur in the hot milk and simmer for 20
.inutes until the sauce is thick. Remove the
an from the heat and stir in 25 g /1 oz of
.e grated Gruyère cheese. Season with salt
ɪd pepper. Allow to become cold.

Heat the oven to 180C /350F /gas 4.

Rinse the aubergine skins and flesh and
ry well on absorbent paper. Brush the skins
ith olive oil and place them in a baking
ɪsh. Cook in the oven for 20–30 minutes.

Meanwhile, heat 30 ml /2 tbls of the
live oil in a frying-pan and sauté the finely
hopped garlic. Add the chopped aubergine
ɪd cook for 10 minutes; add the chopped
ɔmatoes and season with salt and pepper.
eave to cook for 10 minutes. Add the strips
f beef and sauté for 2–3 minutes.

Place the aubergine mixture in the
ubergine shells and spoon over the cheese
auce. Sprinkle the remaining grated
ɔruyère over the aubergines and cook in the
ven for 15–20 minutes until golden.

This recipe is equally good using leftover
ɪmb.

Beef horseradish rolls

making quick meat glaze,
then 1 hour 10 minutes

Serves 6
6 slices rare roast beef
300 ml /10 fl oz beef stock, home-made or
from a cube
40 g /1½ oz butter
30 ml /2 tbls flour
salt and freshly ground black pepper
30–45 ml /2–3 tbls creamed horseradish
sauce
30 ml /2 tbls Quick meat glaze (page 23)
30 ml /2 tbls port
25 g /1 oz shelled pine nuts
125 g /4 oz broccoli florets

1 Heat the oven to 170C /325F /gas 3.
2 In a saucepan, bring the stock to the
boil. In another heavy-based saucepan, melt
25 g /1 oz of the butter and blend in the
flour. Cook, stirring constantly, for a further
2–3 minutes to make a pale roux, and then

Beef horseradish rolls and Mini moussakas

gradually add the boiling stock. Season with
salt and freshly ground black pepper and
simmer gently, stirring occasionally, for
15–20 minutes, or until the sauce has
thickened.
3 Meanwhile, spread the beef generously
with the creamed horseradish and fold the
slices in three. Place them in a shallow
ovenproof dish.
4 Add the quick meat glaze and the port to
the sauce, blend well and cook for a further
20 minutes. Correct the seasoning and add
the sauce to the beef. Cover tightly with foil
and cook in the oven for 15 minutes.
5 In a small frying-pan, melt the remaining butter and sauté the pine nuts until
golden. Reserve.
6 Just before serving, cook the broccoli
florets in boiling salted water for 3–4
minutes or until the broccoli is cooked but *al
dente*. Drain well.
7 Transfer the meat to a serving dish, and
spoon the sauce over the meat. Arrange the
broccoli florets attractively down the sides of
the dish and sprinkle the meat with the
sautéed pine nuts. Serve immediately.

43

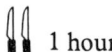

Beef onions

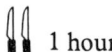
cooking rice,
then 1 hour 5 minutes

Serves 4
4 Spanish onions
salt
30 ml /2 tbls oil, plus extra for greasing
10 ml /2 tsp mild curry powder
50 g /2 oz red pepper, diced
15 ml /1 tbls tomato purée
100 g /4 oz cooked rice (40 g /1½ oz raw rice)
100 g /4 oz cooked beef, finely diced
15 ml /1 tbls fresh coriander leaves, or flat-leaved parsley, chopped
freshly ground black pepper

1 Use a sharp knife to cut off and discard 15 mm /½ in slice from the top of each onio Cut off and discard a thin slice from t. bottom of each onion to make a flat bas With the knife remove the centre of ea onion leaving a 15 mm /½ in thick she Finely chop 75 g /3 oz of the onion scoop out of the centre and reserve.
2 Place the onion shells in a large pa pour over water to cover them and add 2 ml /½ tsp salt. Bring to the boil, cover a simmer for 5 minutes. Remove the onio from the pan with a slotted spoon.
4 Heat the oven to 190C /375F /gas 5.
5 Heat the oil in a frying-pan. Add t chopped onion and sauté for 5 minutes. S in the curry powder and add the peppe Cook for a further 2 minutes. Remove fro the heat and mix in the tomato purée, ric beef, and coriander or flat-leaved parsle Season with salt and pepper to taste.
5 Spoon the filling into the onion shell Brush the outsides of the onions with a lit oil, then place them in a greased ovenpro dish. Cover with foil and bake in the ove for 35–40 minutes, or until the onions a tender when pierced with the point of sharp knife. Serve immediately.

Watercress and beef roulade

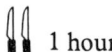 1 hour

Serves 4
175 g /6 oz cooked beef, cut into 5 mm/¼ in dice
1 bunch watercress
75 g /3 oz butter, plus extra for greasing
50 g /2 oz flour
300 ml /10 fl oz milk
2 medium-sized eggs, separated
30 ml /2 tbls chopped fresh parsley
salt and freshly ground black pepper
8 spring onions, trimmed and chopped
225 g /8 oz tomatoes, blanched, skinned an chopped
tomato slices, to garnish

1 Heat the oven to 200C /400F /gas Grease a 34 × 24 cm /13½ × 9½ in Swiss r tin and line with greaseproof paper. Grea

Spiced meat loaf

Serve with a crisp green salad.

 1 hour

Serves 4
50 g /2 oz butter
1 medium-sized onion, chopped
50 g /2 oz wholewheat flour
300 ml /10 fl oz beef stock, home-made or from a cube
5 ml /1 tsp chilli sauce
10 ml /2 tsp Worcestershire sauce
salt and freshly ground black pepper
50 g /2 oz walnuts, chopped
350 g /12 oz cooked beef, finely chopped
500 g /1 lb potatoes
25 g /1 oz butter
milk
pinch of nutmeg
25 g /1 oz cracked wheat
50 g /2 oz Red Leicester, grated

Spiced meat loaf

1 Melt the butter in a pan. Add the onion and cook gently until soft. Stir in the flour and cook for 1 minute. Gradually stir in the stock, chilli sauce, Worcestershire sauce and season with salt and pepper to taste. Cook until the sauce has a smooth, thick consistency, then remove from the heat and set aside to cool.
2 When cool, mix the walnuts and beef into the sauce. Spoon the mixture into a greased 1 L /1½ pt loaf tin and chill.
3 Boil the potatoes until tender, then drain and mash together with the butter and enough milk to make them creamy. Season with salt and pepper and a pinch of nutmeg.
4 Heat the oven to 200C /400F /gas 6.
5 Turn the meat loaf out onto an ovenproof plate and spread over the potato.
6 Mix together the cracked wheat and cheese. Coat the loaf and bake in the oven for 30 minutes until the cracked wheat and cheese topping is crisp and golden brown. Serve immediately.

e paper well.

Discard the watercress stalks, wash oroughly and pat dry with absorbent per. Chop the watercress roughly.

Melt 50 g /2 oz butter in a pan, stir in e flour and cook over a gentle heat for 2 inutes. Blend in the milk and cook for a rther 2 minutes. Remove from the heat.

Beat the egg yolks into the sauce with e chopped watercress and parsley. Add salt d pepper to taste. Whisk the egg whites til they are stiff, then fold them lightly to the mixture.

Pour the mixture into the prepared viss roll tin. Spread it evenly over the base d bake in the oven for 20 minutes.

Meanwhile, melt the remaining butter in pan. Add the chopped onions and cook ntly for 2 minutes. Add the beef and matoes and heat through for a further 2 inutes. Season with salt and pepper.

Remove the roulade from the oven. Turn out of the tin onto a clean sheet of easeproof paper. With a knife, gently ease the roulade away from the lining paper.

8 Spread the beef filling over the surface of the roulade then roll it up like a Swiss roll. Slide the roll onto a warmed serving plate, join side down, garnish and serve.

Roast beef Redbridge

🍴 15 minutes

Serves 4
4 thick slices cold, rare roast beef
25 g /1 oz butter
15–30 ml /1–2 tbls meat juices left over
    from roasting
15 ml /1 tbls Dijon mustard
60–90 ml /4–6 tbls red wine
freshly ground black pepper
15 ml /1 tbls finely snipped chives
bunch of chives, to garnish

1 Melt the butter in a frying-pan large enough to take the beef slices in one layer. Sauté the beef slices for 1–2 minutes each side, or until warmed through, turning them over with a spatula.

2 Remove all fat from the top of the meat juices. In a small bowl, combine the juice with the mustard, whisking until well blended. Pour the mixture over the meat and simmer for a few seconds.

3 Add the red wine and simmer over a high heat for 2–3 minutes or until the sauce has reduced to about 75 ml /5 tbls. Season with freshly ground black pepper to taste.

4 Transfer the beef slices to a heated platter, overlapping each slice slightly. Pour the sauce over and sprinkle with the snipped chives. Garnish with a bunch of chives, and serve immediately.

● It is important to use really rare, moist roast beef for this dish to be successful.

Roast beef Redbridge

BEEF FOR THE FAMILY

Beef need not be a special occasion treat, the cheaper cuts make succulent casseroles, minced beef becomes international and even corned beef is turned into a treat.

Moussaka with yoghurt topping

A topping of yoghurt mixed with grated cheese is a quick and easy substitute for the traditional sauce used for moussaka.

 1 hour 35 minutes

Serves 4–6
2 large aubergines, sliced thinly
salt
approximately 125 ml /4 fl oz oil
2 large potatoes, thinly sliced
1 onion, chopped
1–2 garlic cloves, crushed
450–750 g /1–1½ lb minced beef
4 tomatoes, skinned and chopped
30 ml /2 tbls tomato purée
2.5 ml /½ tsp ground allspice
freshly ground black pepper
600 ml /1 pt yoghurt
30 ml /2 tbls freshly chopped parsley
100 g /4 oz Cheddar cheese, grated
2 eggs, beaten
1.5 ml /¼ tsp grated nutmeg

1 Put the aubergine slices on a plate and sprinkle with salt. Leave to drain for 30 minutes.
2 Meanwhile, heat 30 ml /2 tbls oil in a frying-pan and fry the potato slices in two batches until quite soft and golden brown on all sides, adding more oil when necessary. Drain on absorbent paper.
3 Heat 30 ml /2 tbls oil in a saucepan. Add the onion and garlic and fry gently until lightly coloured. Add the beef and fry until browned, stirring constantly. Add the tomatoes, tomato purée, allspice and salt and pepper to taste. Simmer gently for about 20 minutes until the liquid has evaporated.
4 Heat the oven to 190C /375F /gas 5. Rinse the aubergine slices and pat dry with absorbent paper. Chop roughly. Heat 30 ml /2 tbls more oil in the frying-pan, add the chopped aubergines and fry for about 10 minutes until lightly coloured and soft, adding more oil if necessary. Remove from the pan with a slotted spoon and mix with one-third of the yoghurt.
5 Stir the parsley into the meat mixture, then put half in the bottom of a large, shallow ovenproof dish. Cover with half the potato slices, then half the aubergine mixture. Repeat these layers of meat, potato and aubergine once more.
6 Mix the remaining yoghurt with the cheese, eggs and nutmeg and pour over the mixture in the dish. Bake for 30–40 minutes until golden brown. Remove from the oven and leave to rest for 10 minutes before serving.

Spiced beef in beer

Spiced beef cooked in beer makes a robust family meal. You can vary the flavour by choosing different kinds of beer – from pale ale to stout.

overnight marinating, then 3–3½ hours

Serves 4–6
1–1.4 kg /2–3 lb rolled brisket or boned leg of beef, tied along its length
30 ml /2 tbls olive oil
freshly ground black pepper
2 large onions, chopped
15 ml /1 tbls Dijon mustard
15 ml /1 tbls redcurrant jelly
15 ml /1 tbls black treacle
30 ml /2 tbls brown sugar
salt
15 g /½ oz butter
15 ml /1 tbls flour
For the marinade
425 ml /15 fl oz ale
4 bay leaves
15 ml /1 tbls allspice berries
15 ml /1 tbls coriander seeds
sprig of thyme
2 blades of mace
60 ml /4 tbls olive oil
5 cm /2 in piece root ginger, finely sliced
2 cloves

1 Put the beef in a large bowl and cover with the marinade ingredients. Marinate for 24 hours in a cool place, turning occasionally.
2 Heat the oil in a large frying-pan. Remove the beef from the marinade, pat dry, season with pepper, and add to the pan. Fry over moderate heat on all sides to seal the meat. Transfer to flameproof casserole.
3 Heat the oven to 150C /300F /gas 2.
4 Add the onions to the frying-pan and sauté for about 5 minutes until golden. Add to the casserole. Strain the marinade into a saucepan, bring to the boil and pour into the casserole.
5 Cover the casserole with a tightly fitting lid and cook for 2½–3 hours until tender.
6 Transfer the beef to a large plate, remove the string, and cut into thick slices. Keep warm while you finish the sauce.
7 Skim the casserole juices of fat, add the mustard, redcurrant jelly, black treacle and brown sugar. Season to taste with salt and black pepper.
8 Mash together the butter and flour to make a *beurre manié* and add, a piece at a time, to the casserole, stirring over a low heat, until the butter has melted and the sauce is thickened. Return the meat to the caserole and heat through for a further 10 minutes. Serve immediately.

Meat and potato pie

1 hour 25 minutes

Serves 4
15 ml /1 tbls oil
1 large onion, finely chopped
350 g /12 oz lean minced beef
15 ml /1 tbls flour
175 ml /6 fl oz strong beef stock, home-mad
  or from a cube
1.5 ml /¼ tsp mixed herbs
salt and freshly ground black pepper
300 g /10 oz new potatoes, cubed
225 g /8 oz shortcrust pastry, defrosted if
  frozen

1 Heat the oil in a large frying-pan and fr the onion for 2–3 minutes. Add the bee turn up the heat, and brown well all over.
2 Reduce the heat and add the flour, stoc herbs and salt and pepper to taste. Bring the boil, stirring all the time. Simmer for 1 minutes, add the potatoes and simmer for further 10 minutes or until the potatoes ar soft but not cooked through.
3 Heat the oven to 200C /400F /gas Roll out the pastry and use just over half it to line a 20 cm /8 in flan tin. Fill with th meat and potato mixture and cover with th remaining pastry. Press the edges together seal, then trim and flute with your finger Prick the top with a fork and bake in th centre of the oven for 30 minutes or unt golden brown. Serve at once.

Beef rolls Bellagio

For this dish choose an evenly-shape piece of meat to give neater slices. Be the slices between cling film.

2¼ hours

Serves 4
700 g /1½ lb topside, cut into 4 slices
salt
freshly ground black pepper
30 ml /2 tbls dripping
1 large onion, finely chopped
1 large garlic clove, crushed
4 celery stalks, finely chopped
100 g /4 oz fresh white breadcrumbs
25 g /1 oz butter
15 ml /1 tbls olive oil
400 g /14 oz canned tomatoes, chopped
30 ml /2 tbls tomato purée
5 ml /1 tsp dried basil
1 green pepper, seeded and chopped
5 ml /1 tsp sugar
15 ml /1 tbls wine vinegar
pasta shells, to serve

1 Beat each slice of beef between sheets greaseproof paper with a meat bat to flatte Cut each piece in half to make 8 slice Season them well with salt and pepper both sides.
2 To prepare the stuffing, heat the dri ping in a saucepan and genty fry half t onion with the garlic and celery for 5–

Easy Mexican chilli

inutes until softened. Stir in the
readcrumbs and season with salt and
eshly ground black pepper.

Spread each slice of beef with some
uffing, tuck the edges into neaten and roll
p firmly from the shorter edge. Tie securely
ith fine string.

Heat the butter and olive oil in a
ameproof casserole and sauté the beef rolls,
rning them until browned all over.

Mix together the tomatoes and their
iice, tomato purée, dried basil, green
epper and remaining chopped onion. Add
e sugar and vinegar. Season well and pour
ver the prepared meat.

Cover with a lid and simmer gently for
bout 1½ hours or until the meat is cooked
nd tender.

Remove the beef rolls from the casserole
ith a slotted spoon and cut off the string.
rrange the rolls on a hot serving dish and
oat with the sauce. Serve with freshly
ooked pasta shells.

Easy Mexican chilli

This is an excellent way of making chilli
without soaking beans overnight.

🔪 1 hour

Serves 6–8

30 ml /2 tbls bacon fat, or dripping
2 Spanish onions, finely chopped
2 garlic cloves, finely chopped
450 g /1 lb lean beef, minced
90 ml /6 tbls Mexican chilli powder
15 ml /1 tbls flour
2 bay leaves
5 ml /1 tsp each cumin powder and paprika
2.5 ml /½ tsp dried oregano
salt and freshly ground black pepper
1.1 L /2 pt beef stock, home-made or from a
  cube
150 ml /10 tbls tomato purée
400 g /14 oz canned red kidney beans
flat-leaved parsley, to garnish

1 Heat the bacon fat, or dripping, in a
large flameproof casserole, add the finely
chopped onions and garlic and cook over a
moderate heat until the onions are
translucent. Add the minced beef and sauté
it over a moderately high flame until the
meat is crumbly and well browned.
2 In a small bowl, blend the chilli powder
and flour with a little of the meat juices and
stir into the casserole together with the
crumbled bay leaves, cumin powder, paprika
and dried oregano. Season with salt and
freshly ground black pepper to taste. Cook
the mixture, stirring constantly, for 2–3
minutes.
3 Stir in the beef stock and tomato purée.
Bring to the boil, then reduce the heat and
simmer for 20–30 minutes.
4 Rinse and drain the kidney beans and
add them to the chilli. Stir and cook for a
further 5–10 minutes, or until the beans are
heated through. Serve the chilli with plain
boiled rice or crackers. (Crackers are the
most traditional accompaniment). Finally,
garnish with the flat-leaved parsley.

from the marinade. Grill for 5–7 minut
depending on the thickness of the stea
Turn and grill for another 3–4 minutes.
3   Slice with a sharp knife at an angl
cutting across the grain of the steak.

Spaghetti with mea
balls

1¼ hours

Serves 4
350 g /12 oz spaghetti
freshly grated Parmesan cheese
For the sauce
25 g /1 oz butter
15 ml /1 tbls olive oil
1 Spanish onion, finely chopped
1 garlic clove, finely chopped
100 g /4 oz mushrooms, sliced
400 g /14 oz canned tomatoes
45 ml /3 tbls tomato purée
1 bay leaf
1 small strip of lemon zest
150 ml /5 fl oz beef stock, home-made or
    from a cube
salt and freshly ground black pepper
15 ml /1 tbls Worcestershire sauce
For the meat balls
350 g /12 oz minced beef
350 g /12 oz minced pork
2 slices of bread, crusts removed, soaked in
    milk
2 garlic cloves, finely chopped
30 ml /2 tbls finely chopped parsley
salt and freshly ground black pepper
1 large egg, beaten
45 ml /3 tbls flour
25 g /1 oz butter
30 ml /2 tbls olive oil

1   To make the sauce; heat the butter an
olive oil in a large frying pan. Sauté th
onion and garlic for 7–10 minutes or unt
soft. Add the mushrooms and sauté for
further 3–4 minutes or until lightl
browned. Add the tomatoes, tomato puré
bay leaf, lemon zest and beef stock. Seaso
cover and simmer for 30 minutes, stirrin
occasionally.
2   Meanwhile make the meat balls; in
bowl combine the minced beef and por
bread, and finely chopped garlic and parsle
Season to taste and stir in the egg to bind
Shape into 16 small meat balls.
3   Sprinkle the flour onto a plate and co
each meat ball in flour, shaking off th
excess.
4   Heat the butter and oil in a frying-pa
large enough to take the meat balls in on
layer. Cook the meat balls for 1–2 minut
each side or until evenly browned.
5   Stir the Worcestershire sauce into th
tomato sauce. Transfer the meat balls to th
tomato sauce, using a slotted spoon. Simme
for 20 minutes, turning the meat balls once.
6   Meanwhile, bring a large saucepan o
salted water to the boil, add the spaghet
and cook for 15 minutes. Drain and rinse.
7   Arrange the spaghetti in a large heate
serving dish. Spoon the meat balls and sauc
on top. Serve with Parmesan cheese.

American beef
casserole

2½ hours

Serves 4
1.1 kg /2½ lb rump or topside of beef
salt and freshly ground black pepper
50 g /2 oz butter
30 ml /2 tbls olive oil
700 g /1½ lb tomatoes, blanched, skinned,
    seeded and chopped
30 ml /2 tbls tomato purée
2 sprigs thyme
2 bay leaves
2 garlic cloves
500 g /1 lb potatoes, unpeeled

1   Cut the beef first into thick slices, if you
are using topside, then into 5 cm /2 in
squares. Season generously with salt and
freshly ground black pepper.
2   Heat the butter and olive oil in a large
heavy-based flameproof casserole. Add
enough beef cubes to cover the bottom of the
casserole and sauté until browned all over.
Remove with a slotted spoon and keep
warm. Repeat with the remaining beef.
3   Return the browned beef to the
casserole. Add the prepared tomatoes and
the tomato purée, the sprigs of thyme and
bay leaves. Season to taste with salt and
freshly ground black pepper.
4   Crush the garlic cloves with the flat side

Spaghetti with meat balls

of a knife and add to the casserole. Cover
and simmer for 2 hours.
5   Meanwhile, cook the potatoes in boiling
salted water for 20 minutes. Drain the
potatoes, then peel and cut into thick slices.
Reserve until the beef is tender.
6   Remove the garlic, sprigs of thyme and
bay leaves from the casserole, add the sliced
potatoes and heat through. Correct the
seasoning and serve immediately.

Marinated skirt
steak

3–8 hours marinating,
then 10–12 minutes

Serves 4
2 × 500 g /1 lb beef skirt steak
7.5 ml /1½ tsp ground ginger
7.5 ml /1½ tsp dry mustard
15 ml /1 tbls molasses
150 ml /5 fl oz soy sauce
60 ml /2½ fl oz oil
3 large garlic cloves, crushed

1   Mix together all the ingredients for the
marinade in a large bowl. Add the beef and
leave to marinate for 3–4 hours at room
temperature or 8 hours in the refrigerator,
turning occasionally. Bring to room
temperature before cooking.
2   Heat the grill to high. Remove the meat

Spicy beef stew

Serve this simple but delicious beef stew with plain boiled rice, noodles, pasta or mashed potatoes.

2 hours

Serves 4–6
1 kg /2 lb chuck steak, cut into 25 mm /1 in cubes
15 ml /1 tbls flour
5 ml /1 tsp curry powder
1.5 ml /¼ tsp chilli powder
pinch of salt
25 g /1 oz butter
30 ml /2 tbls olive oil
1 Spanish onion, chopped
300 ml /10 fl oz beef stock, home-made or from a cube
5 ml /1 tsp tomato purée
cauliflower florets

Heat the oven to 170C /325F /gas 3.
Sift the flour, curry powder, chilli powder and salt into a large bowl. Toss the beef cubes in the seasoned flour.
Heat the butter and oil in a flameproof casserole. When foaming subsides, put in enough meat to cover the base of the pan. Sauté the meat until golden brown on all sides. Remove the meat with a slotted spoon to a plate. Repeat with the rest of the meat.
Add the chopped onion to the fat remaining in the pan and sauté for 2–3 minutes until transparent. Pour off the excess fat.
Add the beef stock and tomato purée, stir well and bring the mixture to the boil. Add the browned meat, cover and transfer to the oven. Cook for 1 hour.
Add the cauliflower florets and cook, covered, for a further 30 minutes. Correct the seasoning and serve immediately.

Stewing beef or skirt can be used instead of chuck steak. Be sure to trim the meat of all fat and gristle. Dumplings can be added instead of the cauliflower florets.

New England red flannel hash

This is an old-fashioned New England dish, economically using left-over, boiled, corned beef, although nowadays we use canned corned beef.

boiling potatoes, then 20 minutes

Serves 4–6
75 g /3 oz butter
1 Spanish onion, finely chopped
350 g /12 oz canned corned beef, diced
1 large cooked beetroot, diced
350 g /12 oz boiled potatoes, diced
30–60 ml /2–4 tbls tomato ketchup
10 ml /2 tsp Worcestershire sauce
salt and freshly ground black pepper
30–60 ml /2–4 tbls thick cream

1   Melt 50 g/2 oz butter in a large, heavy-based frying-pan over a moderate heat. Add the onion and cook for 5 minutes.
2   Combine the beef, beetroot and potatoes in a bowl. Add the onion, tomato ketchup and Worcestershire sauce and mix well. Season generously.
3   Turn the corned beef mixture into the frying-pan and cook over a moderate heat, stirring, for 5 minutes. Meanwhile, heat the grill to high.
4   Using a wooden spoon or a spatula, gently pat the hash into a cake in the pan. Dot with the remaining butter and sprinkle with cream. Grill until crisp and golden. Serve immediately.

Chinese mixed fried rice

1 hour, plus cooling rice

Serves 4
225 g /8 oz long-grain rice
125 g /4 oz braising beef, thinly sliced
45 ml /3 tbls sesame seed oil
4 spring onions, thinly sliced
1 green pepper, seeded and sliced lengthways
2 thin slices root ginger, cut into strips
salt
freshly ground black pepper
125 g /4 oz thinly sliced ham, diced
2 slices bacon, diced
4 eggs
2 spring onion 'tassels', to garnish

For the marinade
½ garlic clove, finely chopped
2.5 ml /½ tsp cornflour
2.5 ml /½ tsp sugar
15 ml /1 tbls soy sauce

1   Pour the rice into an 18 cm /7 in soufflé dish. Place the dish on a trivet standing in a heavy-based casserole or saucepan. Fill the dish to the brim with boiling water.
2   Pour boiling water into the bottom of the casserole or pan to come to the base of the bowl. Bring back to the boil, cover tightly and steam the rice over low heat for exactly 30 minutes. Do not remove the lid during the cooking time. Remove from steamer and leave to become cold.
3   Make the marinade. Combine all the ingredients in a bowl and whisk until blended. Add the beef and stir to coat.
4   Heat 30 ml /2 tbls oil in a large, heavy-based frying-pan. Add the spring onions, green pepper and ginger and stir-fry for 2 minutes, using a wooden spoon.
5   Add the rice and season. Stir-fry for a further 2 minutes.
6   Stir in the ham and bacon, together with the beef and marinade. Stir-fry for 3–4 minutes more.
7   In a small bowl, beat the eggs with salt and pepper. Heat the remaining oil in a frying-pan, add the eggs and cook for 1 minute, stirring constantly.
8   Fold the eggs into the rice. Spoon into a warmed serving dish and serve immediately, garnished with spring onions.

Chinese mixed fried rice

STAR MENUS & RECIPE FILE

Farmhouse terrine

Hungarian beef goulash

Polenta

Spinach-stuffed mushrooms

Oranges with almonds

Wine: Klosternenberg or similar red Austrian Wine

Plan-ahead timetable

On the day before the meal

Farmhouse terrine: bone the chicken. Dice the chicken breasts, ham, pork fat, veal and pork. Mince the shoulder of veal, chicken meat, pork fat, ham and pork, or process the meats through a food processor. Make the forcemeat. Assemble the terrine and cook. When cool turn terrine out of the dish. Remove the string and store in refrigerator.

On the morning of the meal

Hungarian beef goulash: make the goulash, cook in the oven for 1–1¼ hours, then remove and allow to cool.

Oranges with almonds: prepare the oranges and make the filling. Assemble the oranges and chill in the refrigerator.

Three hours before the meal

Polenta: mix the cornmeal with the water, tie in muslin and steam for 3 hours.

Farmhouse terrine is a super recipe that makes enough to serve eight as a first course, with some left over to serve later in the week as a light supper or lunch dish for one or two people. This terrine is a combination of minced and cubed meat, flavoured with spices, Madeira and brandy, encased in the body of a boned chicken. It sounds complicated but it is not that difficult to prepare and it is one of those dishes that can be prepared well ahead. Indeed a day or so maturing in the refrigerator will help its flavour. Farmhouse terrine is often served at my dinner parties: it makes the perfect first course of a menu for cooks who like to take a little time and trouble – and is a compliment to guests who know and love good food.

Follow with a lusty Hungarian beef goulash for the main course. Cubes of beef, cooked until meltingly tender, are made rich with the flavours of tomato, paprika and caraway. This dish can also be conveniently prepared ahead – allowing the combination of herbs and spices to mingle and develop. Reheat on top of the cooker just before serving, and add the garnish of soured cream and parsley. Serve the goulash with hearty slices of polenta, a traditional peasant dish from Italy which I serve with a Gruyère cheese topping. Spinach-stuffed mushrooms – succulent mushrooms baked with a tasty spinach stuffing – are simple to prepare and complete this colourful main course.

After this wholesome country fare, a light and refreshing end to the meal is called for. Serve each of your guests with a scooped-out orange, filled with a delicious almond cream and decoratively presented with lids perched on top. A little time and effort are involved in making this attractive and tasty meal, but I am sure you will find the results well worthwhile.

Spinach-stuffed mushrooms: prepare the mushrooms, make the stuffing and cool. Butter the dish and put in the mushrooms. Add the egg to the stuffing and put into the mushrooms, top with breadcrumbs and parsley.

Fifteen minutes before the meal
Hungarian beef goulash: reheat gently on top of the cooker, stirring occasionally to prevent sticking.

Five minutes before the first course
Spinach-stuffed mushrooms: add the dry white wine, bring to a simmer and transfer to the oven.
Farmhouse terrine: remove from the refrigerator, slice and arrange on individual plates.

Between the first and the main course
Polenta: take out of the muslin, cut into slices. Pour over the melted butter, season, sprinkle with Gruyère and serve.
Hungarian beef goulash: add sour cream and serve.

Farmhouse terrine

Serves 8

1.6 kg /3½ lb chicken	**For the forcemeat**
25 g /1 oz butter	350 g /12 oz shoulder of veal
100 g /4 oz cooked ham, cut into 20 mm /¾ in dice	100 g /4 oz chicken meat
100 g /4 oz chicken breasts, cut into 20 mm /¾ in dice	100 g /4 oz cooked ham
100 g /4 oz pork fat, cut into 20 mm /¾ in dice	100 g /4 oz pork fat
100 g /4 oz veal, cut into 20 mm /¾ in dice	100 g/4 oz pork
100 g /4 oz pork, cut into 20 mm/¾ in dice	1 large egg
salt and ground black pepper	salt and ground black pepper
	cayenne pepper
	bay leaf, crumbled
	5 ml /1 tsp dried thyme
	30 ml /2 tbls Madeira
	30 ml /2 tbls brandy

1 Make an incision down the chicken backbone from the neck to the parson's nose. Ease the skin away; cut the meat from the carcass, keeping the knife as close as possible to the bone. Avoid piercing the skin. Cut through the joint where the thigh and wing bones meet the carcass and continue to cut until the chicken is boned, with the thighs and wings still attached. Cut around the top of the thigh and wing bones to loosen the meat and, with the back of the knife, scrape the meat down to the joints. Cut through these joints, then cut around the top of the bone and scrape the meat down to the end of the bone. Cut through where the foot and the drumstick meet. Leave all the meat attached to the chicken skin.
2 Heat the oven to 190C /375F /gas 5. Grease a 1.1 L /2 pt terrine or casserole with half the butter and line it with the boned chicken, so that the breast is on the bottom and the sides hang over the dish.
3 To make the forcemeat, pass the veal, chicken meat, cooked ham, pork fat and pork through the finest blade of your mincer, or use a food processor until smooth. Beat in remaining ingredients.
4 Fold the diced meats into the forcemeat and correct the seasoning. Pack the mixture into the terrine. Bring the chicken flaps up over the forcemeat and sew up with a trussing needle and string.
5 Melt the remaining butter and brush over chicken. Season. Bake for 40 minutes. Reduce heat to 160C /300F /gas 2; cook for 1 hour.
6 Remove the terrine from the oven and allow it to cool. Turn the terrine out of the dish, remove the string and chill overnight.

 boning the chicken, then 3½ hours, plus cooling and chilling overnight

Hungarian beef goulash

Serves 8

1.4 kg /3 lb top rump
50 g /2 oz butter
30 ml /2 tbls olive oil
2 Spanish onions,
   finely chopped
2 garlic cloves,
   finely chopped
90 ml /6 tbls flour
salt and ground black pepper
30 ml /2 tbls paprika

5 ml /1 tsp ground caraway seeds
1 bay leaf
1.5 ml /¼ tsp dried marjoram
1.5 ml /¼ tsp dried thyme
pinch of cayenne pepper
450 g /1 lb button mushrooms,
   sliced
2 red peppers, diced
850 g /1 lb 12 oz canned tomatoes
275 ml /10 fl oz soured cream
finely chopped fresh parsley

1   Heat the oven to 140C /275F /gas 1. Trim the beef and cut into 5 cm /2 in cubes.
2   Heat 25 g /1 oz of the butter and the olive oil in a large flameproof casserole. Add the finely chopped onions and the garlic and cook over a low heat for 10 minutes, or until the onions are transparent, stirring with a wooden spoon. Using a slotted spoon, transfer the onions and garlic to a heated plate and keep warm.
3   Sprinkle the flour onto a plate and season with salt and pepper. Toss the cubes of meat in the flour, shaking off any excess.
4   Heat the remaining butter in the casserole and brown the meat in 4 batches, for 2–3 minutes on each side.
5   Return the onions and garlic to the casserole. Sprinkle with the paprika and ground caraway seeds. Add the bay leaf, dried marjoram and dried thyme and season with cayenne pepper, salt and freshly ground black pepper. Cook for 10 minutes over a moderate heat, stirring constantly with a wooden spoon.
6   Add the sliced mushrooms, diced red peppers and tomatoes. Bring to a simmer. Cover and transfer to the oven and cook for 1–1¼ hours, or until the meat is tender. Correct the seasoning.
7   Transfer the goulash to a warmed serving dish. Pour a little soured cream around the centre, sprinkle with parsley and serve with the remaining soured cream passed separately.

 2–2¼ hours   Klosternenberg or similar red Austrian wine

Polenta

Serves 8

7.5 ml /1½ tsp salt
350 g /12 oz fine cornmeal
120 ml /8 tbls melted butter
salt and freshly ground black pepper
50 g /2 oz Gruyère cheese, freshly grated
For the garnish
flat leaved parsley
1 tomato, finely sliced

1   In a large, heavy saucepan bring 1.2 L /2¼ pt salted water to the boil.
2   Slowly, to avoid the water coming off the boil, pour in the cornmeal, stirring vigorously with a wooden spoon to prevent lumps forming. Continue to cook, stirring vigorously, until the mixture is quite thick and smooth – about 1 minute.
3   Line a metal sieve or colander with a double thickness of muslin. Scrape the polenta mixture into the colander, pull the ends of the muslin neatly together at the top and tie with string. Fit the sieve or colander over a pan of simmering water, cover and steam for 3 hours, topping up the water when necessary, until the polenta is a firm loaf.
4   Turn the polenta out onto a flat dish. Remove the muslin and cut the polenta into 10 mm /½ in slices. Pour 15 ml /1 tbls melted butter over each slice. Season with salt and freshly ground black pepper to taste and sprinkle each slice with 15 ml /1 tbls Gruyère cheese. Garnish with parsley and tomato slices. Serve immediately.

● This fine cornmeal from North Italy is often sold under the name *polenta*, the famous dish made from it. Polenta slices are also delicious fried in butter until crisp and golden. Try them baked in cream and sprinkled with Gruyère cheese until golden and bubbling.

 3½ hours

Spinach-stuffed mushrooms

Serves 8
450 g /1 lb frozen, chopped spinach
85–100 g /3½–4 oz butter
32 button mushrooms, about 450 g /1 lb
8 shallots, finely chopped
2.5 ml /½ tsp dried thyme
salt and freshly ground black pepper
1 large egg, beaten
120 ml /8 tbls fresh white breadcrumbs
30 ml /2 tbls finely chopped fresh parsley
120 ml /8 tbls dry white wine

1   Melt 25 g /1 oz butter in a large saucepan and add the frozen spinach. Cook over medium heat, breaking up the blocks with a wooden spoon.
2   Heat the oven to 190C /375F /gas 5. Remove the mushroom stalks and wipe the caps clean with a damp cloth. Finely chop the stalks.
3   Heat 50 g /2 oz butter in a saucepan and sauté the finely chopped shallots for 5 minutes, or until soft, stirring with a wooden spoon. Add the finely chopped mushroom stalks and sauté for a further 3 minutes. Stir in the drained spinach and the dried thyme. Season with salt and freshly ground black pepper to taste. Remove from the heat and allow to cool.
4   Butter a gratin dish large enough to take the mushroom caps in one layer; use 2 dishes if necessary. Arrange the mushrooms, cap side down, in the prepared dish and season with salt and freshly ground black pepper to taste.
5   Stir the beaten egg into the spinach mixture and spoon it into the mushroom caps.
6   In a small bowl, combine the breadcrumbs and the finely chopped parsley and sprinkle over the mushrooms caps. Pour the dry white wine into the dish and bring to a simmer over a low heat. Transfer to the oven and cook for 15–20 minutes, until the mushroom caps are tender and the breadcrumbs golden. Serve immediately.

● This dish can also be served as an appetizer.

45 minutes

Oranges with almonds

Serves 8
8 large oranges
90 ml /6 tbls curaçao
425 ml /15 fl oz thick cream
180 ml /12 tbls caster sugar
75 g /3 oz finely ground almonds
shiny, green leaves

1   Cut a slice off the top of each orange and reserve. Using a grapefruit knife, remove the pulp from the oranges, being careful not to damage the skins.
2   Squeeze the orange pulp and strain the juice extracted. In a bowl, combine the curaçao, 90 ml /6 tbls strained orange juice and thick cream. Whisk in the sugar and fold in the finely ground almonds. Continue to whisk until the mixture is smooth and stands in peaks.
3   Fill the orange shells with the almond cream and carefully place the tops back on, slightly on the slant. Transfer the oranges to a flat dish and chill.
4   To serve, arrange 2–3 shiny, green leaves under each orange on individual serving dishes.

● This dish must be served the same day it is made.

45 minutes, plus chilling

STAR MENU 2

Beetroot soup
Anchovy dartois

Roast beef provençal
Hash browned potatoes

Baked sultana pudding

Wine: Côtes du Ventoux

Contrast the slightly sweet flavour of my Beetroot soup with the salty tang of Anchovy Dartois for a really unusual first course. The beetroot soup is crystal clear and has a rich, red colour. It is delicious served either chilled or piping hot. Garnish each portion with a thin lemon slice and pass hot, crisp, little puff pastries filled with anchovy butter for a stylish accompaniment.

Follow this intriguing starter with Roast beef provençal, a succulent alternative to plain roast beef. The joint – sirloin or topside – is marinated overnight in the refrigerator with olive oil, red wine, oregano, onion and parsley. It is then roasted in the oven and served with a rich, red wine sauce. Remember to turn it over once or twice while it is marinating and give it plenty of time to come to room temperature before cooking. My favourite Hash browned potatoes are my choice to accompany this succulent joint of beef: fluffy baked potato fried with onion to make a crisp, brown crust.

Provence is the inspiration for the meat course – drink with it a sunny red wine from the South of France, like Côtes du Ventoux – fruity, unpretentious and enjoyable

Plan-ahead timetable

On the day before the meal
Roast beef provençal: marinate the beef.

On the morning of the meal
Beetroot soup: make and chill the soup.

Three hours before the meal
Anchovy Dartois: defrost pastry. Prepare anchovy butter.
Roast beef provençal: bring to room temperature.
Hash browned potatoes: scrub and bake the potatoes. Scoop out flesh and mash. Add onion and seasoning. Reserve.
Gratin of green beans: top and tail the beans.

One hour before the meal
Anchovy Dartois: roll out the pastry and prepare the strips.
Roast beef provençal: transfer the beef to a casserole and roast in centre of the oven. Reserve the marinade.

Thirty-five minutes before the meal
Roast beef provençal: pour the marinade over the beef.
Hash browned potatoes: cook the potato cake. Keep warm.

Twenty minutes before the meal
Beetroot soup: gently reheat the soup, if wished.
Anchovy Dartois: bake on the top shelf. Keep warm.
Baked sultana pudding: prepare the pudding mixture and reserve

Beetroot soup

Serves 4

700 g /1½ lb raw beetroot
1½ chicken stock cubes
1 large onion, stuck with 3 cloves
2 garlic cloves, crushed
bouquet garni
10 ml /2 tsp sugar
1.4 L /2½ pt boiling water
salt and freshly ground black pepper
15 ml /1 tbls wine vinegar or lemon juice
4 thin lemon slices, to garnish

1　Peel and dice the beetroot. Put it in a large saucepan with the chicken stock cubes, the onion stuck with cloves, the crushed garlic, bouquet garni and sugar. Add the boiling water and season to taste with salt and freshly ground black pepper.
2　Bring to the boil, then reduce the heat and simmer, uncovered, for about 1 hour. The beetroot will lose its colour, but the soup itself will turn a beautiful shade of deep red. Strain the soup through a fine sieve and keep hot, or leave to cool and chill.
3　Just before serving, stir in the wine vinegar or lemon juice and correct the seasoning. Garnish with lemon slices and serve hot or chilled.

● This soup is delicious served hot or chilled as you wish, depending on the season and your taste. If you have to reheat it, take great care not to let it come to the boil or it will lose its clear, appetizing colour.
● To give the lemon slices an attractive, frilly edge, groove the lemon lengthways at intervals, using a very sharp knife, before slicing.

1¼ hours, plus chilling (optional)

---

st before the meal

chovy Dartois: cut the anchovy strips and serve.
ast beef provençal: transfer to heated serving platter and leave to
tle in a warm place. Keep the casserole juices warm.

tween the first and the main course

ast beef provençal: finish making the sauce and then transfer it to
auce-boat.
ked sultana pudding: put the mixture in the cake tin and bake.

tween the main course and the dessert

ked sultana pudding: gently heat the cream and serve with the
dding.

Anchovy Dartois

Serves 4
45 g /1¾ oz canned anchovy fillets
60 ml /4 tbls milk
50 g /2 oz unsalted butter
flour for dusting
225 g /8 oz frozen puff pastry, defrosted
1 egg yolk, beaten

1 Heat the oven to 230C /450F /gas 8. Drain the anchovy fillets thoroughly and pat them dry with absorbent paper. Put them in a small, shallow dish, cover with the milk and leave them to soak for about 5 minutes. This will make them less salty.
2 Drain the anchovy fillets again, then chop them roughly. Put them in a mortar with the unsalted butter and pound with the pestle to a smooth paste.
3 Lightly flour a board and roll the pastry out, 3 mm /⅛ in thick. Cut the pastry into 6 strips, 30 × 5 cm /12 × 2 in.
4 Spread half the strips with the anchovy butter, leaving the edges free.
5 Moisten the edges with a little water and cover with the remaining strips, pressing lightly to seal the strips together. Flute the edges lightly with your fingers and a knife, place a thumb on the edge of the pastry and making a small slanting kink with the knife. Brush with beaten egg yolk and make small slits in the top to allow the steam to escape.
6 Using a palette knife, transfer the strips to a baking sheet and bake for about 10 minutes, or until puffed and golden.
7 Cut each strip into 7.5 cm /3 in lengths and serve very hot.

● *Dartois* – 2 thin bands of pastry enclosing a small, tasty filling – are a traditional hot cocktail snack or light appetizer. Serve these Anchovy Dartois – *Dartois aux anchois* in French – with the Beetroot soup (see recipe).

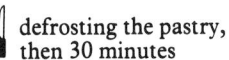 defrosting the pastry, then 30 minutes

Roast beef provençal

Serves 4–6
1.4 kg /3 lb topside or sirloin beef, boned and rolled
1 fat garlic clove, slivered
freshly ground black pepper
5–10 ml /1–2 tsp crushed, dried thyme
salt
watercress, to garnish
For the marinade
60 ml /4 tbls olive oil
25 ml /1½ tbls wine vinegar
pinch of dried oregano

15 ml /1 tbls finely chopped onion
15 ml /1 tbls finely chopped fresh parsley
freshly ground black pepper
150 ml /5 fl oz red wine
½ large bay leaf, crumbled
For the sauce
10 ml /2 tsp cornflour
150 ml /5 fl oz red wine
salt
freshly ground black pepper

1 With the point of a sharp knife, make small slits about 25 mm /1 in deep all over the beef and put in slivers of garlic. Rub the joint all over with freshly ground black pepper and dried thyme, then place it in a shallow dish.
2 Prepare the marinade. In a bowl, combine the oil, wine vinegar, oregano, onion and parsley and a generous pinch of freshly ground black pepper. Stir until well blended and add the wine and bay leaf. Pour the marinade over the meat. Cover and marinate overnight in the refrigerator, turning the meat over once or twice. Leave to come to room temperature before cooking.
3 Heat the oven to 220C /425F /gas 7.
4 Transfer the marinated beef to a flameproof casserole, reserving the marinade juices. Season to taste with salt and freshly ground black pepper. Roast for 25 minutes.
5 Pour the marinade juices over the beef and return to the oven for a further 30 minutes, basting frequently.
6 Reserving the cooking juices, transfer the meat to a heated serving dish. Leave in the turned-off oven with the door open for 15 minutes, to allow the juices to settle and make carving easier.
7 Meanwhile, finish the sauce. In a small bowl, blend together the cornflour, the red wine and 60 ml /4 tbls water. Pour into the casserole and bring to the boil, stirring and scraping the bottom and sides of the casserole with a wooden spoon. Season to taste with salt and freshly ground black pepper and simmer for 1 minute, or until thickened, stirring frequently.
8 Garnish the beef with bouquets of watercress. Serve the meat, with the sauce passed separately in a heated sauceboat.

 marinating overnight, then 1 hour 20 minutes   Côtes du Ventoux

Hash browned potatoes

Serves 4
1.2 kg /2¾ lb large, floury potatoes
1 Spanish onion, finely chopped
salt and freshly ground black pepper
25 g /1 oz butter
30 ml /2 tbls olive oil
15 ml /1 tbls finely snipped chives, to garnish

1   Heat the oven to 200C /400F /gas 6.
2   Scrub the potatoes clean with a stiff brush and place them on a baking tray. Cook them in the oven for about 1 hour, or until soft.
3   Remove the cooked potatoes from the oven. Holding them one at a time in a tea-towel, split them and scoop the flesh out of the skins with a spoon and put it into a bowl.
4   Add the finely chopped onion and mash the potatoes with a fork until free of lumps. Season with salt and freshly ground black pepper to taste.
5   In a heavy-based, medium-sized frying-pan, heat the butter and olive oil. When the foaming subsides, put in the potato mixture. Flatten to a cake with a palette knife. Cook over a low heat for 30 minutes, occasionally shaking the pan and lifting the edges of the cake to make sure the potato mixture is not burning or sticking, until the underside is crusty and well browned.
6   Turn the hash browned potato cake out onto a round, heated serving dish slightly larger in diameter than the pan. Serve as soon as possible, garnished with finely snipped chives.

🕯 1 hour 10 minutes

Baked sultana pudding

Serves 4
butter for greasing
225 g /8 oz flour
salt
5 ml /1 tsp baking powder
75 g /3 oz cold butter, diced
75 g /3 oz sultanas
45 ml /3 tbls sugar
15 ml /1 tbls candied peel, finely shredded
5 ml /1 tsp vanilla essence
2 large eggs, well beaten
175 ml /6 fl oz milk
To serve
275 ml /10 fl oz thick cream
sugar

1   Heat the oven to 190C /375F /gas 5.
2   Grease an 18 cm /7 in square cake tin lightly with butter.
3   Sift the flour, salt and baking powder into a bowl. Rub in the diced butter with your fingertips until the mixture resembles fine breadcrumbs.
4   Pick over and clean the sultanas. Add them with the sugar, shredded candied peel and the vanilla essence to the flour and butter mixture.
5   Make a well in the centre and pour in the beaten eggs and half the milk. Using a wooden spoon, gradually incorporate the flour mixture into the liquid, adding the rest of the milk. Beat until well blended.
6   Spoon the mixture into the prepared cake tin and level off the top with a palette knife. Bake in the oven for 30–35 minutes, or until the pudding is well risen and firm to the touch.
7   Warm the cream in a small saucepan over a gentle heat, taking care not to let it come to boiling point.
8   To serve, cut the pudding into squares, sprinkle with sugar and pass the hot cream separately.

🕯 50 minutes

Beef with Madeira and mushroom sauce

Serves 6

1.8 kg /4 lb topside of beef
100 g /4 oz fat salt pork or
  piece streaky bacon in one,
  chilled
salt and ground black pepper
50 g /2 oz butter
45 ml /3 tbls olive oil
2 large carrots, finely chopped
2 Spanish onions, finely
  chopped
1 sprig of parsley

a sprig of fresh thyme or
  1.5 ml /¼ tsp dried thyme
small bay leaf
4 tomatoes, quartered and seeded
300 ml /10 fl oz beef stock,
  home-made or from a cube
75 ml /5 tbls dry white wine
225 g /8 oz button mushrooms,
  thinly sliced
6 button mushrooms, to garnish
90 ml /6 tbls thick cream
60 ml /4 tbls Madeira

1 Make 25 mm /1 in deep incisions at regular intervals all over the beef with the point of a sharp knife. Cut the fat salt pork or bacon into small strips; push these deeply into the beef. Season generously with salt and freshly ground black pepper.

2 Heat the oven to 160C /300F /gas 2. Heat the butter and olive oil in a heavy, flameproof casserole and brown the meat richly and evenly on all sides over a moderate heat. Remove and keep warm.

3 Add the finely chopped carrots and onions to the casserole; sauté for 10 minutes or until the onions are soft.

4 Add the meat, parsley, thyme, bay leaf and tomatoes. Pour in the stock and dry white wine. Season to taste. Cook, covered, in the oven for 2½ hours, turning the meat and basting occasionally.

5 Remove the meat from the casserole and keep warm. Skim the pan juices of excess fat. Purée the pan juices and vegetables in a blender then sieve into a clean saucepan. Boil vigorously for 10 minutes, stirring, until reduced by a quarter.

6 Return the meat to the casserole together with the sliced mushrooms. Cover and return to the oven for a further 30 minutes or until the meat and mushrooms are tender.

7 Cut a cross in each button mushroom with a sharp knife, then sauté gently until browned. To serve, carve the meat in thick slices, and arrange overlapping, on a heated platter. Stir the thick cream and Madeira into the sauce, and heat through over a low heat. Correct the seasoning. Spoon some of the sauce over the beef slices, garnish with the button mushrooms and serve the remaining sauce separately in a heated sauce boat.

 4 hours

Beef and onion casserole

Serves 4–6

1.1 kg /2½ lb shin of beef
45 ml /3 tbls flour
salt and freshly ground black pepper
60 ml /4 tbls olive oil
100 g /4 oz butter
3 Spanish onions, thinly sliced
2 garlic cloves, crushed
1 strip orange zest, dried out in the oven
2 cloves
bouquet garni
275 /10 fl oz beef stock, home-made or from a cube
bouquet of watercress, to garnish

1 Bring the beef to room temperature. Heat the oven to 110C / 225F /gas ¼.

2 Remove excess fat and gristle from the beef and cut into 5cm /2 in cubes with a sharp knife.

3 On a plate, season the flour with salt and pepper. Toss the beef to coat in the seasoned flour, shaking off any excess.

4 In a flameproof casserole, heat the oil and half the butter. When the foaming subsides, sauté half the beef cubes for 1–2 minutes each side, turning once with a spatula. Remove with a slotted spoon and keep warm. Repeat with the remaining beef.

5 Add the thinly sliced onions and sauté over a moderate heat for 7–10 minutes, or until soft and turning golden, stirring occasionally with a wooden spoon.

6 Add the remaining butter, garlic cloves, dried orange zest, cloves, bouquet garni and beef stock to the casserole. Season with salt and freshly ground black pepper and bring to the boil. Return the meat to the casserole and stir to mix. Cover tightly and cook in the oven for 3½ hours, or until the beef is meltingly tender and the sauce is thick and highly flavoured.

7 Remove the orange zest and the bouquet garni. Skim the sauce. Correct the seasoning and serve immediately from the casserole, garnished with a bouquet of watercress.

 bringing to room temperature, then about 4 hours

Beefsteak with oyster sauce

Serves 4–6
1 rump steak, weighing 700–900 g /1½–2 lb, about 25 mm/1 in thick
freshly ground black pepper
15 g /½ oz butter, softened
For the oyster sauce
12 oysters
25 g /1 oz butter
15–30 ml /1–2 tbls lemon juice
cayenne pepper
2 large egg yolks
90 ml /6 tbls thick cream
Worcestershire sauce

1   Remove the steak from the refrigerator at least 30 minutes before cooking. Slit the fat in several places around the sides to prevent the meat from curling during cooking. Heat the grill to high.
2   Make the oyster sauce: prise the shells open and remove the oysters, saving the liquor. Put the oysters and liquor in a saucepan with the butter and lemon juice, and season with cayenne pepper, to taste. Simmer gently for 1–2 minutes until the oysters begin to curl up; remove the pan from the heat. In a bowl, beat together the egg yolks and thick cream; add a little Worcestershire sauce, and stir into the oyster mixture. Reheat the sauce but do not allow it to come to a boil as the sauce will curdle. Keep warm over hot water.
3   Sprinkle both sides of the steak with freshly ground black pepper and spread with softened butter. Grill for 3–4 minutes on each side for a rare steak, 4–5 minutes each side for medium and 5–6 minutes each side for well done.
4   To serve: place the steak on a hot serving platter and surround with the oyster sauce. Carve the steak into serving portions at the table.

bringing to room temperature,
then 30 minutes

Pan-fried patties with tomato sauce

Serves 4
75 g /3 oz fresh white
  breadcrumbs
150 ml /5 fl oz milk
50 g /2 oz butter
60 ml /4 tbls olive oil
1 onion, finely chopped
125 g /4 oz good quality
  sausage-meat
450 g /1 lb minced beef
2 garlic cloves, finely chopped
30 ml /2tbls chopped parsley
salt and ground pepper
1 large egg, lightly beaten
30 ml /2 tbls flour

For the tomato sauce
60 ml /4 tbls olive oil
2 Spanish onions, finely chopped
2 garlic cloves, finely chopped
60 ml /4 tbls tomato purée
800 g /1 lb 12 oz canned
  tomatoes
2 bay leaves
60 ml /4 tbls chopped parsley
1.5 ml /¼ tsp dried oregano
1 small strip lemon peel
½ beef stock cube, crumbled
salt and ground pepper
5–10 ml /1–2 tsp Worcestershire
  sauce

1   First make the tomato sauce: heat the oil in a heavy-based frying-pan and sauté the onion and garlic until soft but not brown. Add the tomato purée and cook for 1–2 minutes, stirring constantly. Add the tomatoes, bay leaves, parsley, oregano, lemon peel, stock cube and 275 ml /10 fl oz water. Season to taste. Simmer gently for 1 hour, stirring occasionally.
2   Meanwhile, soak the breadcrumbs in the milk. Heat half the butter and oil in a large frying-pan. When the foaming subsides, add the onion and cook over low heat for 10 minutes or until soft.
3   Add the sausage-meat and cook over high heat for 5 minutes or until lightly browned, stirring with a fork to separate the meat. Add the minced beef and mix well.
4   Squeeze out the excess moisture from the breadcrumbs. Add to the mixture, with the garlic and half the parsley. Season to taste. Mix well. Off the heat stir in the beaten egg and leave to cool.
5   Shape the meat mixture into 12 even-sized patties. Sprinkle the flour on to a plate, season with salt and freshly ground black pepper. Toss each patty in the seasoned flour, shaking off excess.
6   Heat the remaining butter and oil in a large frying-pan. When the foaming subsides, fry the patties for 1–2 minutes on each side or until golden. Transfer to a heated serving dish. Check the seasoning for the tomato sauce and add the Worcestershire sauce. Pour over the patties, sprinkle with the remaining parsley. Serve immediately.

making the tomato sauce,
then 1 hour

Baked beef and onions

Serves 4

8 slices of cold roast beef, about 5 mm /¼ in thick
25 g /1 oz butter
30 ml /2 tbls olive oil
2 large onions, thinly sliced
2.5 ml /½ tsp dried thyme
salt and freshly ground black pepper
90ml /6 tbls beef gravy, or 45 ml /3 tbls jellied meat juice left over
   from roasting, diluted with 45 ml /3 tbls water or dry white wine
90 ml /6 tbls freshly grated Cheddar cheese

1   Heat the oven to 200C /400F /gas 6. Cut each slice of roast beef into 3 strips. Arrange the beef strips in a shallow, ovenproof gratin dish.
2   Melt the butter and olive oil in a frying-pan and sauté the thinly sliced onions until they are soft and a rich golden colour. Season generously with the thyme and salt and freshly ground black pepper to taste. Remove the onions from the pan with a slotted spoon and spread them evenly over the beef slices.
3   Moisten the beef and onions with the beef gravy, or diluted roasting juices, and sprinkle with the freshly grated Cheddar cheese. Bake for 15–20 minutes in the oven, or until the beef is hot and the topping is bubbling and golden brown. Serve straight from the gratin dish.

● This supper dish is so good that it is well worth keeping back some of the Sunday joint specially for it. You can make it go further by slicing some left-over boiled potatoes and layering them over the beef before adding the onions.

 35 minutes

Barbecued tournedos de Nîmes

Serves 6

6 × 4cm /1½ in thick tournedos, barded with a thin strip of pork fat
   and tied with string
freshly ground black pepper
6 × 20 mm /¾ in thick aubergine slices, the same diameter as the
   tournedos
salt
olive oil
finely chopped fresh tarragon, to garnish
parsley sprigs, to garnish
For the sauce nîmoise
150 ml /5 fl oz thick cream, whipped
30 ml /2 tbls Dijon mustard
45 ml /3 tbls tomato purée
salt and freshly ground black pepper

1   Wipe the tournedos with absorbent paper and season generously with freshly ground black pepper. Leave to come to room temperature.
2   Place the aubergine slices in a colander and sprinkle generously with salt. Leave to drain for about 30 minutes.
3   Meanwhile prepare the sauce. In a bowl, combine the whipped, thick cream, Dijon mustard and tomato purée. Season to taste with salt and freshly ground black pepper. Heat the grill to high.
4   Rinse the aubergine slices well with cold water and pat dry firmly with absorbent paper to remove any excess moisture. Brush with olive oil and season to taste with freshly ground black pepper.
5   Brush the grill grid with oil, place the aubergine slices on the grid and cook for 3 minutes each side, turning occasionally and basting with more oil.
6   Meanwhile, season the tournedos with salt and more freshly ground black pepper and place on the grid 7.5 cm/3 in from the heat. Cook for 4½ minutes each side for rare meat, 6 minutes each side for medium and 7–8 minutes each side for well done.
7   To serve, place a slice of grilled aubergine on each plate. Remove and discard the pork fat and string from each tournedos. Set a tournedos on each aubergine slice. Top with 15 ml/1 tbls sauce nîmoise. Sprinkle each serving with a pinch of finely chopped tarragon. Garnish with parsley sprigs and serve immediately.

bringing to room temperature,
draining, then 25 minutes

Steak and kidney pie

Serves 4–6

1 kg /2 lb 3 oz braising steak, cut into 4 cm /1½ in cubes
350 g /12 oz veal or lamb's kidneys
150 g /5 oz flour
salt
freshly ground black pepper
50 g /2 oz butter or suet
4 shallots, finely chopped
5 ml /1 tsp Worcestershire sauce
275 ml /10 fl oz beef stock, home-made or from a cube
bay leaf
5 ml /1 tsp chopped fresh parsley
pinch of powdered clove
pinch of dried marjoram
butter for greasing
400 g /14 oz made-weight puff pastry, defrosted
1 large egg, beaten
15 ml /1 tbls dry sherry

1   Clean the kidneys, split them and remove the membrane, fat and the large tubes. Cut the kidneys into 5 mm /¼ in thick slices. Season the flour with the salt and freshly ground black pepper, and roll the steak cubes and kidney slices in the flour until lightly coated.
2   Melt the butter or suet in a thick-bottomed saucepan or casserole and sauté the finely chopped shallots until golden. Add the steak and kidney in batches. Brown them thoroughly and evenly, stirring almost constantly.
3   Return all the steak and kidney to the casserole. Add the Worcestershire sauce, beef stock, bay leaf, chopped parsley, powdered clove and marjoram. Season with freshly ground black pepper to taste. Stir, cover, and simmer over a low heat for 1–1¼ hours or until the meat is tender.
4   At the end of cooking time, if the liquid is too thin, thicken it with a little flour mixed to a smooth paste with water.
5   Heat the oven to 230C /450F /gas 8. Butter a large pie dish (of at least 1.1. L /2 pt capacity), place a pie funnel in the centre of the dish and add the meat and the liquid. Leave to become cold.
6   Roll out the puff pastry and cut a lid for the pie a little larger than the pie dish. Cut a strip from the trimmings and fit this round the moistened edge of the pie dish. Moisten the strip, then transfer the lid to the pie. Knock up and flute the edge. Cut decorations from the remaining trimmings and stick these to the pie with beaten egg. Make a steam vent over the funnel and glaze the top.
7   Bake in the oven for 10 minutes. Then lower the heat to 190C /375F /gas 5. Continue baking for a further 15 minutes, or until the crust is golden brown.
8   Just before serving the pie, pour the dry sherry in through the funnel.

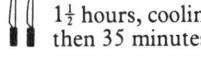 1½ hours, cooling then 35 minutes

Corned beef hash with poached eggs

Serves 6

350 g /12 oz potatoes, scrubbed clean
salt
25 g /1 oz butter
15 ml /1 tbls olive oil
1 Spanish onion, finely chopped
2 green peppers, diced
700 g /1½ lb corned beef
90 ml /6 tbls finely chopped fresh parsley
30 ml /2 tbls Worcestershire sauce
freshly ground black pepper
60 ml /4 tbls white wine vinegar
6 large eggs
sprigs of parsley, to garnish

1   Place the potatoes in a saucepan. Cover with water, add a pinch of salt and bring to the boil. Cook for about 20 minutes, or until the potatoes can easily be pierced, but are not mushy. Drain and leave until cool enough to handle. Peel off the skin and dice the potatoes.
2   In a large frying-pan, heat the butter and olive oil. When the foaming subsides, add the finely chopped onion and diced peppers. Cook over a medium heat for 10 minutes, or until soft, stirring occasionally with a wooden spoon.
3   Meanwhile, scrape any fat from the surface of the corned beef then mash the beef to a paste. Add the mashed corned beef to the cooked vegetables, with the diced potatoes and the finely chopped parsley and Worcestershire sauce. Season to taste with salt and freshly ground black pepper. Cook over a moderate heat for 5 minutes, stirring constantly. Keep hot.
4   To poach the eggs, fill a saucepan with water, add the vinegar, bring to the boil and reduce the heat to a simmer. Break an egg into a cup and slip it into the water. Repeat, quickly and carefully, with the remaining eggs. Raise the heat so that the water bubbles up. Draw the white round the yolk of each egg with a slotted spoon, then reduce the heat and simmer gently for 3–4 minutes. Remove the eggs with a slotted spoon. Rinse under hot water and pat dry with absorbent paper. Trim the edges with scissors if necessary.
5   Turn out the corned beef hash onto a large, heated serving platter. Arrange the poached eggs at even intervals.

 1 hour

Fettucine alla bolognese

Serves 4–6
450 g /1 lb fettucine
salt
freshly grated Parmesan cheese, to serve
For the bolognese sauce
25 g /1 oz butter
15 ml /1 tbls olive oil
1 Spanish onion, finely chopped
225 g /8 oz lean, minced beef
salt and freshly ground black pepper
1.5 ml /¼ tsp dried oregano
150 ml /5 fl oz dry white wine
45 ml /3 tbls tomato purée

1   To make the sauce, heat the butter and olive oil in a large frying-pan. Add the finely chopped Spanish onion and sauté over medium heat for 7–10 minutes or until soft, stirring occasionally with a wooden spoon.
2   Stir in the lean minced beef and sauté for 5 minutes or until browned, stirring constantly. Season with salt and freshly ground black pepper to taste, and the dried oregano.
3   Stir in the dry white wine and tomato purée and simmer gently, uncovered, for 35 minutes.
4   Meanwhile, bring a large saucepan of salted water to the boil, add the fettucine and cook for 8–10 minutes, or until al dente: cooked but still firm.
5   Drain the pasta thoroughly and transfer to a heated serving dish. Pour over the bolognese sauce. Serve immediately with Parmesan cheese, sprinkled on top.

● This Italian starter would make a good lunch or supper dish for 3–4 people.

🍴 1 hour

Boiled beef with mushrooms

Serves 4
1 kg /2 lb 3 oz rolled rib of beef
1 medium-sized onion, stuck with cloves
1 celery stalk, halved
2 carrots, halved
1 turnip, halved
2 large marrow bones
bouquet garni
salt
freshly ground black pepper
For the mushroom sauce
45 ml / 3 tbls olive oil
25 g /1 oz butter
225 g /8 oz button mushrooms, chopped
60 ml /4 tbls tomato purée
salt
freshly ground black pepper

1   Place the rolled rib of beef in a large heavy-based saucepan. Add the onion stuck with cloves, celery, carrots, turnip, marrow bones, bouquet garni, and 1.7–2.2 L /3–4 pt water to cover. Bring to the boil over a very low heat, allowing the scum to accumulate on the surface. When a thick scum has formed, pour in 150 ml /5 fl oz cold water to stop the stock from boiling any further, and skim off the scum with a slotted spoon.
2   Bring to the boil again over a low heat and simmer very gently for 3 hours – the stock should hardly move, otherwise the meat will become tough. After 2 hours, season with salt and freshly ground black pepper to taste.
3   About 20 minutes before the beef is cooked, prepare the mushroom sauce. In a large, heavy-based frying-pan, heat the olive oil and butter. When the foaming subsides, add the chopped mushrooms and sauté over a high heat for 5 minutes or until they are lightly golden in colour, stirring constantly with a wooden spoon. Using a ladle, remove 200 ml /7 fl oz broth from the simmering beef. Add to the mushrooms with the tomato purée and stir to blend. Season with salt and freshly ground black pepper to taste. Cover the pan and simmer gently for 10 minutes, stirring occasionally. Correct the seasoning.
4   Drain the beef, discarding the vegetables and marrow bones, and transfer it to a wooden board. Carve it into 5 mm /¼ in slices. Arrange the beef slices on a long, slim heated serving platter, overlapping them in a single line, and pour over the mushroom sauce. Serve immediately.

🍴 3½ hours

Italian boiled dinner

Serves 8–10

1.8 kg /4 lb chuck steak, in one piece, tied at regular intervals along
    the length to make an even shape
450 g /1 lb salt pork
2 bay leaves
6 peppercorns
1 medium-sized boiling chicken
1 kg /2 lb 3 oz boned and rolled loin of pork
8 large carrots, scraped and halved, weighing about 550 g /1¼ lb
8 small onions, weighing about 450 g /1 lb
8 potatoes, weighing about 700 g /1½ lb
8 small turnips, weighing about 450 g /1 lb
550 g /1¼ lb cabbage, cut into wedges
For the horseradish chantilly
150 ml /5 fl oz thick cream
30 ml /2 tbls iced water
30–45 ml /2–3 tbls horseradish sauce
salt

1   Place the beef in a heavy-based, large casserole with just enough
warm water to cover, bring to the boil and skim off the foam.
2   Add the salt pork, bay leaves and peppercorns. Cover and
simmer over a very low heat for 1 hour. Add the chicken and pork.
Continue to cook for another 2 hours or until all the meats are
tender.
3   Cool slightly and skim off any excess fat. Add the halved carrots
and simmer for 10 minutes. Add the remaining vegetables and cook
for a further 15–20 minutes or until the vegetables are tender but
still crisp.
4   Meanwhile make the horseradish chantilly. Whip the thick
cream until soft peaks form. Add the iced water and continue to
whisk until the sauce is thick and fluffy again. Fold in horseradish
sauce to taste and season lightly with salt. Chill
5   Slice the beef, pork and salt pork, and joint the chicken. Arrange
on a platter garnished with the vegetables. Serve immediately,
accompanied with horseradish chantilly.

● *Bollito misto* is a celebrated Italian dish. Each person gets a
helping of four different meats, all cooked together in a big pot. It is
definitely a dish for a big gathering!

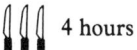 4 hours

Swiss steak casserole

Serves 4–6

1 kg /2 lb 3 oz rump or sirloin steak
1 garlic clove, halved
30 ml /2 tbls seasoned flour
45–60 ml /3–4 tbls lard
2 medium-sized Spanish onions, finely chopped
salt and freshly ground black pepper
400 g /14 oz canned tomatoes
30 ml /2 tbls tomato purée
2.5 ml /½ tsp dried oregano
2.5 ml /½ tsp crushed dried rosemary
125 ml /4 fl oz lager
12 small white onions
sprig of rosemary, to garnish

1   Heat the oven to 110C /225F /gas ¼. Slice the steak lengthways
into 4 or 6 serving pieces and remove any large pieces of fat. Pound
the meat with a mallet or rolling pin to flatten it to about 12 mm /½
in thick. Rub both sides with the cut sides of the garlic halves. Dust
the steak with the seasoned flour.
2   Melt 45 ml /3 tbls lard in a frying-pan over high heat. Sear the
steaks for about 45 seconds on each side to brown and seal them.
Transfer the steaks to a warmed casserole.
3   Add the chopped onion to the fat left in the frying-pan and sauté
until softened and golden brown, adding more lard if necessary.
Season lightly with salt and freshly ground black pepper to taste.
4   Add the peeled tomatoes with their juice, tomato purée, oregano,
rosemary and lager, and stir over a low heat until well blended.
Simmer, uncovered, for 5 minutes, or until the sauce has reduced by
one-third. Add the small white onions.
5   Pour the sauce over the meat. Cover the casserole and bake in
the oven for about 45 minutes, or until the meat is tender. Garnish
with a sprig of rosemary and serve from the casserole.

 1¼ hours

Beer pot roast

Serves 6–8
1.4 kg /3 lb topside of beef, tied at intervals with string
60 ml /4 tbls flour
salt and freshly ground black pepper
50 g /2 oz butter
125 g /4 oz unsmoked streaky bacon, cut into matchstick strips
275 ml /10 fl oz brown ale
1 large onion, finely chopped
1 large carrot, diced
1 celery stalk, diced
1 sprig of parsley
bay leaf

1 Heat the oven to 150C /330F /gas 2.
2 Wipe the meat with a damp cloth or absorbent paper. Season the flour with salt and freshly ground black pepper. Dust the meat all over with the seasoned flour.
3 Melt the butter in a heavy flameproof casserole and add the bacon strips and the meat. Brown the beef over a steady, moderate heat turning it over until the joint is well browned on all sides and the bacon has given up its fat.
4 Remove the beef and bacon from the casserole. Pour in the beer and scrape the bottom and sides of the pan to incorporate the browned flour. Add the vegetables, sprig of parsley and bay leaf.
5 Bring to the boil and replace the beef and bacon, spooning the liquid over the joint. Season generously with salt and freshly ground black pepper, cover the casserole tightly with foil and then with the lid, so it fits very tightly. Put the casserole in the oven and cook for 2½–3 hours, or until the meat is very tender.
6 Transfer the joint to a warmed serving dish. Discard the string and spoon the flavouring vegetables and bacon around it. Skim any excess fat from the sauce and pour the sauce into a heated sauce-boat. Serve immediately.

 3–3½ hours

Mexican stuffed marrow

Serves 4
2 × 450 g /1 lb marrows
butter for greasing
salt and ground black pepper
30 ml /2 tbls olive oil
1 medium-sized onion, chopped
2 garlic cloves, finely chopped
2 fresh green chillies with the stalks and seeds removed
450 g /1 lb lean beef, minced
2.5 ml /½ tsp dried oregano
2 bay leaves
5 ml /1 tsp Tabasco sauce

60 ml /4 tbls fresh white breadcrumbs
225 ml /8 fl oz beef stock, home-made or from a cube
15 ml /1 tbls finely chopped parsley, to garnish
For the sauce
225 g /8 oz cream cheese
150 ml /5 fl oz thick cream
5 ml /1 tsp salt
1.5 ml /¼ tsp of cayenne pepper
50 g /2 oz sultanas or seedless raisins

1 Heat the oven to 180C /350F /gas 4.
2 Slice the marrows in half lengthways. Scoop out the seeds and membrane with a sharp spoon and discard.
3 Generously butter a baking sheet, place the halved marrows on it and season them with salt and freshly ground black pepper. Cover with foil and bake in the oven for about 25 minutes, or until the marrows are a little tender. Remove from the oven and reserve.
4 Meanwhile, heat the olive oil in a large frying-pan. Add the coarsely chopped onion, the finely chopped garlic and the chillies. Cook over a low heat for 7–10 minutes, or until soft.
5 Stir in the minced beef, dried oregano, bay leaves, Tabasco and salt to taste. Sauté for 3–4 minutes, or until the beef begins to brown, stirring frequently.
6 Add the breadcrumbs and the beef stock, bring to the boil, reduce the heat and simmer gently, uncovered, for 30 minutes.
7 Remove the bay leaves and chillies and spoon the mixture into the reserved marrow cavities. Cover with foil and bake in the oven for a further 45 minutes.
8 Meanwhile, prepare the sauce. In a small saucepan, combine the cream cheese and thick cream. Season to taste with the salt and cayenne pepper and cook over a low heat until the mixture is smooth, stirring constantly. Stir in the sultanas or seedless raisins.
9 Remove the foil and pour the sauce over the marrows. Bake for a further 15 minutes or until the sauce is bubbling. Transfer to a large heated serving platter, sprinkle with parsley and serve.

1¾ hours

Veal

ROASTING VEAL

Veal – the meat of young calves that have been specially reared for tenderness – is delicate and requires careful cooking. This chapter shows you which are the best cuts of veal for roasting.

Until fairly recently, veal was not often seen in butchers' shops. One reason for this is that veal does not keep well and must be sold by the butcher within three or four days of purchase. Consequently, butchers without a regular demand for veal were reluctant to stock it. Today, the demand for veal is increasing, partly as a result of foreign travel and partly due to an appreciation of French and Italian food in restaurants. Thus, butchers are happier to stock veal, and it is much more readily available. However, if you want a special cut of veal, you may have to order it in advance.

The size, colour and cost of each cut of veal can vary considerably, depending on the way the calf has been reared and the age at which it has been slaughtered. Veal from calves fed on grass has a slightly darker coloured meat, which some people think has more flavour. However, this is rarely seen in butchers' shops, as raising calves on grass is not an economical proposition these days, and the European method of raising calves indoors has generally been adopted. The animals are reared in enclosed units and fed on a special milk diet. The veal from milk-fed calves, exported by Holland, is the most expensive, and it is particularly prized for its almost white, fine-grained flesh and delicate flavour.

Choosing veal for roasting

The best veal is from young calves. It can be recognized by the fine-grained, firm and smooth texture of the meat, and the white and satiny fat. The meat should be almost white – just faintly tinged with pink. The only drawback with this 'immature' meat is that it has very little fat (or none at all), and so the cooked meat is inclined to be dry.

It is difficult to give exact serving quantities for veal as the amount of bone varies so much with the size of the animal. As a rough guide, allow 175 g /6 oz boneless meat per person, and 225–350 g /8–12 oz per person of meat and bone.

Cuts of veal for roasting

Leg of veal is too large for one family, and is usually divided into two parts; the fillet end, or chump end as it is sometimes called, and the less expensive knuckle or hock end. Fillet end is bought by weight without the bone and may then be stuffed if you wish. The knuckle end removed from a whole leg is not usually used for roasting, but boned and stuffed for braising.
Loin of veal is a prime cut for roasting. It can be roasted either on the bone, boned and rolled or boned and stuffed.
Shoulder from young calves is often boned and rolled for roasting. It can also be bought on the bone, without the foreknuckle, when it is known as an oyster of veal. The oyster can also be boned and stuffed for roasting.

The shoulder from older calves is divided into two or more joints. Boned and rolled shoulder is a good joint for roasting, and cheaper than a leg or loin of veal.
Best end of neck is a fairly inexpensive cut and is good value for money. When the joint is taken from a young calf the bones are ususally chopped but not chined.
Breast from young calves is excellent boned, stuffed and rolled for roasting.

Storing veal for roasting

Unlike large joints of other meat, veal joints do not keep well and should be cooked soon after slaughtering. A joint of veal for roasting can be stored in the refrigerator for up to two days, loosely covered with greaseproof paper or foil.

Remember to remove the veal from the refrigerator and allow it to come to room temperature before you roast it.

Moisturizing the meat

The young meat of veal is largely made up of connective tissue. For the cook, this means not only that the cooking temperature must be kept low to allow the compact tissue of the meat to tenderize gradually, but that the scanty fat must be supplemented by the spreading, larding or barding of additional fat. This is followed, during roasting, by frequent basting with the juices that collect in the roasting tin as a result of this.

Prime cuts of veal, such as loin and fillet, are particularly lean and can become dry and tasteless if proper care is not taken to keep them moist. Breast and shoulder, being slightly fattier, are in less danger of drying out, but still require moisturizing.
Larding: for a large joint you will need long, thin strips of fat salt pork and a *lardoire*. This is a long, needle-like tool with a groove along the top edge (for smaller joints use a larding needle which has a hinged clip to grip the fat). Push the lardoire right through the joint, following the grain, put the fat in the groove and pull the *lardoire* back through the meat. Ease the *lardoire* out, leaving the fat behind. Repeat along the length of the joint. The strips of fat melt during roasting, moisturizing the meat. Larding need not take a long time and is worth the effort for a special roast.
Barding: this is a very simple method of adding fat to a joint. The meat is covered with a 'bard': a thin sheet of pork fat or several thin slices of unsmoked bacon. The bard is simply laid on top of the joint of meat if it contains a bone, or wrapped and tied around the joint if it has been boned and rolled. As the meat roasts the fat melts, keeping the meat moist.
Spreading with fat: the veal can simply be spread with butter or dripping before roasting, then basted with the juices that collect in the roasting tin during cooking.
Stuffing a joint of veal: as well as enhancing the rather mild flavour of the young meat, adding stuffing to a joint of veal helps to keep it moist. The most common flavourings for a veal stuffing are lemon and thyme.
Adding liquid: liquid, as well as fat, can be used to produce a succulent roast of veal. Place the meat on a rack set in a roasting tin and pour a small amount of water, stock or red or white wine into the tin. During roasting, steam is produced around the joint which helps to keep it moist.

Roasting veal

Veal must be seared before roasting. This can be done by sautéing, in a mixture of butter and oil, over direct heat or, more usually, in a hot oven. For a traditional roast, cook the veal joint at 200C /400F /gas 6 for 15–25 minutes, then at 170C /325F /gas 3 for 55–66 minutes per kg /25–30 minutes per lb, having first taken precautions to keep the meat moist.

The tendency towards dryness of some cuts of veal may be counteracted by roasting the joint in a wrapping of aluminium foil. The steam created inside the package helps to keep the meat moist. The veal is spread with butter or dripping, then placed on a trivet standing in the center of a large piece of foil and then both the joint and the trivet are loosely wrapped. If the veal has been marinated, some of the marinade can be added to the package. It is seared at 200C /400F /gas 6 for 15–25 minutes, then the oven temperature is reduced to 170C /325F /gas 3 and the veal is roasted for a further 55–66 minutes per kg /25–30 minutes per lb, opening up the foil for the last 30 minutes so the meat can brown.

To test that roast veal is cooked, stick a skewer into the thickest part of the meat. The juices that run out should be almost colourless.

Carving

All carving will benefit from good preparation. If the butcher hasn't already done so, skewer and tie the meat before cooking. After, remove the skewers and string and let the joint rest in a warm place for 15 minutes to firm up. When carving, secure boneless joints on a spiked dish, and in all instances use a sharp knife and a two-pronged fork with a thumb guard.

Veal is carved in the same way as beef but in slightly thicker slices. Carve across the grain to make it more tender.

Joints of meat that are boned and rolled are simple to carve – place the meat lengthways on a carving dish and cut downwards. Smaller rolled joints are placed upright on the dish and carved across horizontally. Carving a joint on the bone is slightly more complicated and it helps to check where the bones lie before you begin.

Roast breast of veal with spinach stuffing

🍴 bringing to room temperature, then 2¼–2½ hours

Roast breast of veal with spinach stuffing

Serves 6

1.4–1.8 kg /3–4 lb breast of veal, boned
2.5–5 ml /½–1 tsp lemon juice
salt and freshly ground black pepper
about 15 ml /1 tbls flour
25 g /1 oz butter
30 ml /2 tbls olive oil
broccoli, to serve

For the spinach stuffing
50 g /2 oz butter
1 Spanish onion, finely chopped
225 g /8 oz sausage-meat
1.5 ml /¼ tsp ground allspice
1.5 ml /¼ tsp ground nutmeg
2.5 ml /½ tsp dried thyme
15 ml /1 tbls finely chopped fresh parsley
1 medium-sized egg, beaten
275 g /10 oz frozen cut leaf spinach
salt and freshly ground black pepper

For the gravy
150 ml /5 fl oz dry white wine
275 ml /10 fl oz chicken stock

1 Wipe the veal on both sides with a damp cloth. Rub the veal on both sides with the lemon juice, and season generously with freshly ground black pepper. Leave to come to room temperature, then season with salt and more freshly ground black pepper.

2 Heat the oven to 170C /325F /gas 3. Make the stuffing: melt 25 g /1 oz of the butter in a frying-pan and sauté the finely chopped onion until transparent.

3 Add the sausage-meat to the pan and sauté with the onion, stirring constantly and crumbling the sausage-meat, until the meat has started to brown. Transfer the meat and onion to a large mixing bowl. Add the ground allspice, ground nutmeg, dried thyme, finely chopped parsley and beaten egg to the bowl and mix well.

4 Melt the remaining 25 g /1 oz butter in a pan, add the spinach and sauté until it is completely thawed. Press the spinach dry in a fine sieve and add to the mixing bowl. Season the mixture to taste with salt and freshly ground black pepper and mix well.

5 Place the stuffing along the centre of the

veal. Roll up the veal and stuffing neatly then tie the roll securely with fine string. Dust the roll with the flour.

6 Place the 25 g /1 oz butter and the olive oil in a roasting tin, place the tin over a medium heat and brown the meat on all sides.

7 Transfer the roasting tin to the oven and roast the veal for 1½–1¾ hours, basting every 15 minutes with the juices in the tin. Transfer the veal roll to a heated serving dish, remove the string and keep the meat warm.

8 Make the gravy: skim the excess fat from the juices in the tin and pour in the dry white wine and chicken stock. Stand the tin over a medium heat and bring to the boil, stirring and scraping the base and sides of the tin with a wooden spoon to dislodge any sticky bits. Boil the gravy for about 5 minutes, until it is reduced by one-third. Season to taste with salt and freshly ground black pepper, then strain the gravy into a sauceboat and serve immediately with the stuffed breast of veal.

Best end of veal with breadcrumbs

This is a tasty roast that makes the most of a slightly cheaper cut of veal. The bacon and topping both add to the flavour.

bringing to room temperature, then 2¾–3 hours

Serves 4–6
1.8 kg /4 lb best end of neck of veal, boned and rolled
salt and freshly ground black pepper
25 g /1 oz softened butter
6 slices unsmoked bacon
1 Spanish onion, finely chopped
2 carrots, finely chopped
2 stalks celery, finely chopped
425 ml /15 fl oz chicken stock, home-made or from a cube
90 ml /6 tbls fine, white breadcrumbs, toasted
30 ml /2 tbls freshly grated Parmesan cheese
1 medium-sized egg, well beaten

Savoury roast veal

1   Season the meat with plenty of freshly ground black pepper, then spread it with the softened butter. Leave to come to room temperature. Meanwhile, heat the oven to 200C /400F /gas 6.
2   Line a roasting tin with the slices of bacon. Place the veal on the bacon and then surround it with the onion, carrots and celery. Roast for 20–25 minutes, or until the meat is well browned on all sides.
3   Add the stock to the roasting tin, reduce the oven temperature to 170C /325F /gas 3 and continue to roast for 1¾–2 hours, basting frequently until the meat is just cooked.
4   Remove the string from the roast veal. Combine the toasted breadcrumbs and grated Parmesan cheese. Brush the top and sides of the joint with the beaten egg and sprinkle over the breadcrumb and cheese mixture, pressing it on firmly with a palette knife. Return the joint to the oven and cook for a further 15 minutes, or until the topping is golden brown.
5   Transfer the joint to a heated serving dish and keep warm. Place the roasting tin over a high heat and boil until the juices have reduced to a light glaze. Season with salt to taste, strain the gravy into a sauce-boat and serve.

Savoury roast veal

bringing to room temperature, then 1¾–2 hours

Serves 4–6
1.4 kg /3 lb boned and rolled joint of veal (from the fillet end of leg or the shoulder)
freshly ground black pepper
5 ml /1 tsp dried thyme
25–40 g /1–1½ oz softened butter
225 g /8 oz bacon slices
2 whole garlic cloves
4 carrots, thinly sliced
1 Spanish onion, thinly sliced
2 bay leaves
60 ml /4 tbls olive oil
425 ml /15 fl oz chicken stock, home-made or from a cube
For the gravy
150 ml /5 fl oz dry white wine
15 g /½ oz butter
15 ml /1 tbls flour
salt and freshly ground black pepper

1   Season the joint all over with fresh ground black pepper and sprinkle with dri thyme. Spread with the softened butte

leave to come to room temperature. Meanwhile, heat oven to 200C /400F /gas 6.

Cover the top of the veal with the bacon slices and place the meat in a roasting tin. Surround the veal with the whole garlic cloves, thinly sliced carrots and onion and bay leaves. Add the olive oil to the tin, and 150 ml /5 fl oz of the chicken stock. Roast for 15–25 minutes, then reduce the temperature to 170C /325F /gas 3 and roast for 1¼–1½ hours, basting frequently.

Remove the string from the roast veal. Transfer the joint, with its bacon slices, to a heated serving dish and keep warm.

To make the gravy, remove the vegetables from the roasting tin with a slotted spoon and pour off the excess fat. Add the remaining chicken stock and the wine to the tin, place over a high heat and bring to the boil, stirring. Blend the butter and flour together to make a *beurre manié*. Add this to the simmering liquid in tiny pieces, stirring, then simmer the gravy until it has thickened slightly. Adjust the seasonings, strain into a sauceboat and serve immediately with the roast veal.

Garnish with fresh thyme and bay leaves and serve with buttered carrots and sautéed potatoes.

Roast loin of veal with herbs

bringing to room temperature, then 1½–1¾ hours

Serves 6
1.4 kg /3 lb loin of veal, boned, rolled and tied
salt and freshly ground black pepper
bay leaves, roughly crumbled
2–3 sprigs fresh rosemary, finely chopped or 10 ml /2 tsp dried rosemary, crushed
5 ml /1 tsp dried oregano
50 g /2 oz softened butter
150 ml /5 fl oz chicken stock, home-made or from a cube
275 ml /10 fl oz dry white wine

Sprinkle the joint with freshly ground black pepper, the bay leaves, rosemary and oregano. Spread with the softened butter and leave to come to room temperature. Meanwhile, heat oven to 200C /400F /gas 6.

Place the joint on a rack set in a roasting tin and roast in the oven for 15–25 minutes, to sear the meat. Then reduce the oven temperature to 170C /325F /gas 3 and roast for 1¼–1½ hours, basting frequently with the juices in the roasting tin.

Remove the string and pieces of bay leaf from the roast veal. Transfer the joint to a heated serving dish and keep warm. Spoon off any excess fat from the roasting tin. Add the chicken stock and dry white wine to the tin and place over a high heat. Bring to the boil, stirring, and boil for 5–10 minutes, until it is reduced by about one-third. Taste and season, if necessary, then strain the gravy into a sauceboat and serve immediately with the veal.

Stuffed fillet of veal

bringing to room temperature, then 2 hours

Serves 6–8
1.8 kg /4 lb fillet end of veal (top end of the leg), trimmed, boned and tied
freshly ground black pepper
10 ml /2 tsp very finely chopped fresh rosemary, or 5 ml /1 tsp dried rosemary, crushed
25 g /1 oz softened butter, plus extra for sautéing
175 g /6 oz button mushrooms, thinly sliced
melted butter
rosemary sprigs, to garnish
For the sauce
40 g /1½ oz butter
30 ml /2 tbls finely chopped onion
30 ml /2 tbls flour
425 ml /15 fl oz milk, warmed
½ bay leaf
salt
60 ml /4 tbls freshly grated Parmesan cheese
100 g /4 oz cooked ham, cut into 15 mm /½ in cubes

1 Season the joint all over with the pepper and sprinkle with the chopped or crushed rosemary. Spread the meat with the softened butter. Leave to stand, if necessary, to allow the joint to come to room temperature. Meanwhile, heat the oven to 190C /375F / gas 5.
2 Place the meat in a roasting tin and roast in the oven for 1 hour basting frequently. The veal will be crusty on the outside, but rare inside. Add a little hot water to the tin if the juices in the tin look likely to scorch during cooking.
3 Meanwhile, make the sauce: melt the butter over a low heat and add the onion. Sauté for 5 minutes or until the onion has softened. Stir in the flour and cook for 2–3 minutes to make a pale roux. Add the warmed milk and bring to the boil, stirring constantly. Lower the heat, add the bay leaf and season with salt and freshly ground black pepper. Cook the sauce for 10–15 minutes stirring occasionally.
4 Transfer the roast veal to a board. (Do not turn off the oven.) Cut a thin slice from the top of the joint and reserve it to use as a 'lid'. Carefully cut out the rare meat inside, leaving a 15 mm/½ in shell of meat. If there are any holes in the base, line the bottom with a thin slice of veal cut from the removed centre piece.
5 Cut the removed centre of the veal into 15 mm/½ in cubes. Melt some butter in a pan, add the veal cubes and sliced button mushrooms and sauté lightly until the veal is just cooked. Remove the veal and mushrooms from the pan with a slotted spoon and add to the sauce. Add the freshly grated Parmesan cheese and fold in the diced, cooked ham.
6 Fill the meat shell with this mixture, replace the 'lid', brush all over with melted butter and return to the oven for several minutes, to glaze. Serve immediately, garnished with sprigs of fresh rosemary.

Foil-roast veal loin with rosemary

Roasting a veal joint in aluminium foil ensures that the meat will be deliciously moist and tender.

bringing to room temperature, then 1½–1¾ hours

Serves 6
1.4 kg /3 lb loin of veal, boned, rolled and tied
freshly ground black pepper
50 g /2 oz dripping or softened butter
2–3 sprigs of fresh rosemary, finely chopped, or 10 ml /2 tsp dried rosemary, crushed
For the gravy
150 ml /5 fl oz chicken stock, home-made or from a cube
150 ml /5 fl oz dry white wine
15 g /½ oz butter
salt and freshly ground black pepper
lemon juice

1 Season the meat with freshly ground black pepper and spread with the dripping or butter. Sprinkle over the rosemary, then leave the meat to stand, if necessary, to allow it to come to room temperature. Meanwhile, heat the oven to 200C /400F / gas 6.
2 Cut a piece of foil, large enough to cover the joint on a trivet, and allowing for a seam. Place the piece of foil, shiny side up, in a roasting tin. Place a small metal trivet in the centre of the foil, to hold the veal away from the juices that will drip there. Place the veal on the trivet.
3 Bring the foil up over the meat and fold the edges together to seal. Be careful to leave enough space inside the foil for the air to circulate around the veal and take care not to tear or pierce the foil.
4 Place the roasting tin in the centre of the oven and roast for 15–25 minutes, to seal in the juices. Then reduce the temperature to 170C /325F /gas 3 and continue to roast for 1¼–1½ hours, opening out the foil for the last 30 minutes to allow the meat to brown thoroughly. To test that the meat is done, stick a metal skewer into the thickest part of the meat. The juices that run should be almost colourless.
5 Remove the string from the meat and transfer the meat to a heated serving dish. Keep it in a warm place. Remove the trivet from the foil and pour the juices from the foil into the roasting tin to make the gravy.
6 Add the stock and wine to the roasting tin and bring to the boil, stirring. Blend the butter with the flour to make a *beurre manié*. Add the *beurre manié* to the simmering liquid in tiny pieces, then continue to boil, stirring continuously, until the gravy has reduced by about half. Season the gravy with salt and freshly ground black pepper to taste, and a little lemon juice, if liked. Strain the gravy into a sauce-boat and serve immediately with the roast veal. Garnish the veal with a few sprigs of fresh rosemay if available.

GRILLING VEAL

Veal is not at its best grilled plainly in the same way as lamb or beef because it is such a naturally dry meat. However, there are ways of protecting the meat for grilling which make it as delicious.

Veal is such a delicate meat that unless you take steps to protect it while it is grilling it may end up dry and unpalatable. Perhaps with a prime cut of veal and the utmost care you will get good results but to remove any risk I suggest that you marinate or stuff it or add a topping.

What veal to grill

All veal when you buy it should be moist and fine-grained. Milk-fed calves will have a very pale pink or off-white flesh; those fed on grass, a slightly darker pink flesh. Do not buy veal that has a brownish dried-up appearance or any that looks bluish and mottled. Unlike other meats veal quickly goes off, so buy from a butcher who has a good turnover.

Veal chops: loin chops are cut from the middle of the loin, they are meaty and weigh about 350 g /12 oz each. Usually about 25 mm /1 in thick, they have a band of fat running along one side. Chump chops are cut from the leg end of the loin, and often have a bone in the centre. Best end of neck chops are also available; they are good value, being cheaper than loin or chump chops.

Fillet: this is the long tapering muscle that runs beneath the loin of the animal. It can be cut, across the grain, into small medallions. This is the only cut of veal that is really suitable for grilling as you would a piece of lamb or beef. Sometimes slightly thicker slices are cut from the fillet and batted out into small escalopes.

Escalopes: these can be cut from the fillet but they are more likely to be thin slices cut from the top of the leg and batted out into large, thin escalopes. An escalope weighs about 125 g /4 oz.

Shoulder: this cut of veal is ideal for cubing to make brochettes or for mincing for forming into patties.

Preparing veal for grilling

Wipe the meat with absorbent paper and trim off any excess fat, leaving a narrow border on chops. Slash the fat at regular intervals with a sharp knife. Season the meat with freshly ground black pepper and leave to come to room temperature. Just before cooking season again with salt and pepper and brush generously with olive oil and melted butter.

Marinating: veal is excellent marinated; the oil in the marinade prevents it from drying out and the herbs and spices add extra flavour. Chops are particularly good marinated before grilling.

Combine the chosen marinade ingredients in a shallow dish and add the veal, turning it so that it is well coated. Leave to marinate for at least 4 hours in the refrigerator.

Remove the dish from the refrigerator at least 2 hours before grilling to allow the veal

to come to room temperature. Remove the veal from the marinade just before grilling but remember to reserve the marinade to baste the meat while it is cooking.

Stuffing: escalopes are the best cut of veal for stuffing. They should be batted out very thin – this is quite simple to do yourself. Place an escalope between 2 sheets of dampened greaseproof paper or cling film and, with a meat bat or rolling pin, thump the meat fairly hard, starting from one end working towards the other side, 'pushing' the meat in front of the bat. The escalope should at least double in size.

Choose a stuffing which has some moisture or natural fat in it; bacon or finely chopped mushrooms and onions that have been softened in butter are ideal. Spread the stuffing over one side of the veal and then roll it up with the stuffing inside. Secure the veal with strong thread. Brush the oustside of the roll with olive oil before you start grilling.

As you grill the veal the stuffing will release its moisture or fat, keeping the veal moist and adding flavour.

Mincing: this is an excellent way of grilling veal. Shoulder of veal minced with cooked ham, and flavoured with onion, garlic and herbs (see recipe) can be formed into patties to make excellent succulent 'vealburgers' – just as good as hamburgers.

Topping: this idea is a marvellous way of giving added flavour and interest to both veal that has been fried or roasted or to left-over cooked veal. Finishing it off with a topping under the grill makes a delicious dish. For the topping ingredients use a combination of tomato, cheese, cream and herbs. The cheese forms a golden glaze, mingling with the other ingredients.

Grilling veal

Heating the grill: heat the grill to maximum before you start cooking so that the heat will sear the meat immediately, sealing in the juices. Remember not to leave the grid under the grill while it is heating. The grid should be cold when the meat is placed on it. Before putting the veal on the grid, oil it so that the veal does not stick.

Distance from the heat: the grid should be about 7.5 cm /3 in from the source of the heat. The cooking times will vary according to the thickness of the veal and whether it is stuffed, topped or just marinated.

Turning: use tongs or wooden spoons to turn the veal during cooking. Never use a fork because if it punctures the meat the juices will escape – resulting in dry veal.

Grilled veal patties

▮ 30 minutes

Serves 4

500 g /1 lb boned shoulder of veal, trimmed
125 g /4 oz cooked ham
25 g /1 oz butter
½ Spanish onion, finely chopped
2 garlic cloves, finely chopped
2.5 ml /½ tsp dried thyme
60 ml /4 tbls finely chopped fresh parsley
1 large egg, beaten
salt and freshly ground black pepper
olive oil

1 Heat the grill to high.
2 Put the veal and cooked ham through the finest blade of your mincer, or blend in a food processor, until the meat is in tiny pieces. Transfer to a mixing bowl.
3 In a small frying-pan, melt the butter and sauté the finely chopped onion and garlic for 2 minutes. Add to the meat. Add the thyme, parsley and egg and season. Mix well and form 4 patties, 7.5 cm /3 in in diameter and 25 mm /1 in thick.
4 Brush the grid with oil and grill the patties 7.5 cm /3 in from the heat, for 10 minutes, turning once.

Veal avesnoise

20 minutes

Serves 4
large slices cold roast veal
5 g /4 oz Gruyère cheese, finely grated
ml /2 tsp tomato purée
5 ml /½ tsp Worcestershire sauce
ml /2 tbls thick cream
t and freshly ground black pepper
w drops of Tabasco sauce
ve oil
tercress sprigs, to garnish

Heat the grill to high.
In a bowl, mix the cheese, tomato purée,
orcestershire sauce and cream. Season
th salt, pepper and Tabasco.
Brush the grid with olive oil. Spread
ch veal slice with a quarter of the cheese
xture and grill, 7.5 cm /3 in from the heat
r 1–2 minutes until the topping is golden.
arnish with watercress and serve.

Veal rolls with peppers

1 hour

Serves 4
4 × 125–150 g /4–5 oz thin veal escalopes
1 large green pepper
1 large red pepper
125 g /4 oz fat salt pork or bacon, finely
    chopped
60 ml /4 tbls finely chopped fresh parsley
4 garlic cloves, crushed
salt and freshly ground black pepper
olive oil
60 ml /4 tbls thick cream, warmed

1 Quarter the peppers and remove the cores and seeds.
2 Combine the finely chopped salt pork or bacon with the parsley and crushed garlic in a bowl. Season to taste with salt and pepper and blend thoroughly.

3 Spread one side of each escalope with this mixture and roll up tightly, winding a little strong thread round each roll to hold it together. Brush generously with olive oil and leave the rolls to absorb the flavours for 10 minutes.
4 Heat grill, without the grid, to high.
5 Brush the grid with oil and lay the veal rolls and quartered peppers on the grid. Grill 7.5 cm /3 in from heat for 10 minutes, turning twice. The skin on the peppers will blister making them easier to peel. Remove peppers, turn veal rolls again and cook 5 minutes more.
6 Meanwhile, peel the skins off the peppers and brush the flesh lightly with olive oil to make it shine attractively.
7 Remove the strings from veal rolls and arrange them on a heated serving dish. Garnish each roll with a piece of red and green pepper, arranging them red on top of green between the rolls. Pour a little cream over each roll.

Veal avesnoise and Veal rolls
with peppers

Twin grill of veal and beef

🍴🍴 2 hours

Serves 4

4 × 75–100 g /3–4 oz medallions of veal
4 × 50–75 g /2–3 oz filets mignons, cut
   from the tail of the fillet
salt and freshly ground black pepper
75 g /3 oz butter
4 canned artichoke hearts, drained
1.5 ml /¼ tsp dried oregano
4 button mushrooms, stalks removed
4 slices white bread
olive oil

For the tomato concassé

225 g /8 oz tomatoes
5 ml /1 tsp olive oil
1 shallot, finely chopped
1 small garlic clove, unpeeled
bouquet garni

For the bearnaise sauce

4–6 tarragon sprigs, coarsely chopped
4–6 chervil sprigs, coarsely chopped
15 ml /1 tbls chopped shallot
2 black peppercorns, crushed
30 ml /2 tbls tarragon vinegar
150 ml /5 fl oz dry white wine
3 large egg yolks
225 g /8 oz butter, diced then softened
lemon juice
a pinch of cayenne pepper

1 Wipe the meat with absorbent paper. Beat each side with a meat bat and season with freshly ground black pepper.

2 Make a tiny cut in the top of each tomato. Place them in a bowl, cover with boiling water and leave for 10 seconds. Drain and peel. Cut the tomatoes in half and squeeze out and discard the seeds and juice. Chop flesh and season.

3 Heat the olive oil in a saucepan, add the shallot and cook for 4–5 minutes until softened. Add the tomato pulp, garlic and bouquet garni. Lower the heat and simmer for 30 minutes. Remove the garlic and bouquet garni and set sauce aside.

4 For the bearnaise sauce, combine half the herbs with the shallot, peppercorns, vinegar and wine in a saucepan. Bring to the boil and cook until the liquid is reduced to about 30 ml /2 tbls. Remove from the heat.

5 Beat the egg yolks with 15 ml /1 tbls water in the top pan of a double boiler set over hot water. Strain in the reduced liquid. Stir briskly with a wire whisk until light and fluffy.

6 Add the butter a piece at a time, to the egg mixture, whisking briskly until completely incorporated. As the sauce begins to thicken, add more butter, whisking thoroughly. Add more butter, now several pieces at a time, whisking thoroughly as before, until the sauce is thick and all the butter is used. Add salt, lemon juice and cayenne pepper. Strain the sauce through a fine sieve to remove any threads of egg white and to give it a fine gloss. Stir in the remain-

ing herbs. Keep warm over hot water.

7 Heat the grill to high. Melt 15 g /½ butter in a small frying-pan, add t artichoke hearts and sauté for 2 minutes each side. Season with half the oregano, sa and pepper. Keep hot.

8 Melt another 15 g /½ oz butter. Sauté t mushrooms for 3–4 minutes on each sic until tender. Season with the remainir oregano, salt and pepper. Keep hot with t artichoke hearts.

9 Cut the bread slices into neat round slightly larger than the filets mignons. He: 60 ml /4 tbls olive oil and 25 g /1 butt in a clean frying-pan and sauté the bre: slices until crisp and golden on both side Drain on absorbent paper and keep hot.

10 Melt the remaining butter in a sma saucepan. Season the veal and brush wi olive oil and melted butter. Brush the gr grid with olive oil. Grill 7.5 cm /3 in from t heat for 3 minutes on each side. Keep hot.

11 Season the filets mignons and brus with melted butter and olive oil. Grill 7.5 c /3 in from the heat for 2 minutes each sic (rare). Reheat the tomato concassé.

12 Arrange the four croûtons on a heate serving platter. Place a filet mignon on eac one and top with tomato concassé. Plac veal on top of the tomato, and an artichol heart on top of the veal. Spoon bearnaii sauce over each artichoke heart, and top wit a mushroom. Serve immediately with t remaining sauce.

Twin grill of veal and beef

Oriental veal chops

Serve these succulent chops with plain boiled, or fried rice, and a bean sprout salad.

4 hours marinating,
then 20 minutes

Serves 4

4 × 350 g /12 oz veal loin chops, each about
  25 mm /1 in thick
olive oil
bouquets of parsley, to garnish (optional)
For the marinade
15 ml /1 tbls hoisin sauce
30 ml /2 tbls soy sauce
30 ml /2 tbls clear honey
60 ml /4 tbls dry white wine
60 ml /4 tbls peanut oil
1 Spanish onion, finely chopped
pinch of cayenne pepper
few drops of Tabasco

Wipe the chops with absorbent paper. Trim off any excess fat, leaving only a narrow border. With a sharp knife, slash the fat remaining around the edges, at regular intervals, to prevent the chops curling under the grill.

In a shallow dish, combine the marinade ingredients, adding cayenne pepper and Tabasco to taste. Lay the chops in the marinade, and turn to coat well. Cover and leave to marinate for at least 4 hours, turning the chops frequently.

Heat the grill to high.

Brush the grill grid with the olive oil. Remove the chops from the marinade and place them on the grid. Grill 7.5 cm /3 in from the heat for 5 minutes. Turn the chops over with tongs and grill for a further 5 minutes, basting frequently with the marinade.

Arrange the chops on a heated serving platter. Garnish with bouquets of parsley, if wished, and serve immediately.

Peanut oil imparts a delicious flavour to the chops as well as giving them extra moisture during cooking. If you do not have any peanut oil, use a mixture of sesame and olive oil.

Sweetbread and veal brochette

preparing sweetbreads, 1 hour
marinating, then 20 minutes

Serves 6

500 g /1 lb veal sweetbreads, soaked
700 g /1½ lb boned leg of veal
salt
24 button onions
freshly ground black pepper
45 ml /3 tbls finely chopped parsley
150 ml /5 fl oz white wine
15 ml /1 tbls lemon juice
30 ml /2 tbls olive oil
30 ml /2 tbls melted butter
saffron rice with peas, to serve

Oriental veal chops

1 Drain the sweetbreads carefully. Put them in a pan with cold salted water to cover; bring to the boil over a moderate heat and simmer gently for 7–10 minutes. Cool the sweetbreads by leaving the pan under cold running water.

2 Peel the button onions and blanch in the same way as the sweetbreads for 5 minutes. Drain then cool under running water.

3 Cut veal into 24 × 25 mm /1 in cubes, discarding any pieces of skin or gristle. Discard any tubes or membranes from the sweetbreads and divide them into 24 pieces, making them all as near to the same size as possible. If you have small pieces left over, you can thread several of them on to the skewer at a time.

4 Take 6 long metal skewers and thread each one in the following order: a piece of veal, followed by a piece of sweetbread and 1 button onion. Allow 4 sets of ingredients per skewer. Or use 12 short skewers.

5 Lay the brochettes side by side in a large shallow dish or baking tray. Season generously with salt and freshly ground black pepper, and sprinkle with finely chopped parsley. Combine the wine with the lemon juice, pour over the brochettes and leave to marinate for 1 hour, turning the skewers occasionally so that the meat remains evenly coated with the dressing.

6 Heat the grill to high. Combine the olive oil with the melted butter in a small dish. Drain the brochettes thoroughly, reserving the marinade, and brush them all over with the butter and olive oil mixture. Place them on a grill pan under the grill; reduce the heat to moderate and grill the brochettes for about 20 minutes, or until they are cooked through and golden, turning the skewers occasionally. Alternatively you can pan-fry them. Heat the olive oil and butter until hot and proceed as above. Transfer the cooked brochettes to a heated serving dish and keep them warm.

7 Add the reserved marinade to the drippings in the grill pan and bring to the boil by putting it over a moderate heat, scraping up any crusty bits adhering to the bottom and the sides of the pan with a wooden spoon. Strain into a heated sauceboat and serve immediately with the brochettes. A dish of saffron rice tossed with green peas is an excellent accompaniment.

PAN FRYING VEAL

Pan frying is a simple technique which produces many sophisticated and famous dishes. Try Wiener schnitzel, a classic Austrain dish, or Watercress veal, a delightfully presented nouvelle cuisine dish.

When buying veal for frying, choose loin, rib or shoulder chops, or buy the fillet, which can be cut into neat medallions. Another very popular cut of veal for frying is the escalope. This is a thin slice of boneless meat cut across the grain from the leg. The leg is cut into its three main muscles: the topside and flank give the most successful escalopes. As there is no other muscle running through the cut it produces a very tender piece of meat. A weight of 125 g /4 oz is usually allowed per portion. However, each person may be served two or more tiny escalopes, 25–50 g /1–2 oz each, called *scaloppini* or *piccata* in Italy. If you find it difficult to get hold of this particular escalope cut from the leg you can substitute veal fillet or a boneless cutlet which may initially be cut through the width – see recipe for Wiener schnitzel – and then pounded to the right thickness.

Preparing veal for frying

Take the veal out of the refrigerator at least 30 minutes before cooking to allow it to come to room temperature. Pat it dry with absorbent paper and season with freshly ground black pepper. Just before cooking season again with salt and more freshly ground black pepper.

Most cuts should be well trimmed to remove fat, but veal chops need a small layer of fat to help moisturize the meat. It is a good idea to slash this fat with a sharp knife in three or four places round the chop to stop it buckling during cooking.
Preparing escalopes: trim escalopes of veal into neat even-sized rounds or ovals before cooking. Place each trimmed escalope between two sheets of wet greaseproof paper or cling film and beat it with a rolling pin or

meat bat. Beat firmly but not heavily until the meat is 5 mm /¼ in thick all over. You can then coat the meat or use as they are.
Coating escalopes: pat them dry with absorbent paper then season both sides generously with salt and freshly ground black pepper. Coat the escalopes in flour, shaking off the excess.

Professional cooks use fresh breadcrumbs for cooking escalopes. Use bread that is 1 day old, neither stale nor over-fresh. Remove the crusts and grate a chunk on a grater or reduce to crumbs in a food processor or blender. Spread the breadcrumbs on a large plate. Break an egg into a shallow plate and beat with a fork to mix. You may add 15 ml/1 tbls water, beating it in, to make the egg go further. Dip the meat, piece by piece, into the egg, drain it over the plate and then transfer it to the plate of crumbs. Turn the meat escalope to coat the second side. Then shake gently to remove excess crumbs.

Leave the coated escalopes for 30–60 minutes in the refrigerator, if you can, to chill before frying. This dries the coating and helps to stick the crumbs to the meat. Coated escalopes are best fried in generous quantities of butter and oil, because the coating absorbs quite a lot of fat and will burn easily if the pan is allowed to dry out.
Medallions of veal: to make medallions, cut the fillet into even slices, each 25 mm/ 1 in thick. Trim them into neat rounds or ovals and tie a piece of string round each one to hold it nearly in shape (see below).

Equipment and fats for frying

A large, heavy-based frying-pan is the only equipment you will need for this method of cooking. A lid is often a useful addition, especially as veal chops often need extra covered cooking to ensure they are completely cooked through. If your frying-pan does not have a lid, try a saucepan lid.

Butter gives the best flavour to pan-fried food but it burns at a low temperature. Add 30 ml/2 tbls of oil to 25 g/1 oz of butter to stop this happening: oil does not burn until it reaches a very high temperature.

Alternatively use clarified butter which will not burn so readily. Heat the butter in a saucepan until it foams. The foam will sink to the bottom leaving a clear top layer. Carefully pour this off, taking care not to disturb the sediment, and use the clear fat for frying.

Pan frying veal

Thicker cuts of veal, such as chops, need to be quickly seared at a high heat initially. This browns the outside and keeps the precious juices trapped inside. If it is a very thick cut of meat it may take a little longer at higher heat – about 3–4 minutes on each side.

For veal chops it is best to cover the pa[n] after they are well browned and cook slow[ly] for 6–8 minutes or until the juices ha[ve] turned from rose pink to clear. Veal shou[ld] always be well cooked, but still with a hi[nt] of pink in the meat. Be careful not [to] overcook it as this delicate meat is at its be[st] when moist and juicy, not dry.

Medallions of veal, cut from the tend[er] fillet, need only about 2 minutes in the pa[n]. This is a good example of nouvelle cuisin[e] where the finest quality meat is cooked f[or] the shortest possible time to retain t[he] maximum flavour. Escalopes also need ve[ry] little time in the pan, with no initial brow[n]-ing. Cook them over a medium heat so the[y] have time to to cook through witho[ut] becoming dry or tough.

Medallions of veal in lemon sauce

bringing to room temperature, then 20 minutes

Serves 4
8 medallions of veal, 25 mm /1 in thick, from the fillet
30 ml /2 tbls seasoned flour
4 small carrots, cut into sticks
salt and freshly ground black pepper
8 cauliflower florets, about 25 g /1 oz each
8 broccoli florets, about 25 g /1 oz each
25 g /1 oz butter
30 ml /2 tbls olive oil
flat leaved parsley, to garnish
For the lemon sauce
50 g /2 oz butter, softened
15 ml /1 tbls finely chopped parsley
15 ml /1 tbls lemon juice
salt and freshly ground black pepper

1   Tie a piece of string around the middl[e] of each medallion of veal to keep it in shap[e]. Coat the veal in the seasoned flour, shakin[g] off the excess. Bring to room temperature.
2   Put the carrot sticks in a saucepan [of] cold salted water and bring to the bo[il]. Simmer for 10–12 minutes or until tende[r]. Drain, season with pepper and keep warm.
3   Meanwhile simmer the cauliflower an[d] broccoli florets in salted water for 4–[5] minutes or until tender. Drain, season wit[h] pepper and keep warm.
4   Make the lemon sauce. Beat the softene[d] butter in a bowl with a fork until cream[y] then beat in the finely chopped parsley an[d] lemon juice. Season to taste and keep it [at] room temperature.
5   In a heavy frying-pan large enough t[o] take the veal in one layer, heat the butt[er] and olive oil. When the foaming subside[s] fry the medallions of veal for 3–4 minute[s] turning the veal pieces once during cookin[g]. Remove with a slotted spoon and transfer [to] a heated serving platter. Remove the string.
6   Spoon the sauce over the medallions [of] veal and let it melt.
7   Arrange the vegetables around the ve[al] medallions. Garnish with flat leaved parsle[y] and serve immediately.

Medallions of veal in lemon sauce

Making medallions of veal

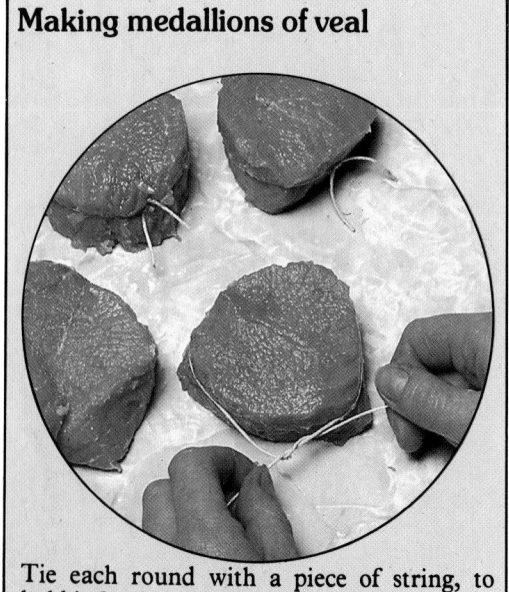

Tie each round with a piece of string, to hold it firmly in shape during cooking.

Veal escalopes with cream and calvados

Flavoured with calvados and cream, the classic ingredients of Normandy cooking, this dish is ideal for a dinner party.

bringing to room temperature, then 15 minutes

Serves 4

4 × 125 g /4 oz veal escalopes, slightly beaten
2 medium-sized red dessert apples
50 g /2 oz butter
salt and freshly ground pepper
30 ml /2 tbls lemon juice
60 ml /4 tbls calvados
200 ml /7 fl oz thick cream
sprigs of parsley, to garnish
For the croûtons
15 ml /1 tbls olive oil
25 g /1 oz butter
2 slices white bread, crusts removed, cut into triangles

1 Make the croûtons: heat the oil and butter in a frying-pan. When the foaming subsides add the bread triangles and sauté for 1–2 minutes, until golden on both sides. Remove from the pan and keep warm.
2 Peel the apples and cut into small cubes. Melt the butter in a heavy-based frying-pan over medium heat. When it starts to foam, add the apple and cook for 2 minutes. Remove with a slotted spoon and set aside.
3 Sprinkle the veal with salt and pepper and the lemon juice. Then add to the frying-pan, over medium heat. Brown the veal quickly on both sides.
4 Heat the calvados in a small pan. Set it alight, then pour it, while still flaming, over the meat, turning the heat up under the frying-pan. Rotate the pan until the flames die down. Lower heat and pour in cream.
5 Add the apple cubes to the meat and cook gently for about 2 minutes, stirring continuously. Don't allow the sauce to boil.
6 When the sauce has thickened, transfer the veal to a warmed serving dish. Arrange the apple cubes on top of the veal and pour the sauce over the apple. Garnish with croûtons and parsley, and serve.

Veal escalopes with cream and calvados

Pojarsky cutlets

20 minutes plus 2 hours chilling, then 25 minutes

Serves 4

500 g /1 lb boned shoulder of veal
salt
freshly ground black pepper
275 ml /10 fl oz thick cream
flour
50–65 g /2–2½ oz butter
175 g /6 oz mushrooms, sliced
150 ml /5 fl oz dry white wine
beurre manié made by mashing together
  15 g /½ oz butter with 15 g /½ oz flour
boiled rice, to serve

1 Trim the meat and cut into small piece Mince the meat in a food processor, or pas twice through blades of a mincer, until ver fine. Season well with salt and pepper an add 150 ml /5 fl oz thick cream. Return t the processor and blend until very fine.

Sprinkle the working surface with flour. [di]vide the minced veal into 8 portions and [for]m each into a miniature cutlet about 5 [cm] /¼ in thick. Chill for 2 hours.

Heat 25 g /1 oz butter in a small pan [an]d sauté the mushroom until just soft.

Melt the remaining butter in a large [fry]ing-pan. When the foaming subsides add [th]e cutlets and sauté them for 4–5 minutes [or] until they are golden brown on both sides. [Lif]t out and drain. Keep warm.

Add the dry wine to the frying-pan and [sti]r. Add the remaining cream and the [mu]shrooms. Stir over a gentle heat.

Add the beurre manié to the pan a little [at] a time, stirring it in well. Heat the sauce [gen]tly for 2–3 minutes.

Serve the cutlets on a bed of boiled rice [wit]h the sauce poured over.

Sauté of veal [P]rovençal

bringing to room temperature, then 1 hour 15 minutes

[S]erves 6
1 kg /2½ lb lean boneless veal (shoulder, leg or loin), in one piece
[sa]lt and freshly ground black pepper
[5]0 g /2 oz butter
[3]0 ml /2 tbls olive oil
[1] Spanish onion, finely chopped
[2] garlic cloves, finely chopped
[4] sage leaves
[2] sprigs of rosemary
[2] green or red peppers, halved, seeded and thinly sliced
[4] small tomatoes, halved and seeded
[2]75 ml /10 fl oz dry white wine
[b]ouquet garni
[1]00 g /4 oz green olives, stoned
[th]in onion rings, to garnish

Cut the veal into thin steaks, about 5 [c]m /¼ in thick. Cut each steak in half. [S]eason generously with salt and pepper.

Heat 15 g /½ oz butter and 15 ml /1 tbls [o]live oil in a large frying-pan. When the [fo]aming subsides, add the onion, garlic, sage [le]aves and sprigs of rosemary, and sauté [o]ver a medium heat for about 10 minutes, or [u]ntil soft, stirring occasionally. Remove and [r]eserve.

Heat the remaining butter and olive oil [in] the frying-pan. When the foaming sub[si]des, sauté the veal steaks in 3 batches, for [1]–2 minutes each side or until lightly [g]olden. Add the reserved onion mixture.

Add the sliced peppers to the pan with [t]he halved and seeded tomatoes, the dry [w]hite wine and the bouquet garni. Season to [t]aste with salt and black pepper.

Cover and simmer for 30 minutes. Stir [i]n the stoned green olives, cover and simmer [f]or a further 15 minutes, or until tender.

Meanwhile, blanch the onion rings for 2 [m]inutes in boiling salted water. Remove, pat [d]ry and keep warm.

Remove the bouquet garni and sprigs of [r]osemary. Arrange the veal steaks overlapp[i]ng on a heated serving dish. Pour the sauce [o]ver the top and garnish with onion rings.

Wiener schnitzel

This is a classic dish from Vienna. The schnitzel should be thin but not transparent.

1 hour including chilling

Serves 4
2 × 275 g /10 oz veal cutlets, boned, or 4 thin slices veal fillet
25 g /1 oz flour
1 medium-sized egg, beaten
75 g /3 oz fine dry white breadcrumbs
100–175 g /4–6 oz butter
30 ml /2 tbls olive oil
salt
freshly ground black pepper
For the garnish
4 anchovy fillets
4 stuffed olives
1 lemon, cut in wedges
parsley sprigs

Wiener schnitzel

1 If boned cutlets are used, cut each one into 2 thin slices, horizontally so that you cut as much across the grain as possible. Lay the pieces of veal between 2 sheets of greaseproof paper and pound them until thin using a meat mallet or a rolling pin.
2 Sprinkle a little flour on each schnitzel. Put the beaten egg in a wide shallow dish and the breadcrumbs in a similar dish or on greaseproof paper. Dip the veal in beaten egg and drain off the excess. Coat with breadcrumbs, patting them firmly with a palette knife or the palm of your hand. Chill in the refrigerator for at least 30 minutes.
3 Use 1 very large frying-pan or 2 smaller ones which will hold all the veal pieces comfortably in one layer. Heat the butter with the olive oil until foaming, and sprinkle lightly with salt and freshly ground black pepper. Add the veal pieces and fry over a moderate heat for 3–5 minutes on each side, turning once, until the breadcrumb coating is golden and the veal cooked but juicy.
4 Transfer the veal to a large heated serving dish. Wrap an anchovy fillet around each olive and place one in the centre of each cutlet. Garnish and serve.

● For a delicious summer luncheon, V
chops with sauce niçoise combir
admirably with freshly boiled nood
accompanied by a crisp green salad.

Veal scaloppini

**The lemon juice and butter in this Itali
dish, emphasise the flavour of the mea**

bringing to room temperature,
then 30 minutes

Serves 6
6 veal escalopes, 100 g /4 oz each
salt and freshly ground black pepper
75 g /3 oz butter
45 ml /3 tbls olive oil
45 ml /3 tbls lemon juice
*30 ml /2 tbls finely chopped parsley, to
garnish*

1   Put each slice of veal between 2 sheets
wet greaseproof paper or cling film and be
with a meat bat or rolling pin until each o
is double the original size. Season on ea
side with salt and black pepper and cut ea
escalope in half.
2   Heat 15 g /½ oz butter and 15 ml /1 t
of the oil over medium-high heat, in
frying-pan large enough to take 4 of the v
pieces in a single layer. When the foami
subsides, put in 4 of the veal pieces and 1
for 1 minute each side, turning them witl
fish slice. Transfer to a serving di
overlapping the pieces slightly, and ke
warm. Repeat with the remaining veal slic
adding 15 g /½ oz butter and 15 ml /1 tbls
for each new batch.
3   Add the remaining butter to the p
with the lemon juice. Heat gently, scrap
the bottom and sides of the pan with
wooden spoon. Correct the seasoning.
4   Pour the pan juices over the v
escalopes, and sprinkle with finely chopp
parsley. Serve immediately.

● The escalope 'scaloppini', should be c
across the grain from a leg of veal. You m
find it difficult to persuade your butcher
do this, in which case you can substitute
fillet or boned veal cutlet - pounded to t
right thickness.

Veal chops with ham

bringing to room temperature,
then 45 minutes

Serves 4
4 veal chops, weighing approximately 225
8 oz each
salt and freshly ground black pepper
65–75 g /2½–3 oz butter
4 large slices bread, trimmed of crusts
4 thin slices York ham
30 ml /2 tbls armagnac
30 ml /2 tbls dry Madeira
12 button mushrooms
60 ml /4 tbls thick cream
lemon twists and watercress, to garnish

Veal chops with sauce niçoise

**This thick, country-style sauce is really
perfect with veal chops**

bringing to room temperature,
making sauce, then 25 minutes

Serves 4
4 veal chops, about 225 g /8 oz each
15 ml /1 tbls flour, for dusting
salt and freshly ground black pepper
30 ml /2 tbls olive oil
24 stoned black olives, to garnish
60 ml /4 tbls chopped fresh basil, to garnish
For the sauce niçoise
½ Spanish onion, finely chopped
*400 g /14 oz canned tomatoes, with their
juice*
30 ml /2 tbls tomato purée
6 fresh basil or sage leaves, finely chopped
salt
freshly ground black pepper

1   Season the flour with salt and freshly
ground black pepper. Lightly dust the veal

Veal chops with sauce niçoise

chops with the seasoned flour, shaking off
any excess.
2   Heat the olive oil in a large, heavy-based
frying-pan and fry the chops for about 5
minutes, turning once, until they are lightly
browned on both sides. Remove the cooked
chops from the pan with a slotted spoon and
keep warm.
3   Add the finely chopped onion and garlic
to the oil remaining in the pan and cook
over a medium heat for 10 minutes, until
they are soft and transparent.
4   Add the canned tomatoes and their juice,
tomato purée, finely chopped basil or sage
and salt and freshly ground black pepper to
taste. Bring to the boil, then reduce the heat
to low and simmer, uncovered, for about 10
minutes.
5   Return the veal chops to the pan, and
stir together to coat with the sauce. Cover
the pan and simmer gently for 15 minutes,
or until the chops are tender and well heated
through.
6   Transfer the chops and sauce to a heated
serving platter and sprinkle with the stoned
black olives and chopped fresh basil. Serve
immediately.

Season the veal chops with salt and
freshly ground black pepper to taste. Heat
[ ]g /2 oz butter in a large frying-pan.
[W]hen the foaming subsides, put in the chops
[an]d sear them on both sides.

Then reduce the heat and sauté for 10
[m]inutes, or until cooked through. Remove
[w]ith a slotted spoon and keep warm.

To make four large croûtons, fry the
[tr]immed bread slices in the frying-pan.
[Ad]ding 15–25 g /½–1 oz more butter if
[ne]cessary, fry until golden on both sides.
[R]emove from the pan, drain on absorbent
[pa]per and keep warm.

Lightly sauté the thin slices of York ham
[in] the frying-pan until heated through.
[R]eserve the pan juices. Trim the sautéed
[ha]m to fit the croûtons. Place the croûtons
[on] a warmed serving platter, cover each
[cr]oûton with a slice of sautéed ham and
[pl]ace a veal chop on each one. Keep warm.

Add the armagnac, Madeira and button
[m]ushrooms to the pan juices, and sauté until
[th]e mushrooms are tender. Stir in the thick
[cr]eam and pour the hot sauce over the veal
[ch]ops. Serve immediately, garnished with
[le]mon twists and watercress.

Pan-fried veal chops grandmère

bringing to room temperature,
then 20 minutes

[Se]rves 4
[4] × 350 g /12 oz thick veal chops
[fr]eshly ground black pepper
[sa]lt
[1]6 button onions
[1]25 g /4 oz bacon, diced
[50] g /2 oz butter
[30] ml /2 tbls olive oil
[1]25 g /4 oz button mushrooms, cut into
    quarters
[6]0 ml /4 tbls beef stock, home-made or from
    a cube
[3]0 ml /2 tbls finely chopped parsley, to
    garnish

Trim the veal chops, leaving only a
[na]rrow border of fat. Slash the remaining
[fa]t in 3 or 4 places so that the chop does not
[cu]rl up during cooking. Wipe the meat with
[ab]sorbent paper and season with freshly
[gr]ound black pepper. Leave to come to room
[te]mperature. Just before cooking season
[ag]ain with salt and pepper.

Place the button onions and diced bacon
[in] a saucepan of cold water and bring to the
[bo]il. Drain.

Heat 25 g /1 oz butter and the olive oil
[in] a heavy frying-pan over a high heat.
[W]hen the foaming subsides, brown the veal
[ch]ops for 2 minutes on each side. Reduce the
[he]at to medium, cover the pan and cook the
[ch]ops gently for 6–8 minutes.

Meanwhile, melt the remaining butter in
[an]other heavy frying-pan and sauté the
[on]ions and bacon for 5 minutes. Add the
[m]ushrooms and cook for a further 2–3
[m]inutes.

When cooked, transfer the veal chops to
[a] heated serving dish and keep warm.

6 Stir the beef stock into the veal pan
juices. Add the onion, bacon and mushroom
mixture and season with salt and freshly
ground black pepper to taste. Pour the
mixture over the veal chops. Sprinkle with
finely chopped parsley and serve
immediately.

Watercress veal

bringing to room temperature,
then 45 minutes

Serves 4
4 × 175 g /6 oz veal escalopes,
    thinly beaten out
50 g /2 oz shelled, halved walnuts
1 bunch of watercress, washed
50 g /2 oz butter
1 small onion, finely chopped
150 ml /5 fl oz thick cream
salt and freshly ground black pepper
lemon juice
milk (optional)
new potatoes, to serve
broccoli florets, to serve

1 Put the halved walnuts in a small bowl
and pour over enough boiling water to
cover. Leave to stand for 10 minutes.

2 Discard the stalks from the watercress;
chop the leaves.
3 Drain the walnuts and remove the thin
brown skin that covers the nuts. Chop them
finely.
4 In a heavy-based frying-pan, melt half
the butter. When the foaming subsides, add
the finely chopped onion and sauté, stirring
occasionally, for about 5 minutes or until
soft. Add the chopped watercress leaves,
thick cream and chopped walnuts. Season
with salt, freshly ground black pepper and
lemon juice to taste. Cover the pan tightly
and simmer gently over a very low heat for
7–10 minutes. (Add a little milk if the sauce
reduces and thickens too rapidly.)
5 Remove the sauce from the heat and
purée in a blender until smooth. Return the
sauce to a pan and keep warm over a low
heat.
6 Meanwhile, melt the remaining butter in
a frying-pan. Cut each beaten escalope into
2 evenly-shaped, smaller escalopes. Sauté in
batches over a medium heat until cooked
through, 3–4 minutes.
7 To serve, arrange the veal on individual
heated plates and spoon the sauce over.
Serve with tiny new potatoes and florets of
broccoli.

Watercress veal

CASSEROLING & POT-ROASTING VEAL

Casseroling and pot-roasting are two straightforward methods of cooking veal with delicious results. Long, slow cooking develops the flavours of all the ingredients, blending succulent meat in a rich sauce.

Casseroling and pot-roasting are two methods of cooking which have much in common. Both involve cooking meat very slowly in a liquid in a container with a tightly-fitting lid, either on top of the stove or in the oven.

Marinating the meat before it is cooked will improve its flavour. Use wine, olive oil and herbs and marinate for at least a few hours or, preferably, overnight. Use the resulting liquid in the cooking. Alternatively, sear the surface of the meat in a little butter and olive oil to seal it and then flavour it with aromatic herbs and a touch of garlic before simmering it gently in a good stock.

What cuts to use

Casseroling: veal shoulder, breast, knuckle and shin all take kindly to long, gentle cooking in a well-flavoured sauce and so make wonderful casseroles. Veal chops and cutlets are also excellent cooked in this way, and look extremely attractive served as a dinner party dish. Remember, though, they will cook much more rapidly than less tender cuts.

Don't use fillet of veal in casseroles – it may disintegrate with long, slow cooking.

Pot-roasting: leg or loin are the best joints to use, but most veal will cook well using this method as it makes sure the meat stays moist and succulent.

The cooking pot

The ideal pot for casseroling and pot roast-ing on top of the stove is a flameproof casserole or a heavy-based saucepan. cooking in an oven, use ovenproof cookwar Whichever you use, it should have a heav base and a tightly fitting lid, so that r steam escapes. Do not choose one that is to large or the liquid will be dissipated over th surface of the pan and will boil away. On th other hand, the pan must be large enough hold all the ingredients and still be only tw thirds full.

If the lid does not fit as tightly as yo would like, cover the top of the ope casserole with a piece of buttere greaseproof paper and then put the lid o top of this – it serves the double purpose making the lid fit more tightly and keepir the top of the meat from touching the lid.

If you do not have a flameproof casserole, own the meat in a frying-pan first and then transfer it to an ordinary ovenproof casserole for the final cooking, but be sure to oil the cooking liquid in the frying-pan, scraping the bottom and sides of the pan thoroughly.

Preparing the meat

Boneless meat should be cut into 25 mm – 4 cm /1–1½ in cubes, making them all the same size so that they will cook evenly.

Bring the meat to room temperature, and make sure it is thoroughly dry. If necessary, dry it on absorbent paper. (This applies to meat which has been marinated, too.) If the meat is wet it will steam in the pan and not brown properly when you fry it. If the meat is to be dusted with flour, do so only at the last moment. (Flour seems to draw out any moisture and make the meat damp.)

Browning the meat

For both casseroling and pot-roasting start

by browning the meat all over – it improves the flavour of the finished dish. For this I like to use a mixture of butter and olive oil. This combination gives good, even browning with a buttery flavour. Don't use butter on its own as it burns. Alternatively, you can use fresh beef or pork dripping, bacon fat or lard.

Add the meat to the heated fat in batches. This way, the steam from the meat escapes. If it doesn't, the meat simmers in its own juices and won't brown. Make sure that the meat browns steadily and thoroughly and that it doesn't burn.

When the first batch is ready, remove it from the dish or pan with a slotted spoon and reserve. The fat is then reheated and the rest of the meat browned, again in batches.

Finally, brown any flavouring vegetables that are to be added to the casserole or pot roast. Usually, like the meat, they are evenly diced first. Stir them occasionally during cooking so they brown evenly.

Adding the liquid

When both meat and vegetables have been browned, return the meat to the pan and add the liquid. Choose a good, rich stock and add a little wine for extra flavour – it need not be a fine wine, of course, but choose something that is smooth and matured. Since you don't need to use a lot, one glass from the bottle you are going to drink will hardly be missed. The extra flavour of a spoonful or two of brandy, poured over the hot meat and flamed to burn off the alcohol and concentrate the flavour, also works wonders. Beer or cider can be used instead of wine.

Whichever liquid you choose, always bring it to the boil before adding it to the meat in the casserole or saucepan. If you add the liquid to the dish or pot cold and bring it to the boil with the meat, it extracts flavour and moisture from the meat.

Another tip to make the most of your casserole – make sure that the sediment and morsels left in the pan after the meat and vegetables have been browned are scraped up and added to the casserole or pot-roast. To do this, once all the meat and vegetables have been removed from the pan, take the pan off the heat and add 45–60 ml /3–4 tbls of the liquid from the recipe, stir in and scrape the bottom and sides of the pan clean with a wooden spoon.

Cooking a casserole or pot roast

Whether you cook on top of the stove or in the oven, cover the casserole tightly to prevent evaporation and control the heat to keep it just at a gentle simmer. If cooking in the oven, a setting of 140C /275F /gas 1 or 150C /300F /gas 2 is usually about right. If cooking on top of the stove, a heat diffuser helps, but do watch the casserole carefully to see that it doesn't start to bubble.

A casserole can be ruined by too much heat and if the liquid is allowed to boil, the meat will harden and the liquid is likely to boil away before cooking is complete. It is much better to cook the casserole or pot roast very slowly and, if there is too much

Fricassée of veal

liquid left at the end, to reduce it down.

To do this, remove the meat from the pan, boil the sauce briskly over a high heat, stirring constantly, until the liquid is reduced to the desired consistency, then return the meat to the pan. This method is suitable for casseroles and pot roasts which aren't too highly seasoned and which already have some thickening agent in them, such as flour.

Apart from the casserole or pot-roast being too liquid, whether you thicken it or not depends on your own taste, as well as the recipe; many braised and pot-roasted recipes do not really need extra thickening in any special way, and the flavouring vegetables disintegrate in the stock, thickening it during cooking.

If you do add thickening, it is usually in the form of *beurre manié*, added piece by piece, or a paste of flour or cornflour blended with cold water and added at the last minute. Always boil a sauce thickened with flour, in order to remove the unpleasant taste of raw flour.

Blanquettes and fricassées

Blanquettes and fricassées are simple, white stews made from meat or poultry simmered in a white stock and finished with a velouté sauce. Delicious to eat and simple to prepare, they have enjoyed long-standing popularity and have become classic recipes in many countries.

Blanquette or fricassée?

The finished dishes may look similar but there are differences between a blanquette and a fricassée. For a blanquette the meat, poultry, or other ingredient is first soaked in acidulated water to whiten it, then simmered in a light veal or chicken stock. (It can be made with a stock cube, although a real stock will give the finished velouté sauce a much subtler flavour.) In a fricassée the meat or poultry is lightly seared in hot butter to seal it and then simmered in stock until tender. (You can use beef stock instead of chicken or veal stock if you want a stronger flavour.)

In both cases the meat is cut into even-sized pieces first, and, after simmering, the cooking liquid is used to make a velouté sauce. Flour may be used to help to thicken it and a liaison of egg yolks and thick cream both enriches it and gives it a lovely, velvety texture.

The final garnishing again distinguishes the two dishes: blanquettes are traditionally garnished with button onions and mushrooms; fricassées can be garnished with a selection of vegetables, if wished.

Variations

Blanquettes are particularly appropriate for lower calorie nouvelle cuisine recipes. The sauce can be thickened by reduction rather than with a roux. The result is a lighter, more subtly-flavoured sauce with a finer texture.

Fricassées may be made from cooked meat left over from another dish. It is possible to vary the sauce by adding vegetables which have been puréed or sliced and cooked to the finished velouté.

of the liquid may be sufficient to cook th
eggs and thicken the sauce. If not, heat
through over the lowest possible hea
without letting the mixture come to the boil
10 Carefully stir the cooked mushroo▮
caps and leeks into the fricassée. Adjust th
seasoning and grate a little fresh nutme▮
into the sauce. Serve immediately, garnishe▮
with fried bread triangles which have eac▮
had chopped herbs sprinkled over on▮
corner.

Mediterranean veal stew

⫟⫟ 2½ hours

Serves 4
900 g /2 lb boned shoulder of veal, cut into
 25 mm /1 in cubes
75 g /3 oz butter
45 ml /3 tbls olive oil
salt
freshly ground black pepper
1 Spanish onion, thinly sliced
2 garlic cloves, finely sliced
1 green pepper, seeded and sliced
125 g /4 oz mushrooms, sliced
400 g /14 oz canned tomatoes
225 ml /8 fl oz dry white wine
10 ml /2 tsp dried oregano
5 ml /1 tsp dried rosemary
grated zest of 1 lemon
500 g /1 lb courgettes, trimmed and cut int▮
 5 mm /¼ in slices

1 In a flameproof casserole heat 25 g /1 c
butter and 30 ml /2 tbls olive oil. Season th
veal cubes with salt and freshly groun▮
black pepper. When the foaming subside▮
put in enough meat to cover the base of th
pan and sauté it until it is lightly browne▮
on all sides. Remove the veal with a slotte▮
spoon and set it aside on a plate; repeat wit
the rest of the meat.
2 To the fat remaining in the casserole ad▮
15 g /½ oz butter and 15 ml /1 tbls oil. Ad▮
the sliced onion, sliced garlic and gree▮
pepper and sauté for 7–10 minutes, until th
onion is soft and translucent but n▮
browned. Stir in the mushrooms an▮
tomatoes with their juice and cook th
vegetables for a further 3 minutes.
3 Add the dry white wine, dried oregan▮
and rosemary, grated lemon zest and seaso▮
to taste with salt and freshly ground blac▮
pepper. Bring to the boil and stir to remov▮
any sediment from the sides of the casserol▮
then add the meat. Bring the mixture bac▮
to the boil, reduce the heat to very lo▮
cover the casserole and simmer for 1 hour 2▮
minutes, or until the veal is tender.
4 Meanwhile, melt the remaining butter i▮
a frying-pan and sauté the courgette slice▮
until they are slightly coloured but still ▮
dente. Remove the cooked courgettes with ▮
slotted spoon and drain them well.
5 Remove any grease from the casserol▮
with a spoon or absorbent paper. Add th
courgettes, adjust the seasoning and cook f▮
a further 2–3 minutes, until the courgette▮
are heated through. Serve immediately.

Fricassée of veal

🕐⫟⫟ overnight soaking the meat,
then 1¾ hours

Serves 6
1.4 kg /3 lb rump or shoulder of veal
juice of 1 lemon
40 g /1½ oz butter
30 ml /2 tbls olive oil
2 Spanish onions, chopped
4 large carrots, sliced
30 ml /2 tbls flour
600 ml /1 pt chicken stock, home-made or
 from a cube
425 ml /15 fl oz dry white wine
salt and freshly ground black pepper
1 bouquet garni
4 leeks, cut into thin strips
12 button mushrooms, stalks removed
 (about 100 g /4 oz)
4 large egg yolks
375 ml /13 fl oz thick cream
freshly grated nutmeg
fried bread triangles, to garnish
15 ml /1 tbls each finely chopped fresh
 tarragon, chervil and parsley, to garnish

1 Cut the veal into 4 cm /1½ in cubes and
soak for 12 hours covered in cold water with
lemon juice, changing the water twice.
2 Heat the oven to 140C /275F /gas 1.
3 Drain the veal well in a colander and
then blot the pieces well with absorbent

Mediterranean veal stew

paper. Heat 25 g /1 oz of the butter and the
olive oil in a large flameproof casserole and
sauté the blanched veal cubes. Remove the
cubes from the casserole with a slotted spoon
and reserve.
4 Add the chopped onions and sliced
carrots to the pan and sauté until the onion
is transparent and the carrots golden.
5 Sprinkle the flour into the pan and, stirring constantly, cook for 4–5 minutes, or
until a pale roux forms. Gradually stir in the
chicken stock and the dry white wine, and
bring to the boil, stirring constantly.
6 Return the veal cubes to the pan and
season with salt and freshly ground black
pepper to taste. Add the bouquet garni,
cover and cook in the oven for 1½ hours, or
until the veal is tender.
7 Meanwhile, cook the leek strips in
boiling, salted water for 1–2 minutes, or
until tender but firm. Drain and keep warm.
8 Melt the remaining butter in a small
saucepan. Add 30 ml /2 tbls lemon juice and
the mushroom caps and cook for 3–4
minutes, or until the mushrooms are tender.
Add them to the leeks.
9 In a bowl whisk the egg yolks with the
thick cream. Remove the casserole from the
oven when cooked and ladle a little hot
sauce into the egg and cream mixture,
whisking constantly to prevent the eggs from
curdling. Return the egg mixture to the
sauce in the casserole and stir well. The heat

Veal paprika

The caraway seeds in this recipe give an authentic Hungarian flavour.

1¼ hours

Serves 4–6

1 kg /2 lb stewing veal, cubed
30 ml /2 tbls oil
15 g /½ oz butter
1 large onion, sliced
5 ml /1 tsp caraway seeds
30 ml /2 tbls mild paprika
400 g /14 oz canned, peeled tomatoes
salt and freshly ground black pepper
450 g /1 lb tagliatelle verdi
150 ml /5 fl oz soured cream

Heat the oil and butter in a large frying-pan over moderate heat and, in batches, sear the meat. Reserve with a slotted spoon. Add the sliced onion and cook it gently to soften for 5 minutes.

Add the caraway seeds and paprika to the pan and cook for 3 minutes, stirring the ingredients well with a wooden spoon. Add

Veal paprika

the veal cubes to the contents of the pan.
3 Pour in the tomatoes and season with salt and freshly ground black pepper to taste. Stir well, cover and cook over a low heat for 1 hour.
4 Fifteen minutes before the veal is cooked, prepare the tagliatelle verdi. Bring a pan of salted water to the boil, add the tagliatelle and boil for 10 minutes or until *al dente* – firm to the bite. Drain and transfer the tagliatelle to a large platter and then keep warm.
5 Stir the soured cream with a fork, then add it to the cooked veal mixture. Stir the veal paprika to distribute the soured cream, and allow it to warm through but not boil.
6 Spoon the veal onto the centre of the tagliatelle and serve immediately.

Osso buco with orange

The Italian name of this dish means marrow bones. Choose shin of veal bones with marrow inside and plenty of meat round the outside.

1 hour 50 minutes

Serves 4–6

4–6 thick slices shin of veal, with bone
salt and freshly ground black pepper
25–50 g /1–2 oz flour
60–90 ml /4–6 tbls olive oil
3 garlic cloves, finely chopped
1 Spanish onion, finely chopped
150 ml /5 fl oz hot chicken stock, home-made or from a cube
150 ml /5 fl oz dry white wine
90 ml /6 tbls tomato purée
4–6 anchovy fillets, finely chopped
30–45 ml /2–3 tbls finely chopped fresh parsley
grated zest of ½ orange
grated zest of ¼ lemon

1 Season the veal slices generously on both sides with salt and pepper and dredge with flour. Select a flameproof casserole large enough to hold the slices in a single layer. Heat the oil in the casserole, add the meat and cook for 5 minutes until browned.
2 Arrange the slices with the bone pointing upwards in the pan. Add 2 of the garlic cloves and the chopped onion; pour over the stock and wine and stir in the tomato purée. Cover and simmer gently for 1½ hours.
3 Add the chopped anchovy fillets and remaining garlic to the dish. Adjust the seasoning and add the parsley and zest.

Veal stew with asparagus

🔪🔪🔪 1½ hours

Serves 4
900 g /2 lb stewing veal
60 ml /4 tbls flour
salt and freshly ground black pepper
60 ml /4 tbls olive oil
1 Spanish onion, finely chopped
150 ml /5 fl oz chicken stock, home-made or
    from a cube
300 ml /10 fl oz dry white wine
500 g /1 lb fresh asparagus
beurre manié (made with 15 g /½ oz butter
    and 15 ml /1 tbls flour)
150 ml /5 fl oz thick cream
juice of 1 lemon

1 Trim the veal of any fat or gristle and cut into 25 mm – 4 cm /1–1½ in cubes.
2 Season the flour with salt and freshly ground black pepper and coat the pieces of meat in the seasoned flour.
3 In a medium-sized flameproof casserole, heat the olive oil. When hot, add enough meat to cover the base of the pan and sauté until the meat is lightly golden on all sides. Remove with a slotted spoon. Repeat with the remaining veal.
4 Add the chopped onion to the pan and cook for 2–3 minutes, or until transparent. Add the chicken stock and white wine, stir and bring to the boil. Season with salt and freshly ground black pepper to taste. Add the meat, reduce the heat and simmer for 45 minutes, or until the veal is tender.
5 Meanwhile, trim the asparagus and cook for 5–10 minutes in boiling, salted water, or until al dente. Drain, refresh under cold, running water and drain again on absorbent paper.
6 When the veal is tender, remove it to a heated serving dish with a slotted spoon. Bring the cooking liquid to the boil and stir in the beurre manié a little piece at a time, until the sauce has thickened.
7 Stir in the thick cream and the lemon juice to taste. Add the asparagus and heat through gently.
8 Spoon the sauce and the asparagus over the veal and serve immediately.

Veal chops in herbs

🔪🔪 ¾–1 hour

Serves 4
4 veal chops, each 350 g /12 oz
50 g /2 oz butter
30 ml /2 tbls olive oil
salt and freshly ground black pepper
150 ml /5 fl oz chicken stock, home-made or
    from a cube
90 ml /6 tbls white wine
2 shallots, finely chopped
15 ml /1 tbls finely chopped fresh parsley
15 ml /1 tbls finely chopped fresh chervil
15 ml /1 tbls finely chopped fresh tarragon

1 In a large frying-pan heat 25 g /1 oz butter and 15 ml /1 tbls olive oil. Season the chops with salt and freshly ground black pepper. When foaming subsides, brown 2 of the chops on both sides. Transfer the chops to the flameproof casserole. Add the remaining butter and oil to the frying-pan and brown the other 2 chops. Transfer them to the casserole.
2 Add the stock and wine to the frying-pan, stir to remove the sediment from the base of the pan, bring to the boil and pour over the chops. Sprinkle over the shallots, cover the casserole and cook, over a low heat, for 20–30 minutes, until tender.
3 With a slotted spoon, transfer the chops to a heated serving dish and keep warm. Boil the juices left in the casserole to half their original quantity. Stir in the herbs, and pour over the sauce.

Veal creole

🔪🔪 2¼ hours

Serves 4–6
1 kg /2 lb stewing veal, in 25 mm /1 in cubes
30 ml /2 tbls seasoned flour
30 ml /2 tbls oil
25 g /1 oz butter
4 medium-sized carrots, diced
100 g /4 oz mushrooms, caps separated from
    stalks
2 medium-sized onions, chopped
1 garlic clove, crushed
1 calf's foot or 2 pig's trotters
150 ml /5 fl oz dry sherry
1 bay leaf
a sprig of fresh thyme or 5 ml /1 tsp dried
    thyme
15 ml /1 tbls tomato purée
1 leek, sliced
30 ml /2 tbls thin cream
For the garnish
paprika
freshly chopped parsley

1 Dust the veal lightly with the seasoned flour. Heat the oil and butter in a frying-pan and brown the veal over high heat. Remove the meat from the pan with a slotted spoon and put it into the casserole.
2 Lower the heat and gently sauté the carrots, mushroom stalks, onions and garlic for 2–3 minutes. Transfer to the casserole.
3 Brown the calf's foot or pig's trotters in the fat remaining in the pan. Add to the casserole with 600 ml /1 pt water, the sherry, herbs and tomato purée. Bring to the boil, then simmer gently for 1 hour. Add the leek, simmer for 15 minutes, then add the mushroom caps.
4 Continue cooking for a further 30 minutes, or until the meat is tender. Remove the calf's foot or pig's trotters and skim off any fat. Stir in the cream, sprinkle with paprika and the parsley. Serve at once.

Hungarian goulash

🔪🔪 1¼ hours

Serves 6
1.1 kg /2½ lb boned shoulder or leg of veal
2 Spanish onions, finely chopped
2 garlic cloves, finely chopped
25–40 g /1–1½ oz lard
1.5 ml /¼ tsp caraway seeds
30–45 ml /2–3 tbls paprika
1 bay leaf
a generous pinch of dried marjoram
a generous pinch of dried thyme
salt and freshly ground black pepper
250 g /8 oz button mushrooms, sliced
2 red peppers, seeded and diced
2 green peppers, seeded and diced
400 g /14 oz canned, peeled tomatoes
300 ml /10 fl oz soured cream

1 Heat the oven to 150C /300F/ gas. Sauté the onions and garlic in 25 g /1 o lard in a large flameproof casserole unt transparent. Remove from the pan.
2 Cut the veal into 5 cm /2 in cubes. Ad to the casserole and sauté until golder Return the onion and garlic to the cassero and sprinkle with the caraway seeds an paprika to taste. Add the bay leaf and drie herbs and cook gently for 10 minutes.
3 Season with salt and freshly groun black pepper to taste. Top with th mushrooms, peppers and tomatoes.
4 Cover and bring gently to boil, the transfer to the oven and cook gently fe about 1 hour. Serve with soured cream.

Pot-roasted veal à la suisse

Chill the meat thoroughly before slicing and inserting the cheese.

bringing to room temperature, then 2¼ hours

Serves 8

1.4 kg /3 lb boned and rolled leg or loin of veal
salt and freshly ground black pepper
freshly grated nutmeg
2 very thin slices, about 50 g /2 oz, raw ham: prosciutto, Westphalian or Bayonne
2 thin slices, about 175 g /6 oz, Gruyère cheese
125–150 g /4–5 oz streaky bacon, cut into long, thin strips
125 g /4 oz butter
carrots, finely chopped
medium-sized onions, finely chopped
300 ml /10 fl oz dry white wine
garlic clove, finely chopped
45 ml /3 tbls brandy
20 baby onions, peeled
15 ml /1 tbls caster sugar
24 small button mushrooms, thickly sliced
150 ml /5 fl oz thick cream
sprigs of flat-leaved parsley, to garnish

1   Choose a long, thin joint of veal, rather than a short one with a large diameter. Lay it on a board and, with a sharp knife, cut it into 13 even-sized slices without separating them completely – just as you would a French loaf for garlic bread. Open the slices out carefully and season them generously with salt, freshly ground black pepper and a pinch of freshly grated nutmeg.
2   Lay a slice of raw ham and Gruyère cheese neatly in each of the 12 cuts.
3   Put the joint back together again. Cover it with long, thin strips of streaky bacon and tie securely with string, first lengthways and then horizontally, in several places.
4   In a heavy, flameproof casserole which will hold the joint comfortably, melt half the butter and sauté the joint until it is browned all over. Remove from the casserole and keep warm.
5   In the same fat, sauté the finely chopped carrots and onions until golden brown.
6   Meanwhile, combine the dry white wine and the chopped garlic clove in a small pan and bring to the boil.
7   Lay the veal on top of the sautéed vegetables. Warm the brandy, pour it over the veal, and flame it.
8   As soon as the flames have died down, moisten the veal with boiling wine and garlic. Cover the casserole and simmer, over the lowest possible heat, for 1–1¼ hours, or until the veal is tender.

Pot-roasted veal à la suisse

9   Meanwhile, fit the baby onions into the bottom of a heavy pan that will take them in one layer. Add the caster sugar, 15 g /½ oz butter and season with salt and freshly ground black pepper. Cook, shaking the pan frequently, for 12–15 minutes, until the onions are *al dente* and evenly golden-coloured.
10   In another pan, melt 25 g /1 oz butter and sauté the thickly sliced mushrooms for 4–5 minutes until tender and golden. Sprinkle with salt and freshly ground black pepper and put aside.
11   When the veal is tender, remove it from the casserole. Discard the strings and the bacon and keep the meat hot on a heated serving dish while you finish the sauce.
12   Strain the sauce through a fine sieve, pressing some of the flavouring vegetables through as well. Return the sauce to the casserole. Stir in the thick cream and reheat gently without boiling. Taste and adjust the seasoning.
13   Heat the remaining butter in a large frying-pan and toss the glazed onions and sautéed mushrooms for 2–3 minutes to heat them through.
14   To serve, garnish the veal with the parsley, onions and mushrooms. Spoon some of the sauce over the meat and serve the remainder in a heated sauce-boat.

Loin of veal with artichokes

Loin of veal with artichokes

In Brittany, where artichokes are plentiful, this dish is made with fresh artichoke hearts, the outer leaves and the inner chokes being discarded.

about 2½ hours

Serves 4–6
1.8 kg /4 lb loin of veal, boned and rolled
75 g /3 oz butter
2 medium-sized onions, chopped
4 medium-sized carrots, sliced
275 ml /10 fl oz Muscadet or other dry white wine
275 ml /10 fl oz chicken stock, home-made or from a cube
1 calf's foot
1 bouquet garni
salt and freshly ground black pepper
8 canned artichoke hearts, or 8 frozen artichoke hearts
crusty bread to serve

1 Melt 50 g /2 oz of the butter in a large flameproof casserole, add the onion and carrot and stir over moderate heat for 2 minutes
2 Push the vegetables to the sides of the pan and place the joint in the centre. Brown over high heat, turning, until golden on all sides. Pour in the wine and stock, add the calf's foot and bouquet garni and season generously with salt and pepper. Bring the ingredients to the boil, then cover and simmer them for 2 hours. Remove the bouquet garni.
3 Just before the meat is ready, drain the canned artichoke hearts or cook the frozen ones in boiling, salted water until tender and drain.
4 Melt the remaining butter in a clean pan, then toss the artichoke hearts in this and cook them until they are piping hot and just turning golden.
5 Place the veal on a dish and slice. Serve with portions of the meat from the calf's foot, some of the vegetables and stock from the casserole and the artichoke hearts. Hand round the rest of the stock separately in a sauce-boat, together with a large basket of crusty bread.

● Serve with roast potatoes.

Veal blanquette with celeriac

Serve this creamy blanquette with plain boiled potatoes or buttered noodles.

2½ hours, plus soaking

Serves 4
750 g /1½ lb pie veal, in 20 mm /¾ in dice, soaked
350 g /12 oz celeriac, peeled
4 celery stalks
2 sprigs of fresh thyme
2 sprigs of fresh parsley
2 thinly pared strips of lemon zest
250 g /8 oz carrots, sliced
1 large onion, thinly sliced
600 ml /1 pt chicken stock, home-made or from a cube
a pinch of ground mace
salt and white pepper
25 g /1 oz butter
45 ml /3 tbls flour
2 medium-sized egg yolks
25 g /1 oz freshly grated Parmesan cheese
freshly chopped parsley, to garnish

Royal korma

$2\frac{1}{4} - 2\frac{1}{2}$ hours

Serves 6
450 g /1 lb very lean veal, cut into 4 cm /1½
  in cubes
2 large onions
6 garlic cloves
25 mm /1 in piece of fresh root ginger
30 ml /2 tbls clarified butter or margarine
2.5 ml /½ tsp chilli powder
5 ml /1 tsp ground coriander
2.5 ml /½ tsp ground cumin
6 cardamom pods, crushed
salt
400 ml /14 fl oz milk
5 ml /1 tsp sugar
5 ml /1 tsp poppy seeds, ground in a mortar
  and pestle
15 ml /1 tbls ground almonds
a pinch of saffron
sprigs of coriander, to garnish
pilau rice or chapatis, to serve

1 Finely grate 1 of the onions, the garlic and the ginger onto a plate. Crush them together with the flat side of a knife to make a smooth paste.

2 Slice the other onion thinly. Heat the clarified butter or margarine in a frying-pan over medium heat and fry the onion slices until they are golden brown. Remove them with a slotted spoon, drain thoroughly on absorbent paper and then reserve them.

3 Add the onion paste to the pan with the chilli powder, coriander and cumin. Fry for 3–4 minutes, sprinkling a little water into the pan when the spices begin to stick.

4 Add the meat and cardamom pods to the pan and season with salt. Stir the mixture for 5–10 minutes, turning the meat, until it is golden brown on all sides and all the liquid has evaporated.

5 Add the milk and sugar; simmer covered, over low heat until the meat is half-tender, 50–60 minutes. Add the ground poppy seeds and the fried onion slices and continue cooking for about 1 hour, or until the meat is tender and the liquid has thickened.

6 Add the ground almonds and saffron, and cook for 5 minutes. Garnish with coriander sprigs and serve hot with pilau rice or chapatis.

● Pilau or pulao rice can be bought from supermarkets and is made from basmati rice. To this is added a wide variety of spices, which may include cloves, cinnamon, cardamom pods, turmeric, cumin, ginger and saffron. Raisins, almonds and bay leaves may also be added. If making your own pilau rice, allow 400 g /10 oz of rice for 6 people.

● Chapatis are a flat bread made from wholemeal flour, salt and clarified butter. They are available from supermarkets and Indian stores.

Royal korma

Cut the celeriac and celery into large, regular-sized pieces. Tie the thyme and parsley sprigs and lemon zest together to make a bouquet garni.

Put the veal, celeriac, celery and bouquet garni into a large saucepan with the carrots and onion. Pour in the stock and add the mace, salt and pepper. Bring to the boil over a medium heat, cover and simmer for 1 hour.

Strain off and reserve the stock. Discard the bouquet garni. Return the veal and vegetables to the saucepan.

Melt the butter in a medium-sized saucepan over a medium heat. Stir in the flour and cook for ½ minute. Stir in 425 ml /15 fl oz of the reserved stock and bring it to the boil, stirring. Simmer the sauce for 2 minutes, then take the pan from the heat.

Beat the egg yolks with the cheese and gradually add about 100 ml /3½ fl oz of the hot sauce. Stir this mixture back into the rest of the sauce. Reheat very gently, without boiling, so the mixture thickens.

Mix the sauce into the veal and vegetables and let the blanquette stand for 1 hour to let the flavours blend.

Just before serving, reheat gently – do not allow the sauce to boil – and sprinkle with the chopped parsley.

VEAL OFFAL

Much prized for its superior flavour, veal offal – kidney, liver and sweetbreads – make a delectable, if rather expensive, dish. It is often difficult to obtain, so order from your butcher first.

Sweetbreads

Sweetbreads come from the thymus gland and should be pale, creamy, moist and plump if you are buying fresh ones. Frozen sweetbreads are often available in larger supermarkets.

Sweetbreads used to be sold in pairs but are now more often sold by weight. Allow 100–175 g /4–6 oz per person. You will find that one pair of sweetbreads will serve two adequately.

To prepare, soak in cold water for 2–3 hours, changing the water several times, until no traces of blood remain. Drain and rinse under the cold tap. Place the sweetbreads in a saucepan, just cover with cold water, add 15 ml /1 tbls lemon juice, 5 ml /1 tsp salt and a bay leaf (optional) and bring slowly to the boil. Simmer gently for 7–10 minutes, drain and plunge into cold water to firm. Remove the tubes and outer membrane.

Calf's liver with raspberries

If a neat shape is required, the sweetbreads can be pressed between two plates or pieces of foil, covered with a weight and left in the refrigerator for 3 hours or overnight before cooking.

Kidneys

Veal kidneys are larger and more expensive than lamb's or pig's kidneys and different in shape and structure, consisting of numerous segments joined to a central core. Their size varies according to the age of the calf. They are considered the choicest kidney of all, as they are very tender and mild, but are often scarce and difficult to obtain. If the kidneys are to be baked whole, leave a little of the surrounding fat in place to keep them moist in the oven. Otherwise remove any fat and the thin covering of membrane. Then cut across into 5 mm /¼ in slices. Do not overcook veal kidneys, otherwise they harden and their delicate flavour is lost. Slice then fry, or bake them whole in their suet covering. Allow 100 g /4 oz per portion.

Liver

Calf's liver is the finest and the most expensive kind of liver, but is often difficult obtain. It has an excellent flavour and smooth texture and is exceptionally tender It is best fried or grilled and it should moist and slightly pink in the centre, never overcooked, which will make it unpleasant hard and tough.

Pan-fried veal kidney with port

Pan-fried veal kidney with port takes on minutes to prepare for a quick late-night supper dish.

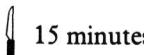 15 minutes

Serves 4
1 veal kidney
8 thick slices of white bread, 1 day old
65 g /2½ oz butter
30 ml /2 tbls olive oil
30 ml /2 tbls seasoned flour
90 ml /6 tbls port
50 g /2 oz mushrooms, thinly sliced
salt
freshly ground black pepper
sprigs of parsley, to garnish

Cut a 7 cm /2¾ in round from each slice bread.

Heat 25 g /1 oz butter and the olive oil a heavy frying-pan. Fry the bread rounds til golden brown on both sides. Drain em on absorbent paper. Place 2 croûtons each of 4 heated plates and keep warm.

Cut the veal kidney into eight 15 mm /½ slices – do not remove the core or the ces will collapse. Coat the kidney slices in asoned flour, shaking off the excess.

Heat the remaining butter in a clean avy frying-pan. Fry the kidney slices for) seconds on each side, carefully turning em over. Remove with a slotted spoon and ace a kidney slice on each croûton. Keep arm.

Add the port and sliced mushrooms to e pan juices. Season and cook for 1 inute, stirring occasionally. Top each rving of kidney with mushrooms and pour /er the port sauce. Garnish with parsley d serve immediately.

Calf's liver with raspberries

he sweet taste of raspberries comple-ents the smooth flavour of calf's liver eautifully.

⏱ 15 minutes

erves 4
2 very thin slices of calf's liver
0 ml /4 tbls flour
llt and freshly ground black pepper
0 g /2 oz butter
5 ml /1 tbls olive oil
50 g /5 oz fresh raspberries, puréed and sieved
5–30 ml /1–2 tbls Quick meat glaze (page 23) or 120 ml /8 tbls beef stock, home-made or from a cube
0–45 ml /2–3 tbls framboise liqueur
uice of 1 lemon
aspberries, flat-leaved parsley and lemon slices, to garnish

Sprinkle the flour on a plate and season /ith salt and black pepper. Coat the liver lices with the seasoned flour.

Heat half the butter and the olive oil in a arge frying-pan. Sauté 2 servings (6 slices) f liver for 30 seconds on each side, turning hem with a fish slice. Remove the liver slices rom the pan and place on a heated serving platter; keep warm. Add the remaining utter and repeat with remaining servings.

To the juices left in the pan add the aspberry purée and the meat glaze or the beef stock. Stir in the framboise liqueur and emon juice and pour over the liver. Garnish nd serve immediately.

Sweetbreads anisette

⏱ preparing sweetbreads, then 15 minutes

Serves 4
700 g /1½ lb calf's sweetbreads
600 ml /1 pt chicken stock, home-made or from a cube
150 ml /5 fl oz medium-dry white wine
700 g /1½ lb fresh spinach, washed, trimmed and coarsely chopped, or 500 g /1 lb frozen spinach, defrosted
150 g /5 oz butter
salt
freshly ground black pepper
15 ml /1 tbls lemon juice
15 ml /1 tbls anisette

1 Soak the sweetbreads in cold water to cover, for 2–3 hours.
2 Drain the sweetbreads, rinse well and put them in a heavy-based saucepan. Cover with the chicken stock and white wine and bring slowly to the boil.
3 Simmer them until they become white and firm, about 7–10 minutes. Be careful not to overcook them – they should just lose their raw pink colour.
4 Remove from the pan with a slotted spoon, reserving the cooking liquid. Cool them quickly under cold running water, then remove any hard bits and little tubes, being careful not to take off too much of the thin transparent membrane that holds them together. Put them between two plates with a weight on top and press overnight or for at least 3 hours in a cool place.
5 Put the fresh spinach (if using) in a large

Pan-fried veal kidney with port

saucepan with only the water clinging to its leaves. Cook for about 5–10 minutes over a low heat or until the spinach is tender when pierced with a fork.
6 Drain the spinach and return to the pan together with 75 g /3 oz butter. Season with salt and pepper and stir in the lemon juice. If using frozen spinach, put in the pan with butter and seasonings. Simmer the spinach gently while you finish cooking the sweetbreads.
7 Bring the reserved cooking liquid to the boil and reduce rapidly until it is a scant 175 ml /6 fl oz. Reserve this.
8 Cut the sweetbreads into 15 mm /½ in slices. Melt the remaining butter in a sauce-pan and add the sweetbreads. Sauté for 3–5 minutes until golden.
9 Add 50 ml /2 fl oz of the reduced cooking liquid to the sweetbreads, and simmer until well reduced. Continue adding liquid and reducing until it is all used up. This will make a rich glaze.
10 Put the spinach in an even layer in a shallow serving dish. When there is just a little glaze left in the sweetbread pan, remove the sweetbreads and put them on top of the spinach. Keep warm.
11 Add the anisette to the sweetbread pan, stir it around and scrape all the pan sedi-ments into the sauce. Pour over the sweetbreads and serve immediately.

VEAL FOR THE FAMILY

An appetizing selection of recipes using the cheaper cuts of veal, from a spectacular traditional veal, ham and egg pie, to a warming homely stew. Eat well and save money with these super dishes.

Veal, ham and egg pie

🕐🍴 3¾ hours, plus standing and chilling time

Serves 8
275 g /10 oz flour
2.5 ml /½ tsp salt
1 medium-sized egg yolk
75 g /3 oz lard
1 medium-sized egg, beaten
For the filling
700 g /1½ lb pie veal, chopped
175 g /6 oz lean ham, chopped
50 g /2 oz lean bacon, chopped
15 ml /1 tbls grated onion
1.5 ml /¼ tsp dried sage
salt and freshly ground black pepper
3 medium-sized eggs, hard-boiled
For the jelly
150 ml /5 fl oz hot chicken stock, home-made or from a cube
7.5 ml /1½ tsp gelatine
salt and freshly ground black pepper

1 Sift the flour and salt together into a bowl. Make a well in the centre, drop in the yolk and sprinkle on some of the flour.
2 Place the lard and 150 ml /5 fl oz water in a pan, heat gently until the fat melts then bring to boiling point. Remove from heat and pour immediately into the dry ingredients and egg yolk. Mix to a dough.
3 Turn out on a floured surface and knead thoroughly for 1 minute, until the dough is smooth and pliable.
4 Cover and leave in a warm place for 20 minutes before using.
5 Heat the oven to 200C /400F /gas 6. Cut off two-thirds of the pastry, leaving the remainder covered in a warm place to prevent it from drying out. Roll out the pastry to a rectangle about 30 × 20 cm / 12 × 8 in. Place in a greased 1.7 L /3 pt loaf tin and mould with your fingers up the sides of the tin, taking care in the corners to avoid a double thickness of pastry. Aim to get an even thickness of 5 mm /¼ in and allow the pastry to overlap the top edge of the tin all round. Leave in a cool place until firm, about 1 hour.
6 Meanwhile, make the filling. Mix together the veal, ham, bacon, onion, sage, salt and pepper.
7 Place about a third of the meat mixture in the pastry case. Shell the eggs and arrange them in a line in the tin. Pack more meat mixture round the eggs, put in the remaining mixture and level the top.
8 Roll out the rest of the pastry to a thickness of about 5 mm /¼ in to make a lid. Dampen the pastry edges, put on the lid and pinch the join well. Trim off pastry neatly

above the join and crimp the edges.
9 Brush the pie with beaten egg. Cut two 5 cm /2 in crosses in the pastry lid and fold back the points to leave square holes in the pie. To make pastry roses divide the trimmings in 8 and roll out into 8 layers. Flouring between the layers, put four layers one on top of each other. Cut the 2 piles into two 5 cm /2 in squares. Pinch the corners together well. With a sharp knife cut a deep cross through each square. Place one decoration over each hole in the pie and open out the petals (*see picture*). Insert a rolled card in each hole to keep it open during baking. Brush all over with beaten egg.
10 Bake for 25 minutes then reduce the heat to 180C /350F /gas 4, lay a sheet of greaseproof paper or foil lightly on top of the pie and cook for a further 2¼ hours.
11 Leave the pie to cool in the tin for 1 hour then turn out. Turn upright and leave to cool completely.
12 Put half the hot stock in a bowl and sprinkle over the gelatine. Leave to stand for 5 minutes then add the remaining stock and stir until the gelatine has completely dissolved. Season carefully and leave until almost cold.
13 Remove the rolled cards from the pie. Using a small funnel, pour the jellied stock in each hole to fill the spaces in the pie. Chill the pie for at least 4 hours before serving.

Veal with aubergines

🍴 1¾ hours

Serves 6
1.4 kg /3 lb boneless shoulder of veal
3 medium-sized aubergines
salt
freshly ground black pepper
25 g /1 oz butter
45 ml /3 tbls olive oil
1 garlic clove, finely chopped
275 ml /10 fl oz dry white wine
150 ml /5 fl oz chicken stock, home-made or from a cube
oil for deep frying
25 g /1 oz flour
30–60 ml /2–4 tbls finely chopped parsley
finely grated zest of 1 lemon
flat-leaved parsley, to garnish
For the tomato sauce
2 streaky bacon slices, rinds removed and chopped
1 large onion, finely chopped
400 g/14 oz canned tomatoes
1 bay leaf
bouquet garni
salt
freshly ground black pepper

1 Peel the aubergines and cut into 5 mm ¼ in thick rounds. Sprinkle with salt. Lea[ve] in a colander for 30 minutes to drain.
2 Cut the veal into even-sized chunks a[nd] season with salt and freshly ground bla[ck] pepper. Heat the butter and oil in a lar[ge] flameproof casserole and and sauté the ve[al] in 2 batches for 3 minutes each side.
3 Return the first batch of veal to the pa[n] and add the garlic, wine and chicken stoc[k]. Cover and simmer over the lowest possib[le] heat for 1 hour.
4 Meanwhile, make the tomato sauc[e]. Sauté the bacon in a frying-pan until the f[at] runs. Add the onion and sauté for 5–[?] minutes until golden. Add the tomatoes, ba[y] leaf and bouquet garni. Season, cover an[d] simmer for 15 minutes.
5 Press the sauce through a fine sieve, the[n] reheat it and keep hot.
6 Heat the oil in a deep-fat frier to 190C 375F. Rinse the aubergine slices in co[ld] water, then dry with absorbent paper. Du[st] with flour and fry in batches in hot oil unt[il] golden on both sides. Drain and keep hot.
7 Transfer the veal to a heated servir[g] dish. Keep hot. Boil the remaining ve[al] juices until reduced by half. Stir into t[he] tomato sauce, then spoon over the veal.
8 Arrange the aubergine slices around th[e] edge of the dish, sprinkle with parsley an[d] lemon zest and garnish with parsley.

Veal chops with chervil and parsley

45 minutes

Serves 4

veal loin chops
salt and freshly ground black pepper
10 ml /2 tsp chopped fresh chervil or 5 ml /1
* tsp dried chervil*
100 g /4 oz butter
small onion, finely chopped
garlic clove, crushed
150 ml /5 fl oz dry white wine or cider
150 ml /5 fl oz chicken stock, home-made or
* from a cube*
50 g /2 oz fresh parsley sprigs
a few extra fresh parsley sprigs, to garnish

Season the chops with salt, pepper and the fresh or dried chervil.

Melt half the butter in a large, heavy-based frying-pan over a moderate heat. Add the onion and garlic and cook for 3–4 minutes, until soft. Add the chops and fry for 3 minutes on each side.

Pour the wine and stock over the chops, check the seasoning, bring to the boil, reduce the heat and simmer for 25–30 minutes, or until the chops are tender.

4   Using a slotted spoon, transfer the chops to a heated serving dish. Pour over the sauce, cover and keep warm.

5   Just before serving, melt the remaining butter in a small saucepan until it sizzles, but do not allow it to turn brown. In it toss the 50 g /2 oz fresh parsley sprigs and fry briskly for about 30 seconds.

6   Garnish with fresh parsley and serve the fried parsley separately.

Farmer's veal hock

2¾ hours

Serves 4

1 kg /2 lb 3 oz meaty veal hock (or knuckle
* end of leg), cut into 4 thick slices*
100 g /4 oz streaky bacon with rind, cut in
* 15 mm /½ in squares*
30 ml /2 tbls oil
1 medium-sized carrot, coarsely chopped
1 medium-sized onion, coarsely chopped
25 g /1 oz butter, plus extra for greasing
150 ml /5 fl oz medium-dry still cider
salt and freshly ground black pepper
150 ml /5 fl oz condensed cream of chicken
* soup*
flat-leaved parsley, to garnish

1   Heat the oven to 150C /300F /gas 2. Drop the bacon pieces in boiling water and simmer for 2 minutes, then drain and dry on absorbent paper.

2   Pour the oil into a flameproof casserole which will just hold all the ingredients. Place over a moderate heat and, when it is hot, add the bacon, carrot and onion. Cook, stirring, for 2 minutes until softened slightly, without letting them colour.

3   Add the butter and, as soon as it melts, put in the veal. Cook for 5 minutes, turning to colour the slices on both sides. Pour in the cider and cook, uncovered, for 5 minutes. Season with salt and freshly ground black pepper, then pour the soup over the veal. Cover with a piece of buttered paper, then with a lid.

4   Cook in the oven for 2 hours, basting the meat with the cooking juices twice while cooking. Remove the casserole lid after 1 hour, leaving the buttered greaseproof paper on top for the second hour.

5   Remove the paper, raise the oven temperature to 220C /425F /gas 7, and cook the veal for a further 10–15 minutes, until the surface of the dish is lightly glazed. Skim any excess fat from the top, garnish with a sprig of flat-leaved parsley and serve at once, from the casserole.

Veal, ham and egg pie

STAR MENUS & RECIPE FILE

Green consommé

~

Veal escalopes
with orange and sherry

Pommes amandines

Tomatoes
with buttered breadcrumbs

~

Chocolate granita

Wine: Côte Chalonnaise

I am not a cook who smiles readily when a classic recipe is tampered with; I believe in respecting tradition. But I believe, too, in creativity. So if you find the idea of meats cooked with fruit a little unusual, let me remind you of some classic dishes: duck with oranges, *à l'orange*; fillets of sole with grapes, *Véronique*; and calf's liver with blackcurrants, *au cassis*.

On this theme I have created a dish of veal escalopes with orange that I like enormously – and it is a dish that has found favour with friends who have dined with me at my home. This is not a complicated recipe by any means. The paper-thin escalopes are dusted with flour, dipped in beaten egg and then coated with fine breadcrumbs before being lightly browned in butter and olive oil. The buttery pan juices are flavoured with a hint of onion, garlic, orange and lemon juice, and dry sherry. Pommes amandines make an exciting accompaniment, and Tomatoes with buttered breadcrumbs add a splash of colour.

Before the veal, try a delicious soup of shredded lettuce, spinach and sorrel (if available), blanched for one minute and then stirred into hot beef or chicken consommé. The consommé should preferably be home-made – remember to prepare it on the day preceding the party if you intend to make your own.

Follow the main course with the dark, cool note of Chocolate granita, sparked with a splash of coffee liqueur and dressed for the party with a thin half round of orange, unpeeled of course, and a ripe, red strawberry.

And to drink choose a light red or a white from the Côte Challonaise – open red wine to bring out the flavour, or chill the white before serving.

Plan-ahead timetable

Four hours before the meal
Chocolate granita: make the granita, put in the freezer and freeze until required.
Pommes amandines: cook the potatoes, purée and season, leave to cool. Make the choux paste and blend into the potato purée.
Green consommé: prepare the lettuce, spinach and sorrel leaves, blanch and drain.

Two hours before the meal
Veal escalopes with orange and sherry: pound and coat the escalopes and put in the refrigerator to set.
Tomatoes with buttered breadcrumbs: slice the tomatoes and place them in a buttered dish with seasoning and oil; make the breadcrumb mixture and sprinkle it over the tomatoes. Dot them with butter.
Pommes amandines: pipe out the potato-paste and roll the lengths in the chopped almonds. Set aside.

Green consommé

Serves 4
40 g /1½ oz lettuce leaves
40 g /1½ oz spinach leaves, weighed after stalks removed
40 g /1½ oz sorrel leaves, weighed after stalks removed (if available)
1.1 L /2 pt beef or chicken consommé, home-made or from a can

1   Wash the lettuce, spinach and sorrel leaves carefully. Pat them dry in a cloth, discarding any discoloured leaves, and then shred them finely with a sharp knife.
2   Put the shredded leaves in a pan. Pour over enough boiling water to cover them, bring back to the boil and simmer the leaves for 1 minutes.
3   Pour the consommé into a pan and reheat gently. Drain the leaves thoroughly and stir into the hot consommé. Serve immediately.

● If sorrel is not available, then you can flavour the consommé with a few drops of lemon juice.
● Allow extra time if making your own consommé.

 10 minutes

Forty minutes before the meal
Tomatoes with buttered breadcrumbs: put in the oven to bake.
Veal escalopes with orange and sherry: brown the veal escalopes and remove from the pan. Sauté the onions, add the sauce ingredients and simmer.
Pommes amandine: fry the potato rolls in batches and keep hot.

Ten minutes before the meal
Green consommé: reheat the consomme and add the leaves.
Veal escalopes with orange and sherry: cook the escalopes in the sauce, add the orange slices and cook. Remove the veal and the orange slices, keep hot. Reserve the sauce.
Tomatoes with buttered breadcrumbs: keep hot.

Between the first and the main course
Veal escalopes with orange and sherry: add the cream to the sauce and heat gently, pour over the escalopes and serve.
Chocolate granita: put in the refrigerator to soften.

Between the main course and dessert
Chocolate granita: spoon into glasses and decorate.

Veal escalopes with orange and sherry

Serves 4

4 veal escalopes, each 100 g /4 oz
25 g /1 oz seasoned flour
1 egg, lightly beaten
75 g /3 oz fresh white
   breadcrumbs
50 g /2 oz butter
30 ml /2 tbls olive oil
4 spring onions, trimmed
   and thinly sliced
1 garlic clove, finely chopped

juice of 2 oranges, about
   150 ml /5 fl oz
30 ml /2 tbls lemon juice
90 ml /6 tbls medium sherry
1 large, seedless navel orange
a pinch of freshly grated
   nutmeg
90 ml /6 tbls thick cream
salt and ground black pepper
flat-leaved parsley, to garnish

1   Lay the veal escalopes between 2 sheets of greaseproof paper and pound them with a rolling pin until very thin.
2   Dust each escalope with the seasoned flour. Dip them in the beaten egg, draining off any excess and then coat with breadcrumbs, patting them on firmly with a palette knife or the palm of your hand. Chill the escalopes in the refrigerator for at least 30 minutes.
3   In a large frying-pan, heat the butter and olive oil over a high heat. Cook the veal escalopes, in 2 batches, for 1 minute on each side, so they are lightly and evenly browned. Remove the veal from the pan and pour off all but 30 ml /2 tbls of the butter and olive oil.
4   Reduce the heat and add the thinly sliced spring onion and finely chopped garlic. Cook, stirring occasionally, for 2–3 minutes, or until the spring onions are soft and translucent but not brown.
5   Add the orange juice, lemon juice and sherry to the pan and bring the liquid to the boil, stirring occasionally. Reduce the heat to low and simmer the mixture gently for 10 minutes.
6   While the sauce is simmering, trim off the 2 ends of the orange. Cut the unpeeled orange into 8 thin rounds. Return the veal pieces to the pan, add the grated nutmeg and continue to simmer for a further 7 minutes. Add the orange rounds to the pan and continue to simmer for 3 more minutes, or until the veal is cooked and tender.
7   Transfer the veal escalopes to a large, heated serving dish, arrange the orange slices around the dish and keep warm. Add the thick cream to the frying-pan and simmer, stirring occasionally, for 2 minutes, or until the sauce is heated through. Correct the seasoning and spoon the sauce over the escalopes. Garnish with parsley and serve immediately.

🔪🔪 1½ hours   🍾 White Côte Chalonnaise

Pommes amandines

Serves 4–8

500 g /1 lb floury potatoes
salt
25 g /1 oz butter
1 egg yolk, lightly beaten
freshly ground black pepper
freshly grated nutmeg
50 g /2 oz flour
2 small eggs
oil for deep frying
75 g /3 oz blanched almonds, finely chopped

1   Peel the potatoes and cut into even-sized pieces. Cook in simmering, salted water until soft when pierced with a fork. Drain them thoroughly, return to the pan and toss over a low heat to evaporate any remaining moisture. Remove from the heat.
2   Press the potatoes through a sieve into a bowl. With a wooden spoon beat in half the butter and the egg yolk, season with salt, freshly ground black pepper and nutmeg to taste; leave to cool.
3   Meanwhile make the choux paste. Sift the flour onto a sheet of greaseproof paper. Place the remaining butter in a heavy-based saucepan with 25 ml /1 fl oz water, stand it over a low heat until the butter has melted, then bring the mixture quickly to the boil.
4   Remove the saucepan from the heat and immediately pour all the flour in at once. Beat with a wooden spoon, return to a low heat and continue beating for 2–3 minutes until the paste leaves the base and sides of the pan.
5   Remove the pan from the heat, let the paste cool for 1–2 minutes, then beat in the eggs. Continue beating until the paste is smooth and shiny.
6   Blend the cool potato pureé with the paste, correct the seasoning, then spoon into a piping bag fitted with a 20 mm /$\frac{3}{4}$ in plain nozzle. Pipe the mixture into 25 mm /1 in lengths onto a sheet of lightly oiled greaseproof paper standing on a baking sheet. Chill the mixture if you have time.
7   Heat the oil in a deep-fat frier to 180C/350F, or until a stale bread cube browns in 60 seconds. Meanwhile, roll the potato-paste rolls in the finely chopped almonds until coated on all sides.
8   Carefully drop in 8–10 little rolls at a time and deep fry for 4–5 minutes, or until they are puffed and golden. Repeat with the remaining rolls. Drain thoroughly on absorbent paper and serve piping hot.

🔪🔪 50 minutes

Tomatoes with buttered breadcrumbs

Serves 4
4 large tomatoes
salt and freshly ground black pepper
15 ml /1 tbls olive oil
30 ml /2 tbls fresh white breadcrumbs
15–30 ml /1–2 tbls finely chopped fresh parsley
1 garlic clove, finely chopped
butter for greasing and dotting

1 Heat the oven to 190C /375F /gas 5. Slice the tomatoes thickly, discarding the ends. Season with salt and freshly ground black pepper and dribble over the olive oil.
2 In a bowl, mix the breadcrumbs, the finely chopped parsley and the garlic. Sprinkle this breadcrumb mixture over the tomatoes. Lay the slices in a buttered, rectangular gratin dish, dot with butter and bake in the oven for 20–25 minutes, or until the topping is golden. Serve immediately.

30 minutes

Chocolate granita

Serves 4
60 ml /4 tbls cocoa powder
175 g /6 oz caster sugar
15–30 ml /1–2 tbls strong black coffee
4 ice cubes
For the decoration
20–40 ml /4–8 tsp Tia Maria or another coffee liqueur
150 ml /5 fl oz thick cream, whipped
thin slices unpeeled orange, halved
ripe strawberries or white grapes

1 In a saucepan, blend the cocoa with a little water; add the sugar, 300 ml /10 fl oz water and the strong black coffee. Bring slowly to the boil and boil for 5 minutes. Remove from the heat, add a further 300 ml /10 fl oz water and the ice cubes. Stir with a wooden spoon until the ice is melted. Pour the mixture into 2 shallow freezerproof containers, or a loaf tin, and freeze for 1½ hours until it is firm to a depth of 25 mm /1 in around the sides of the containers.
2 Turn the chocolate ice into a large bowl and whisk until smooth. Pour it back into the containers and return it to the freezer for 1 hour, or until the granita is firm.
3 To serve, stir the granita and spoon it into tall glasses. Top each serving with 5–10 ml /1–2 tsp coffee liqueur. Top with the whipped cream and garnish with a halved slice of unpeeled orange and a ripe strawberry or a few white grapes.
4 Transfer the granita to the refrigerator for 10–20 minutes before serving.

3 hours, including freezing

STAR MENU 2

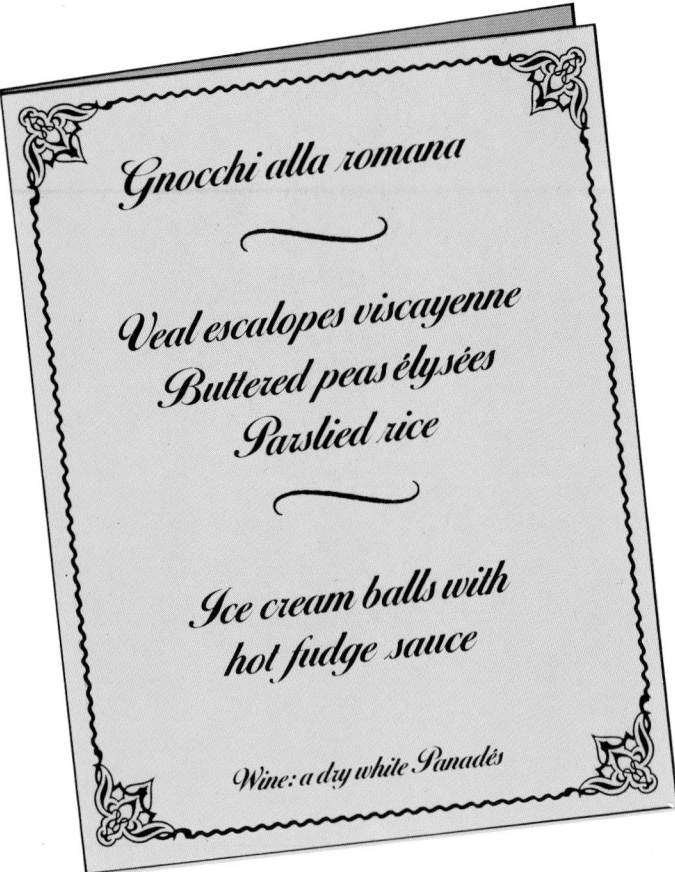

Gnocchi alla romana

Veal escalopes viscayenne
Buttered peas élysées
Parslied rice

Ice cream balls with
hot fudge sauce

Wine: a dry white Panadés

Plan-ahead timetable

One and a half hours before the meal
Ice cream balls with hot fudge sauce: transfer the ice cream to the refrigerator to soften slightly. Crumble the macaroons.
Veal escalopes viscayennes: season the veal escalopes. Prepare the vegetables for the sauce. Make and simmer the sauce.

One hour before the meal
Ice cream balls with hot fudge sauce: scoop the ice cream into balls. Coat with macaroon crumbs. Put in the freezer.
Parslied rice: prepare the vegetables. Heat the water, then boil the rice.

Forty-five minutes before the meal
Gnocchi alla romana: sieve the cottage cheese. Make the gnocchi mixture and spoon into a pastry bag.
Buttered peas élysées: cook the peas for 1 minute. Drain, refresh and drain. Prepare the lettuce.
Veal escalopes viscayennes: remove the sauce from the heat and reserve.

Thirty minutes before the meal
Gnocchi alla romana: boil the water; cut the gnocchi into the

This dinner party menu, to serve four, has an international flavour. It starts with a satisfying appetizer which is as Italian as spaghetti – little poached dumplings from Rome. Gnocchi alla romana are small cork-like shapes, rich in butter and cheese, gently poached, then coated with yet more Parmesan cheese and butter and grilled to a luscious golden brown.

Veal escalopes viscayenne, which follow, are very lightly sautéed – just flashed in and out of the pan and still rosy in the centre. The viscayenne sauce, which takes its name from the district of Vizceya in the Pyrenees, is a mixture of green peppers and tomatoes enriched with garlic, cream and white wine. To serve with it, I have chosen two simple vegetable dishes: Parslied rice and Buttered peas élysées. For the Parslied rice use either white, long-grain rice or a nutritious brown rice. The rice is combined with sautéed spring onion and celery and then mixed together with finely chopped parsley, for a colourful, summer accompaniment. Buttered peas élysées soak up all the flavour of the butter and chicken stock in which they are simmered, as well as the shredded lettuce which accompanies them. A mixture of cream and egg yolks are stirred into the peas and lettuce at the end of cooking to add extra richness.

Everybody loves ice cream, so for dessert I have chosen an unusual way of serving a creamy vanilla ice, Ice cream balls with hot fudge sauce. Balls of ice cream, shaped with an ice cream scoop, are rolled in macaroon crumbs for a good, crunchy coating. They are then chilled and served with a warm, fudgy sauce. This is a very grown-up version of a childhood favourite. The ice cream and macaroons can either be made well in advance or bought from most supermarkets. Do buy the best quality ice cream, as the texture and flavour are far superior to inexpensive makes. Whichever you prefer – home-made or store-bought – it makes this mouthwatering dessert a very convenient one for the busy hostess.

To go with the Spanish-inspired main veal course, what could be more appropriate than a dry white wine from Spain? I have chosen one from the Panadés area of Catalonia in north-east Spain.

ater. Poach and drain on absorbent paper.
arslied rice: cook the spring onions and celery. Drain the rice,
nse and drain again. Reserve both.

ifteen minutes before the meal

nocchi alla romana: heat the grill. Arrange the gnocchi in a
reased gratin dish. Add the butter and Parmesan cheese; grill
ntil golden brown. Keep warm.
uttered peas élysées: cook the peas with the lettuce. Blend the
g and cream together.
eal escalopes viscayenne: season and sauté the veal. Keep warm
n a serving platter. Complete the sauce.

ive minutes before the meal

uttered peas élysées: stir the egg and cream mixture into the
eas. Transfer to a heated serving dish and keep warm.

n between the first and main courses

Veal escalopes viscayenne: spoon the sauce over the veal.
arslied rice: add rice to spring onions and celery; heat through.

n between the main course and dessert

ce cream balls with hot fudge sauce: make the sauce. Arrange
he cake balls on plates. Pour some of the sauce over, serve the
emainder separately.

Gnocchi alla romana

Serves 4
225 g /8 oz cottage cheese
175 g /6 oz butter, melted
120 ml /8 tbls freshly grated Parmesan cheese
3 large egg yolks
60 ml /4 tbls flour
salt and freshly ground black pepper
freshly grated nutmeg
flat-leaved parsley, to garnish

1   Press the cottage cheese through a sieve with a wooden spoon
into a mixing bowl.
2   Beat 60 ml /4 tbls melted butter, 60 ml /4 tbls freshly grated
Parmesan cheese and the egg yolks together in a separate bowl with
a wooden spoon. Stir in the sieved cheese alternately with the flour.
Season with salt and freshly ground black pepper and freshly grated
nutmeg to taste. Meanwhile, fit a pastry bag with a 15 mm /$\frac{1}{2}$ in
nozzle. Stand this in a bowl and fold back the top like a cuff. Spoon
in the cheese mixture. Twist over the top of the pastry bag and hold
it securely with your thumb.
3   Bring a large saucepan of salted water to the boil, then reduce to
simmering.
4   Hold the bag over the saucepan. Squeeze the top of the bag to
force the mixture through the nozzle. With scissors cut it off in 25
mm /1 in lengths.
5   Poach the gnocchi in the gently simmering water for 6–7
minutes. When they are cooked through they will rise to the top of
the pan, so remove them in sequence with a slotted spoon. Drain on
absorbent paper.
6   Heat the grill to high. Grease a gratin dish large enough to take
the gnocchi in one layer with some of the melted butter. Arrange the
gnocchi in the dish and spoon the remaining melted butter over the
top. Sprinkle with the remaining grated Parmesan cheese.
7   Place under the grill for 10 minutes, or until the cheese is
bubbling and the gnocchi are golden brown. Garnish with flat-
leaved parsley and serve.

 40 minutes

Veal escalopes viscayenne

Serves 4
4 × 150 g /5 oz veal escalopes
freshly ground black pepper
100 g /4 oz butter
60 ml /4 tbls olive oil
1 Spanish onion, finely chopped
4 garlic cloves, finely chopped
4 small green peppers, seeded and sliced
8 tomatoes, blanched, skinned, seeded and quartered
salt
150 ml /5 fl oz thick cream
60–90 ml /4–6 tbls dry white wine

1 Season the escalopes generously on both sides with freshly ground black pepper and leave to come to room temperature.
2 In a large frying-pan, heat 25 g /1 oz butter and 30 ml /2 tbls olive oil. Sauté the finely chopped onion and garlic for 7–10 minutes, or until soft and transparent, stirring occasionally with a wooden spoon.
3 Add the sliced peppers and quartered tomatoes. Season to taste with salt and freshly ground black pepper and simmer gently for 30 minutes, or until the pepper is soft and the tomato is reduced to a pulp.
4 Stir the thick cream and 50 g /2 oz butter into the pan.
5 Meanwhile, heat the remaining butter and olive oil in a clean frying-pan until the foaming subsides. Season the veal with salt. Sauté the veal escalopes in two batches, 1 minute on each side, turning with a spatula. Transfer to a large, heated serving platter and keep warm. Repeat with the remaining veal escalopes.
6 Stir the dry white wine into the pan juices and boil to reduce to half the original quantity over a high heat. Add this to the sauce and bring to simmering point, stirring. Correct the seasoning, spoon a little sauce over each veal escalope and serve immediately.

● This dish, with its pepper, tomato and onion garnish, comes from Vizcaya, one of the provinces in north-west Spain, close to the Pyrenees.

Bringing to room temperature, then 45 minutes   a dry white Panadés

Buttered peas élysées

Serves 4
salt
500 g /1 lb frozen peas
50 g /2 oz butter
60 ml /4 tbls chicken stock, home-made or from a cube
freshly ground black pepper
2.5 ml /½ tsp sugar (optional)
4 lettuce leaves, cut into thin strips
1 large egg yolk
60 ml /4 tbls thick cream

1 Bring a saucepan of salted water to the boil, add the peas and simmer for 1 minute. Drain, place under cold, running water to refresh, and drain again.
2 Replace the peas in the saucepan and add the butter and chicken stock. Season with salt and freshly ground black pepper to taste and sugar, if used. Cover with the lettuce strips and simmer over a low heat for 10 minutes, or until the peas have absorbed the liquid.
3 In a small bowl, blend the egg yolk and thick cream together with a whisk. Stir into the peas and lettuce. Correct the seasoning, transfer to a heated serving dish and serve immediately.

● This dish can, of course, be made using fresh shelled peas. You will need to buy 1.4 kg /3 lb of peas in the pod. The cooking time must be increased by 15–20 minutes.

15 minutes

Parslied rice

Serves 4
salt
225 g /8 oz long-grain rice
50 g /2 oz butter
1 bunch spring onions, sliced
4 large celery stalks, sliced
25 g /1 oz finely chopped fresh parsley
freshly ground black pepper

1 Bring a large saucepan of salted water to the boil. Sprinkle the rice gradually into the pan through your fingers so that the water does not come off the boil.
2 Stir once to dislodge any grains stuck to the bottom of the pan and boil the rice for 15–18 minutes, or until just tender.
3 Meanwhile, melt 25 g /1 oz butter in a large, heavy saucepan and cook the sliced spring onions and celery for 7–10 minutes, or until just tender, stirring occasionally.
4 Drain the rice in a colander and rinse thoroughly under hot, running water. Shake out excess moisture.
5 Add the rice to the cooked spring onion and celery, together with the remaining butter and finely chopped parsley. Season to taste with salt and freshly ground pepper and heat through, stirring constantly. Transfer to a heated serving dish and serve.

● Instead of white long-grain rice, try nutritious brown rice in this dish. Brown rice has a nutty flavour and, as the germ of the grain is retained, it contains large amounts of vitamins, minerals and protein. It needs to be cooked longer than white rice, up to 40 minutes.

20 minutes

Ice cream balls with hot fudge sauce

Serves 4–6
850 ml /1½ pt good quality vanilla ice cream
2 macaroons
For the hot fudge sauce
175 ml /6 fl oz thick cream
50 g /2 oz unsalted butter
15 ml /1 tbls sugar
60 ml /4 tbls soft, dark brown sugar

1 About 1½ hours before serving, transfer the vanilla ice cream to the main cabinet of the refrigerator to soften slightly.
2 Crumble the macaroons finely onto a large plate.
3 About ½–1 hour before serving, use an ice cream scoop to shape 8–12 even-sized balls of vanilla ice cream. Roll the balls in the crumbled macaroons to coat, shaking off the excess. Place the balls on a baking tray and put in the freezer or freezing compartment of the refrigerator.
4 Meanwhile, make the hot fudge sauce. In a large, heavy-bottomed saucepan combine the thick cream and unsalted butter. Place the pan over a moderate heat and simmer, stirring constantly with a wooden spoon, until the butter has melted and the cream just comes to a low boil. Add the sugars to the pan and continue cooking over a low heat until the sugars have dissolved. Bring to the boil and boil for 2 minutes, or until thick and glossy.
5 To serve, arrange 2–3 ice cream balls on each of 4–6 individual serving plates and pour a little hot fudge sauce over the top of each ice cream ball. Serve the remaining sauce separately.

20 minutes, plus chilling

Calf's liver and bacon

Serves 4
about 500 g /1 lb calf's liver, cut into 4 thin slices, 5 mm /¼ in thick
salt and freshly ground black pepper
30–60 ml /2–4 tbls flour
50 g /2 oz butter
4 thin slices of streaky bacon
parsley sprigs, to garnish
For the green butter
50 g /2 oz butter, softened
1 garlic clove, crushed
15 ml /1 tbls finely chopped parsley
15 ml /1 tbls lemon juice
salt and freshly ground black pepper

1   Make the green butter, using a wooden spoon, cream the
softened butter with the crushed garlic and finely chopped parsley.
Season with the lemon juice and salt and freshly ground black
pepper to taste. Place in greaseproof paper and roll up into a firm
sausage shape, twisting up the ends. Chill in the refrigerator.
2   Remove the thin white skin covering the liver. Season the liver
slices on both sides with salt and freshly ground black pepper. Dust
the slices with flour, shaking off the excess.
3   Melt the butter in a large frying-pan. Fry the bacon slices gently
for a few minutes on both sides. Lift out with a slotted spoon, drain
on absorbent paper and keep hot.
4   Heat a serving dish. Fry the liver slices in the butter left in the
frying-pan for just 2–3 minutes on each side. Drain well and
arrange on the serving dish. Cover each slice of liver with a slice of
bacon.
5   To serve, cut the green butter into 4 slices and place a slice on
each piece of bacon. Garnish with parsley sprigs and serve
immediately.

● Calf's liver is a tender luxury and this dish is a far cry from the
usual grilled or fried liver and bacon. Take great care not to
overcook the liver; once it becomes tough, no amount of further
cooking will soften it again. Serve with plain boiled potatoes and a
salad.
● Green butter is a useful item to have ready-frozen in the freezer.
Use it for baked potatoes and grilled chops as well.

 15 minutes plus chilling for
the butter, then 20 minutes

Veal escalopes Parmigiana

Serves 4

4 × 150 g /5 oz veal escalopes
oil for deep frying
30 ml /2 tbls flour
salt and ground pepper
1 large egg, lightly beaten
60 ml /4 tbls thin cream
25 g /1 oz fresh white
  breadcrumbs
120 ml /8 tbls grated Parmesan
  cheese
100 g /4 oz Mozzarella sliced
30 ml /2 tbls finely chopped
  parsley
bouquet of watercress, to garnish

For the raw tomato sauce
250 g /8 oz fresh, ripe tomatoes
30 ml /2 tbls chopped fresh
  chervil
30 ml /2 tbls chopped fresh
  parsley
15 ml /1 tbls chopped fresh
  tarragon
15 ml /1 tbls Dijon mustard
1.5 ml /¼ tsp Worcestershire
  sauce
45 ml /3 tbls olive oil
5 ml /1 tsp lemon juice
salt and ground pepper

1   First make the tomato sauce. Skin the tomatoes: place them in a
bowl, pour over boiling water and leave to stand for 10 seconds.
Drain and peel. Cut the tomatoes in half and squeeze out the seeds
and juice: reserve for another recipe. Dice the flesh finely.
2   Place the diced tomatoes in a bowl with the remaining
ingredients and mix well. Place the bowl over a pan of hot water and
let the sauce heat through gently.
3   Heat the oven to 230C /450F /gas 8. Heat the oil in a deep-fat
frier to 190C /375F; or until a crouton turns golden in 50 seconds.
4   Place the veal escalopes between sheets of cling film and flatten
until thin with a meat bat or rolling pin.
5   Sprinkle the flour onto a plate and season to taste. In a shallow
bowl, combine the egg and cream and mix to blend with a fork. Mix
the breadcrumbs and half the Parmesan in another dish.
6   Toss each escalope in seasoned flour to coat, then in the egg and
cream mixture, draining off any excess. Coat in the breadcrumb and
cheese mixture. Lay the prepared escalopes flat on a tray.
7   Deep fry 2 escalopes at a time, for 30 seconds on each side.
Drain well on absorbent paper and place in a gratin dish. Spread
tomato sauce evenly over each one and sprinkle with the remaining
Parmesan. Top with Mozzarella and sprinkle with parsley.
8   Bake for 10 minutes. Garnish with the bouquet of watercress.

 making sauce,
then 45 minutes

Veal chops La Coupole

Serves 4
4 veal loin chops
salt and freshly ground black pepper
50 g /2 oz butter
10 ml /2 tsp finely chopped spring onion
100 g /4 oz button mushrooms, sliced
60 ml /4 tbls port
90–120 ml /6–8 tbls thick cream
60 ml /4 tbls finely chopped ham
spring onions, to garnish
flat leaved parsley, to garnish

1   Season the veal to taste with salt and freshly ground black
pepper. Melt the butter in a large frying-pan and when the foaming
subsides put in the chops. Fry them for 6–10 minutes on each side.
2   When the chops are cooked, sprinkle them with the finely
chopped spring onions. Remove from the pan and keep warm on a
serving dish.
3   Add the sliced mushrooms to the pan and cook for 3–4 minutes
or until tender. Stir the port, and cream to taste, into the
mushrooms. Spoon the mushrooms over the veal on the serving dish
and pour the remaining sauce on top.
4   Sprinkle with finely chopped ham, garnish with spring onions
and flat leaved parsley and serve immediately.

● This dish is particularly good served with sauté potatoes.
● The French are very fond of veal chops, *côtes de veau* – La
Coupole is a restaurant in the south of Paris on the Boulevarde
Montparnasse.

30 minutes

Calf's liver with red wine sauce

Serves 6
12 large thin slices calf's liver
30–60 ml /2–4 tbls seasoned flour
50 g /2 oz butter
2 Spanish onions, finely chopped
15 ml /1 tbls chopped fresh tarragon, or parsley
275 ml /10 fl oz dry red wine
15 ml /1 tbls French mustard
salt and freshly ground black pepper

1   Dust the liver slices with seasoned flour. In a frying-pan melt 25
g /1 oz of the butter and sauté the finely chopped onions until
golden; cover the pan and simmer until the onions are very soft and
melting, about 10–15 minutes, taking care not to let them brown.
Remove the onions from the pan with a slotted spoon and keep
warm.
2   Melt the remaining butter in the same frying-pan, adding a little
tarragon or parsley. When the butter is foaming add 4 of the liver
slices and sear quickly: this will not take more than 2–3 minutes on
each side. Transfer the liver slices to a heated serving dish and keep
warm while you cook the remaining liver slices.
3   To make the sauce pour the wine into the frying-pan and bring
to the boil over a high heat, scraping the bottom and sides of the pan
with a wooden spoon. Reduce the wine to a third of its original
quantity. Lower the heat and add the French mustard, stirring until
the sauce is smooth. Simmer for 1 minute, then return the onions to
the pan and mix well. Correct the seasoning.
4   Pour the onion mixture over the liver slices; sprinkle the entire
dish with the remaining fresh tarragon, or parsley, and serve
immediately.

40 minutes

Veal medallions Macaire

Serves 4

4 veal medallions, about
   25 mm /1 in thick
freshly ground black pepper
salt
60 ml /4 tbls flour
25 g /1 oz butter
15 ml /1 tbls olive oil
90 ml /6 tbls port
chicken stock, made with
   ⅓ stock cube and
   75 ml /3 fl oz water

30 ml /2 tbls sultanas, soaked
   2 hours in 45 ml /3 tbls port
4 sprigs of parsley, to garnish
For the Macaire potato cakes
550 g /1¼ lb medium-sized
   potatoes
salt and ground black pepper
25 g /1 oz softened butter
1 large egg yolk
25 g /1 oz butter
15 ml /1 tbls olive oil

1 Trim the medallions into a neat shape. Pat dry with absorbent paper. Season generously with freshly ground black pepper.
2 Meanwhile, prepare the potato cakes. Peel the potatoes and cut them into even-sized pieces. Bring a saucepan of salted water to the boil and cook the potatoes for 20 minutes, or until tender but not disintegrating. Drain. Using the back of a wooden spoon, press the potatoes through a sieve into a bowl. Beat in the softened butter, then add the egg yolk and beat it into mixture. Season to taste with salt and feshly ground black pepper. Divide into 4 and shape into 10 cm /4 in rounds.
3 In a large frying-pan, heat the butter and olive oil. With a spatula, lay the potato rounds side by side in the hot fat. Sauté for 2–3 minutes each side, turning with the spatula. Carefully transfer to a heated serving plate and keep warm.
4 Season the veal generously with salt. Sprinkle the flour onto a plate and toss each medallion to coat, shaking off the excess.
5 In a large frying-pan, heat the butter and olive oil and sauté the medallions for 5 minutes each side, or until cooked through, turning with a spatula. Drain on absorbent paper. Keep warm.
6 Drain the fats from the pan and discard. Pour in the port and stock. Bring to the boil, stirring and scraping with a wooden spoon. Season to taste with freshly ground black pepper. Boil rapidly until reduced by ⅓, stirring frequently, then strain the sauce into a small saucepan. Stir in the soaked sultanas and heat through.
7 To serve, arrange the potato cakes on the heated serving plate, top with the medallions, mask with sauce, garnish, and serve.

 soaking, bringing to room
temperature, then 1¼–1½ hours

Calf's liver with mushrooms

Serves 4

16 ×3 mm /⅛ in thick small slices calf's liver, about 500 g /1 lb
   weight
45 ml /3 tbls flour
salt and freshly ground black pepper
225 g /8 oz button mushrooms
25 g /1 oz butter, plus extra, if necessary
30 ml /2 tbls olive oil, plus extra, if necessary
lemon juice
For the garnish
5 thin twists of lemon
5 small sprigs of watercress

1 Season the flour with 2.5 ml /½ tsp salt and a good sprinkling of freshly ground black pepper, mixing them well on a plate.
2 Wash or wipe the button mushrooms clean. Trim the stalks and cut the mushrooms into thin slices.
3 In a heavy frying-pan, heat half the butter and oil with 15 ml /1 tbls lemon juice. Add the sliced mushrooms. Toss until well coated in the lemony fat and sauté over a moderate heat for 5–7 minutes, or until soft, stirring occasionally with a wooden spoon. Season to taste with salt and freshly ground black pepper. Keep hot.
4 Dry the liver on absorbent paper. Coat each slice with seasoned flour, shaking off any excess.
5 In a large frying-pan, heat the remaining butter and olive oil. Add half the liver slices to the sizzling fat in a single layer. Sauté on one side for 1 minute, or until droplets of blood appear on the uncooked surface.
6 With a spatula, turn the slices over and sauté for 1 minute on the other side. The liver should be nicely browned on the surface but still faintly pink inside. Transfer to a heated serving dish and keep warm while sautéeing the remaining liver in the same way, using more butter and oil, if necessary.
7 Garnish with the sautéed mushrooms and their juices. Arrange the lemon twists along one side of the liver slices and place a small sprig of watercress on each lemon twist. Serve immediately.

25 minutes

Veal escalopes Holstein

Serves 4

4 × 100 g /4 oz veal escalopes
50 g /2 oz seasoned flour
2 eggs, beaten
175 g /6 oz breadcrumbs
175 g /6 oz butter
30 ml /2 tbls olive oil
150 ml /5 fl oz chicken stock
30 ml /2 tbls softened butter
juice of ½ lemon

2.5–5 ml /½–1 tsp jellied
 meat juices (optional)
salt and freshly ground pepper
For the garnish
25 g /1 oz butter
4 eggs
8 anchovy fillets
16 capers
4 lemon twists
4 sprigs of watercress

1   Lay each piece of veal between 2 sheets of cling film or wet greaseproof paper and beat until very thin, about 5 mm /¼ in.
2   Put the flour in a shallow dish, the beaten eggs in another shallow dish, and the breadcrumbs in a third dish. Coat each escalope with flour, then dip in the beaten eggs, draining off the excess. Coat with breadcrumbs, patting them on firmly with a palette knife or the palm of your hand. Chill for at least 30 minutes.
3   In a frying-pan large enough to hold 2 escalopes comfortably in one layer, heat half the butter and olive oil until foaming. Add 2 escalopes and fry over a steady moderate heat for 1½ minutes on each side, turning them over once with a fish slice, until the casing is crisp and golden and the veal inside cooked but still very juicy.
4   Remove the escalopes from the pan and place them on a large heated serving dish. Keep hot. Add the remaining butter and oil to the pan and fry the remaining 2 escalopes in the same way.
5   In a large frying-pan, heat 25 g /1 oz butter until sizzling. Break an egg into a cup, season it with salt and freshly ground black pepper and slide it gently into the sizzling butter. Repeat with the remaining eggs and fry for 2–3 minutes until cooked to your liking. Lift the eggs out with a fish slice, draining them over the pan. Trim them to a neat shape and keep warm.
6   Meanwhile, to the juices in the veal pan, add the stock, softened butter, lemon juice, and jellied meat juices, if wished. Bring to the boil, scraping the pan thoroughly with a wooden spoon. Simmer for 1 minute. Season lightly with salt and freshly ground black pepper.
7   Pour the pan juices into a sauce-boat. Place a fried egg on top of each escalope. Lay 2 anchovy fillets across over each egg. Garnish with capers, lemon twists and watercress. Serve immediately.

 30 minutes,
plus chilling

Veal fingers with sage

Serves 4
6 escalopes of veal, each about 90 g /3½ oz
freshly ground black pepper
salt
25 g /1 oz butter
30 ml /2 tbls olive oil
2 garlic cloves
6 sage leaves
90 ml /6 tbls dry white wine
a sprig of sage, to garnish

1   Place escalopes between sheets of cling film or wet greaseproof paper. Beat firmly but not heavily with a rolling pin or meat bat until the meat is about 5 mm /¼ in thick all over. Remove the wrappings, and cut the veal into strips 25 mm /1 in across. Season generously with freshly ground black pepper and leave to come to room temperature. Sprinkle with salt when ready to cook.
2   In a large frying-pan, heat half the butter and olive oil, add 1 garlic clove and 3 sage leaves, and gently cook for a few minutes over a low heat to impregnate the fat with the flavours.
3   Add half the veal strips, and sauté over a high heat, tossing with a spatula, for 3–4 minutes, or until the veal strips turn pale in colour but are still slightly pink in the middle. With a slotted spoon, transfer the veal to a heated serving dish and keep warm.
4   Drain and reserve the juices. Heat the remaining butter and oil and flavour with garlic and sage as before. Sauté the remaining veal strips in the same way. Transfer the veal to the serving dish.
5   Return the reserved juices to the pan, mix with the juices from the second batch and remove the garlic cloves and sage leaves. Pour in the white wine and boil briskly over a high heat for 3 minutes, or until the sauce has reduced to a syrupy consistency, stirring well.
6   Pour the sauce over the cooked strips of veal.
7   Garnish with a sprig of sage and serve immediately.

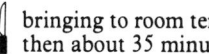 bringing to room temperature,
then about 35 minutes

Veal escalopes with mushroom sauce

Serves 4
4 veal escalopes, about 125 g /4 oz each
salt and freshly ground black pepper
30 ml /2 tbls flour
30 ml /2 tbls olive oil
50 g /2 oz butter
4 shallots, finely chopped
90 ml /6 tbls brandy
250 g /8 oz white button mushrooms, sliced
90 ml /6 tbls chicken stock or dry white wine
150 ml /5 fl oz thin cream
finely chopped parsley

1　Place the escalopes between 2 pieces of cling film or wet greaseproof paper. Beat them out thinly with a flat meat bat or a rolling pin. Season with salt and freshly ground black pepper and dust with flour.
2　Sauté the escalopes in the olive oil and 25 g /1 oz butter for 5 minutes on each side, or until just cooked. Be careful not to overcook them or they will dry out. Remove from the pan and keep hot on a large, shallow serving dish.
3　Add the remaining butter to the pan and sauté the shallots over a moderate heat about 5 minutes, or until they are soft and lightly coloured.
4　Stir in 75 ml /5 tbls brandy and simmer, stirring from time to time. When the mixture is reduced by half, add the mushrooms and chicken stock or dry white wine. Bring to the boil and simmer gently for a further 10 minutes.
5　Stir in the thin cream. Season with salt, freshly ground black pepper and the remaining 15 ml /1 tbls brandy. Simmer for 3–4 minutes.
6　Cover the escalopes with the mushroom sauce sprinkled with finely chopped parsley and serve immediately.

 bringing to room temperature,
then 35 minutes

Veal steaks with wine sauce

Serves 6
6 veal medallions, 25 mm /1 in thick
freshly ground black pepper
salt
15–30 ml /1–2 tbls flour
30 ml /2 tbls olive oil
25 g /1 oz butter
6 shallots, chopped
125 ml /4 fl oz dry white wine
125 ml /4 fl oz port
125 ml /4 fl oz chicken stock
25–50 g /1–2 oz cold butter, diced
parsley sprigs, to garnish

1　Wipe the meat dry with absorbent paper and season with freshly ground black pepper. If the meat has been in the refrigerator, allow it to come to room temperature. Season with salt just before cooking and dust lightly with flour.
2　Heat the olive oil and butter in a heavy-based frying-pan until foaming subsides. Add the veal and cook for 1–2 minutes on each side, turning the meat carefully with tongs.
3　Transfer to a heated serving dish and keep warm.
4　Add the shallots to the pan juices, sauté for about 5 minutes or until they soften. Add the dry white wine and port. Increase the heat and boil rapidly to reduce the liquids to half their original quantity. Add the chicken stock. Reduce the heat and when the sauce is hot but not boiling, remove the pan from the heat and whisk in the diced butter in small pieces, to thicken and emulsify the sauce. Pour over the steaks and serve immediately, garnished with fresh parsley.

bringing to room temperature,
then 20 minutes

Sautéed veal with Madeira

Serves 4
600 g /1¼ lb loin or fillet of veal, sliced 5 mm /¼ in thick
salt and freshly ground black pepper
30 ml /2 tbls olive oil
50 g /2 oz butter
60 ml /4 tbls Madeira
flat leaved parsley, to garnish
onion rings, to garnish

1 Cut the veal in to 5 cm /2 in pieces. Season generously with salt and freshly ground black pepper.
2 Heat the oil with 25 g /1 oz butter in a large frying-pan. Sauté the veal pieces in two batches, 1 minute each side, or until cooked but still just pink in the middle. Turn each square over with a fish slice. Transfer the cooked veal to a heated serving platter with a slotted spoon, and repeat with the remaining batch.
3 Add the remaining butter to the pan juices together with the Madeira. Heat gently, scraping the sediment from the bottom of the pan with a wooden spoon.
4 Pour the pan juices over the veal, garnish and serve immediately.

Calf's liver with apple

Serves 6
12 very thin slices calf's liver, about 550 g /1¼ lb
40 g /1½ oz butter
30 ml /2 tbls olive oil
1 onion, thinly sliced
60 ml /4 tbls seasoned flour
15 ml /1 tbls wine vinegar
150 ml /5 fl oz dry white wine
salt and freshly ground black pepper
2 crisp green eating apples, quartered, cored and sliced
15 ml /1 tbls finely chopped parsley, to garnish

1 Heat 15 g /½ oz butter and 15 ml /1 tbls olive oil in a large frying-pan. When the foaming subsides, add the thinly sliced onion and cook over a high heat for about 7 minutes or until lightly golden, turning with a spatula. Transfer the cooked onion slices onto a plate with a slotted spoon and keep warm.
2 Coat the liver slices with seasoned flour, shaking off the excess.
3 Heat the remaining butter and olive oil in the frying-pan. When the foaming subsides, sauté 6 slices of liver for about 30 seconds on each side over a high heat, turning them with a spatula. Remove the sautéed liver slices from the pan and arrange them on a heated serving dish. Keep hot. Repeat with the remaining 6 slices.
4 Return the onion slices to the pan. Pour in the vinegar and boil over a high heat for 1 minute to evaporate it slightly. Add the wine and boil for 2–3 minutes, or until reduced by a quarter, stirring occasionally with a wooden spoon and scraping the bottom and sides of the pan. Season to taste with salt and freshly ground black pepper. Remove from the pan with a slotted spoon and keep warm.
5 Stir the sliced apples into the pan juices and heat through. Remove from the pan with a slotted spoon.
6 Strain a little sauce over the sautéed liver slices and arrange the apples and onion around the outer edges of the dish. Sprinkle the finely chopped fresh parsley in a line over the dish and serve immediately.

20 minutes

20 minutes

Beef: basic information

Cattle were first domesticated about 10,000 BC from the wild ox. Selective breeding has developed cattle farming to what it is today. Now, there are about 227 breeds, of which 33 are the best beef-producing strains, lean and tender. The farmer aims at an optimum time to keep his beasts – usually 1½–2 years; 1 year is too short, resulting in steers (young males) with little flavour, and more than 2 years can become uneconomic.

Choosing beef

More than other meats, the quality of beef is dependent on how the butcher handles it, from hanging the carcasses in his cold store to cutting up and preparing the joints – so try to find a reliable butcher.

Beef should be hung for at least 8–10 days before it is sold. Without hanging, the meat will lack flavour and can never be very tender no matter how carefully it is cooked.

Buy the prime joints for quick cooking methods, such as roasting or grilling, and cook the economical cuts which require longer, slower cooking with added liquid by methods such as braising or casseroling. It is a waste of time and money to cook any cut of beef by an unsuitable method (see chart).

When choosing beef, remember that colour is not a reliable indicator of quality, as the flesh darkens upon exposure to air. The appearance can also be affected by the shop lighting. The meat should look fresh and moist but not watery. There should be very little gristle between the fat and the lean if the meat is from a young animal, and the fat should be firm, dry and cream or white in colour. The lean or prime cuts should look smooth and velvety while more economical cuts will have a coarser texture.

Storing beef

Remove the shop wrapping, put the beef on a plate, loosely cover with foil or cling film, and store in the refrigerator. Joints and steaks can be kept for up to 4 days, stewing meat for up to 2 days and mince for 1 day. Without a refrigerator, the storage times are halved. The more cut surfaces the meat has, the shorter time it should be kept, so if you are chopping or mincing at home, do it just before cooking. Cooked meat can be kept for 1–2 days in a cool place (maximum 13C / 55F), 2–3 days in the refrigerator and 3–6 months in the freezer. If there is bacon in the dish it can only be kept in the freezer for up to 6 weeks.

Preparing and cooking beef

To prepare a joint of beef for cooking, remove it from the refrigerator and wipe with a clean, damp cloth. Season with freshly ground black pepper – no salt at this stage as it tends to draw out the meat juices. Bring to room temperature for 2–3 hours before cooking.

Quantities: for meat with a large amount of bone, allow 275–350 g /10–12 oz per person. Meat with a small amount of bone should be calculated at 225–275 g /8–10 oz per person. Steaks for grilling or frying should be 175–225 g /6–8 oz per portion, while for stewing beef, boned and rolled roasts, or minced beef you will need 125–175 g /4–6 oz per person.

Buying beef for the freezer

Buy beef from a well-tried, reliable source and check that the beef has been well hung. With a large quantity get the butcher to freeze it for you, packaged into cuts suited your particular needs and labelled. Chec the weight includes bones and trimmed or whether it is the prepared joint, in wh case the price will be higher.

On the slab: sirloin on the bone and fore ri In trays, top row: cubed shin, silverside an topside. Middle row: entrecôte steaks, cub top rump, fillet and rolled brisket. Bottom row: blade both sliced and cubed, rump steak, sliced leg and cubed clod

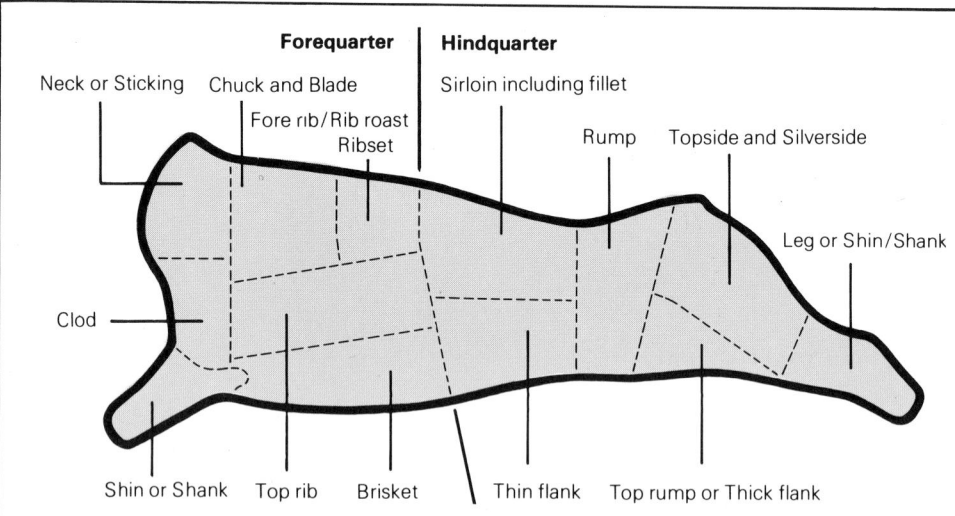

Forequarter — Neck or Sticking, Chuck and Blade, Fore rib/Rib roast Ribset, Clod, Shin or Shank, Top rib, Brisket

Hindquarter — Sirloin including fillet, Rump, Topside and Silverside, Leg or Shin/Shank, Thin flank, Top rump or Thick flank

Buying and cooking beef: the first five listed are the quality cuts

Cut and weight	Butchering
Sirloin sold with or without the fillet; tender, prime beef with a thin covering of fat; 6.5–9 kg /15–20 lb	Joint on the bone; 2.7–3.6 kg /6–8 lb Joint boned and rolled; 2–2.5 kg / 4¼–5½ lb Sliced into steaks; 20 mm /¾ in
Fillet undercut from the sirloin; very tender, lean, prime beef; often sold barded; 1–1.8 kg /2–4 lb	Whole Sliced into steaks; 25 mm /1 in Minced
Rump lean, prime cut with a narrow border of fat; less tender than sirloin or fillet but good flavour 5 kg /11 lb	Sliced into steaks; 15 mm /¼ in
Topside very lean cut; about 7.3 kg / 16 lb	Joint, often sold rolled and barded average joint; 1.4–1.8 kg /3–4 lb
Rib roast or Fore rib traditional roast beef joint; about 4 kg /9 lb	Joint on the bone; 1.8–2.3 kg /4–5 lb (sometimes sold with bone cut short) Joint boned and rolled; 1.4–1.8 kg /3–4 lb
Leg (hind leg) lean meat, high proportion of connective tissue; 2.7 kg /6 lb	Cubed or thickly sliced for cutting up
Shin (fore leg) lean meat, high proportion of connective tissue; 1.4 kg /3 lb	Cubed or thickly sliced for cutting up

Cooking methods	Cut and weight	Butchering	Cooking methods
oast	**Silverside**		
oast	streaky, coarse-grained meat; about 6.5 kg /15 lb	Joint, fresh	Pot roast or braise
		Joint, salted; 1.8 kg /4 lb	Boil with dumplings
rill or fry			
	Top rump (thick flank)		
oast	lean mt similar to topside but not as tender; 5.9 kg /13 lb	Boneless joint	Pot roast
rill or fry		Sliced	Braise
teak tartare		Cubed	Casserole, stew, use in pies or puddings
	Thin flank		
rill or fry	coarse-grained meat layered with fat; about 4.5 kg /10 lb	Joint on the bone, fresh	Pot roast
		Joint boned and rolled, fresh	Pot roast or braise
		Joint boned and rolled, salted	Boil and press to serve cold
	Brisket		
oast (best rare)	coarse-grained meat layered with fat; about 5.4 kg /12 lb	Joint boned and rolled, fresh	Braise
pot roast		Joint boned and rolled, salted	Boil and press to serve cold
	Top rib		
Roast	lean, medium-quality meat; about 6.5 kg /15 lb	Joint boned and rolled	Pot roast or braise
Roast		Thickly sliced	Braise
	Chuck and blade (braising steak)		
ow, slow cooking in asserole or stew	lean, medium-quality meat with good flavour; about 12 kg /27 lb	Cubed	Casserole, stew, use in pies or puddings
		Sliced	Braise
ong, slow cooking in asserole or stew	**Neck and clod**		
	good flavour; produces rich gravy during long, slow cooking	Cubed	Casserole or stew
		Minced (2nd quality)	Pâtés, stuffings, etc.

Thawing times for frozen beef

Cut	In a refrigerator	At room temperature
Large joints – 1.5 kg /3¼ lb or more	12–14 hours per kg /6–7 hours per lb	4–5 hours per kg /2–3 hours per lb
Small joints – under 1.5 kg /3¼ lb	6–8 hours per kg /3–4 hours per lb	2–4 hours per kg /1–2 hours per lb
Steaks or stewing steaks – 25 mm /1 in thick (not diced)	5–6 hours	2–4 hours

Roasting frozen beef joints: at 180C /350F /gas 4

Weight	Cooking	Minutes per kg	Minutes per lb	Thermometer
under 1.8 kg /4 lb	well done	75 + 35 extra	35 + 35 extra	79C /170F
	medium/rare	65 + 30 extra	30 + 30 extra	71C /160F
1.8–2.7 kg / 4–6 lb	well done	90 + 40 extra	40 + 40 extra	79C /170F
	medium/rare	75 + 35 extra	35 + 35 extra	71C /160F

Roasting prime quality beef

Cut of meat	220C /425F /gas 7		170C /325F /gas 3		How well done
	Minutes per kg	Minutes per lb	Minutes per kg	Minutes per lb	
fillet	18–22	8–10			very rare–rare
	30	14			medium rare–medium
rib roast and **sirloin on the bone** 2–3 rib joint (2.3 kg /5 lb)	15 minutes initially, then		35	16	rare
	15 minutes initially, then		45	20	medium
	15 minutes initially, then		65	30	well done
rib roast 4 rib joint (5 kg /11 lb)	15 minutes initially, then		33	15	rare
	15 minutes initially, then		45	20	medium
	15 minutes initially, then		55	25	well done
rolled sirloin	15 minutes initially, then		33	15	rare
	15 minutes initially, then		55	25	medium
	15 minutes initially, then		72–75	30–35	well done
topside	15 minutes initially, then		33	15	rare
	15 minutes initially, then		42	20	medium

The best time to buy a side or quarter of beef is in the autumn when prices are generally lowest, as grass-fed cattle are often slaughtered rather than kept on through the winter. If, however, you are buying on a smaller scale, look for bargain packs of stewing or casserole steaks in the summer when demand is low.

Bulk buying can be a considerable saving but there are three things to consider: the financial outlay will be large, a minimum of 100 L /3½ cu ft of freezer space will be needed (for a quarter carcass), and will the family happily eat all the various cuts supplied? For large families accustomed to eating a lot of meat bulk buying can be a sound investment, but for many homes smaller packs of favoured cuts of meat are more practical then large amounts.

Ordering frozen beef

Most beef for the freezer is sold boned and trimmed. If any cuts are required on the bone, this should be made clear when ordering the meat from the butcher.

Hindquarter: includes a quantity of prime roasting, grilling and frying cuts, with about 20% braising and stewing beef.

Forequarter: 15% roasting cuts, 55% pot roasting or braising meat with 30% for casseroles, stews and mincing.

Smaller bulk buys: the possibilities are rump, usually sold on the bone with fat and trimmings, approximately 9–13.5 kg /

Beef freezer facts

Space: allow 30 L /1 cu ft for every 15 kg /30 lb of meat (boned and trimmed).
Storage times: at – 18C /0F:
uncooked joints, steaks and cubed stewing meat – up to 12 months
uncooked mince and salted joints – up to 3 months
cooked joints, and pies – up to 3 months
casseroles without bacon – up to 6 month
casseroles with bacon – up to 6 weeks
curry – up to 4 months.
How supplied: jointed and on the bone a
hindquarters: leg, topside, silverside, sirloin including fillet, rump, thin flank
forequarters: fore rib, rib roast, chuck and blade, brisket, neck, clod and shin
customer's selection: rump steaks, rump and loin, silverside, casserole and stewing beef, mince.

20–30 lb in weight; rump and loin, which the rump plus sirloin and flank; and t piece which consists of the topsid silverside, thick flank and leg. Alternative make your own choice of sirloin, topsid rump steaks, casserole or stewing packs, et

Cooking frozen beef

Defrost frozen joints of beef in t refrigerator (see chart). Bring them up room temperature for 2 hours prior cooking. Cook in the normal way. Bon and rolled meat, and larger joints, shou always be fully thawed before cooking, should pot roast and boiling joints.

Cooking still-frozen beef: to roast a joi of beef, first decide how well-done you li your meat and calculate the cooking tin from the chart. Use a meat thermometer pressing it into the meat once sufficient thawed – so that cooking time can b extended, if necessary, until the corre internal temperature is reached.

To grill frozen steaks, brush the me with oil and place about 5 cm /2 in furthe away from the heat than usual. When th meat is almost cooked, move nearer to th heat and continue cooking until brown.

To fry frozen steaks, sausages or han burgers, put a little fat in the pan and sta cooking at a lower than usual temperatur When cooking is almost complete, raise th temperature to brown the meat. Turn onc to brown both sides of the meat.

Timing for both grilling and frying wi depend on the thickness of the meat and ho well you like it cooked, but expect it to tak 5–10 minutes longer.

To cook frozen mince, place the block in dry pan over a gentle heat. Keep turnin and scraping as the outer layer thaw pushing the thawed mince to the side of th pan. When the block has thawed, continu cooking at once, as for fresh mince.

To cook frozen stewing meat, put th cubes of meat into a casserole together wit vegetables and liquids and cook for 3 minutes longer than usual.

Thawing and refreezing: meat taken fron the freezer and thawed may then be cooke and refrozen, provided it is cooled quickl before freezing.

Veal: basic information

al is calf's meat, the best coming from ef 2½ to 3 months old. There are 3 types of al: unweaned 'bobby' calves, marketed thin 2 to 4 weeks from birth, have almost ite flesh and a very mild flavour, but the casses yield little meat. This veal, almost ariably, is cubed and sold as 'pie veal'. ass-fed meat from weaned calves is darker colour than any other, as well as being igher and more strongly flavoured. The rd type, until recently mainly exported by lland but now a standard European way raising veal, comes from relatively large ves which are kept indoors and fed on a et of milk replacer. The veal they yield is fine-grained and almost as pale and gently voured as bobby veal.

uying veal

al is becoming more popular than it was, d frozen, Dutch-style veal in particular is sier to get than a few years ago; escalopes, instance, are sometimes available in permarkets, although if you want a large nt or a particular European cut you will ve to order it in advance from one of the ger supermarkets or a specialist butcher.

Veal tends to be expensive, so make sure you buy the best quality: look for finely grained flesh which is white or only just very pale pink. Never buy wet or flabby veal, or meat which is brownish or mottled.

You will need 225–275 g /8–10 oz per serving of veal on the bone; 100–175 g / 4–6 oz of boneless veal.

Storing and freezing veal

Refrigerate veal, loosely covered, as soon as you get it home, and use it within 2 days.

Veal tends to lose flavour when frozen so it is not, as a rule, a good meat to freeze except for some special reason. If you do freeze it, double wrap it and freeze for up to 6 months. You can, however, successfully freeze uncooked veal in a mild marinade and cooked veal, without garlic.

1 boneless fillet end, 2 boned breast, 3 boned oyster, 4 hind shin, 5 best end of neck, 6 loin, 7 fillet with one medallion cut off, 8 hock, 9 boned and rolled loin, 10 escalope from topside, 11 chump chop, 12 chop, best end of neck, 13 boned scrag, 14 boned and rolled scrag

Cooking veal

Veal's delicate flesh and flavour demand close attention because the meat can become rubbery and tasteless if it is overcooked, yet it must be well cooked through. Since young veal, especially, has much less natural fat than other meats, it needs handling in ways which keep it moist or which provide extra fat to supplement its own scanty supply.

Marinating the meat is one way of giving some cuts extra moisture, while larding and barding are good ways to moisturize large cuts, and a moist or fatty stuffing is also helpful. Thin pieces of veal such as escalopes are usually coated with beaten egg and soft breadcrumbs or flour to hold in such natural

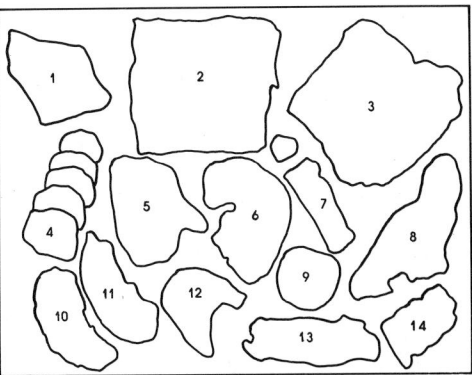

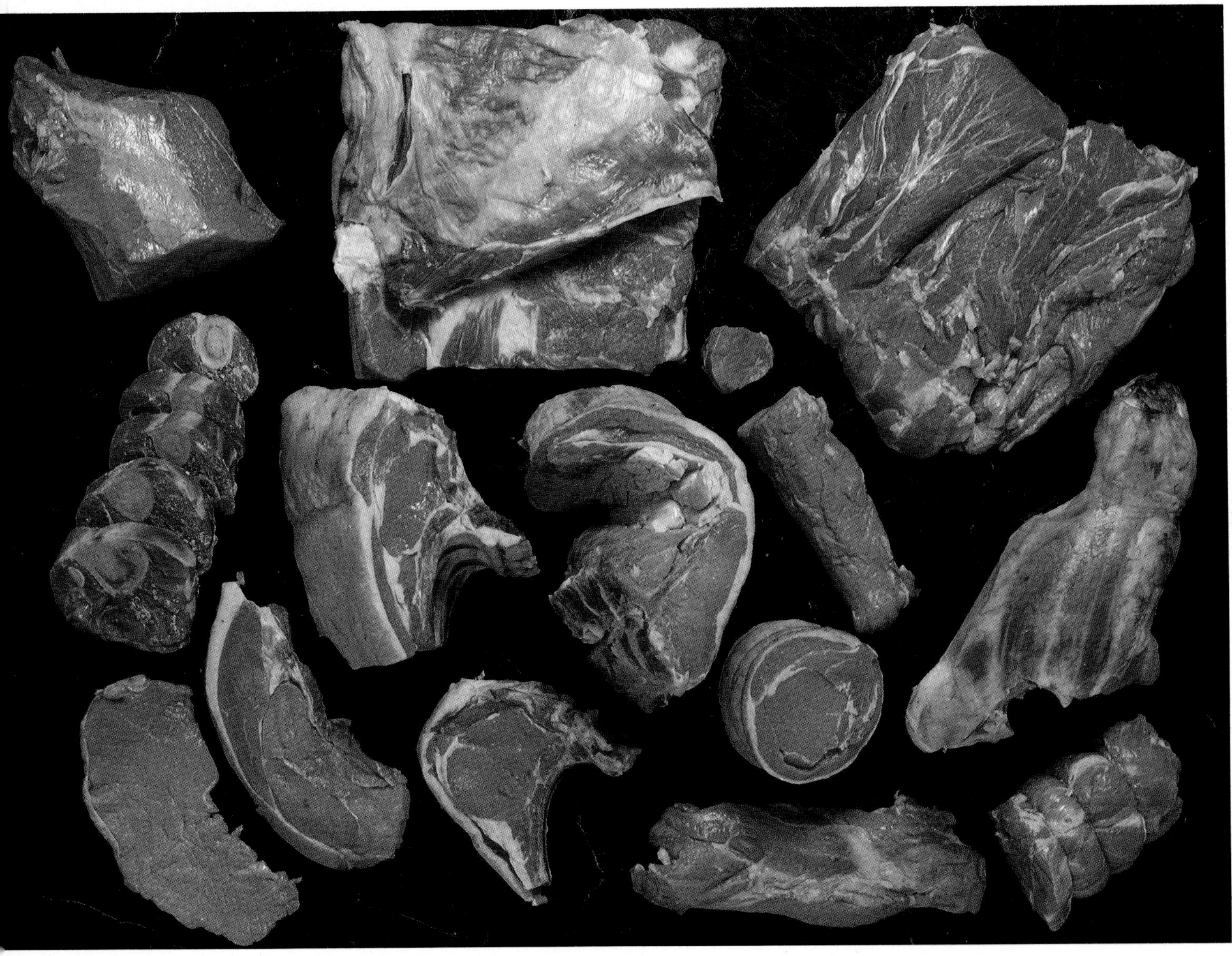

Buying and cooking guide to veal

Cut and weight (Dutch-style veal)	Butchering	Cooking methods
Leg Prime cut; lean with a thin layer of outside fat; 18 kg /40 lb	Hind knuckle and shin Hock or knuckle end Topside Fillet end (boneless) Escalopes and scallopine	Braise, make into pies and patties Braise Braise Roast – can be rolled or stuffed Fry
Fillet Tenderest and most expensive cut; 1.1 kg /2½ lb	Whole Steaks or medallions	Lard and roast or pot roast Fry or grill
Loin Succulent; lean with an outside layer of fat; 5.4 kg /12 lb	Whole – on bone or boned and rolled Chump (rear end of loin) Chops	Roast or pot roast Braise if whole; fry, grill or bake chops Fry or bake
Best end of neck Medium-quality cut; 4 kg /9 lb	Whole Cutlets	Roast, pot roast or braise Fry, grill or braise
Breast Lean but coarse textured; needs slow, moist cooking; 6 kg /13¼ lb	Whole, boned	Stuff and roast, braise, stew or make into a galantine
Shoulder Tender, lean meat slightly marbled with fat. Difficult to carve so usually boned and rolled; 10 kg /22 lb	Oyster (shoulder with fore-knuckle removed) Joints	Roast or pot roast Roast; or cube for brochettes, pies, stews
Neck Coarse textured, very bony meat with a good flavour; 10 kg /22 lb	Middle neck Scrag	Fry, grill, braise or stew cutlets; make boned meat into pies and patties Stew, make into pies, patties, soups

moisture as the piece of meat possesses.

A skewer can be used to test large oven-cooked joints for readiness; pierce them to see if the meat juices run clear. However, a meat thermometer is a better guide for oven-cooked joints: it should give an interior reading of 80–82C /176–179F.

Some people find the natural flavour of veal rather bland, and certainly it welcomes herbal flavourings and rich, flavoursome sauces. Rosemary, basil and marjoram go particularly well with veal, and so do paprika, sweet peppers and tomatoes. Wine, cheese and cream marry well with it also.

Basic veal stock
A light stock can be made from leg, neck or rib bones that have plenty of meat left on them (add a knucklebone for extra gelatine). These are placed in a pan, covered with cold water and brought to the boil very, very slowly (it may take as long as an hour). Once the liquid has boiled, the scum that forms on top is removed. This sequence of boiling and skimming is then repeated until only a white froth appears on the surface.

At this stage vegetables and salt are added for flavour and the liquid is once again brought to the boil and skimmed. Next it is simmered gently for 4 hours. During this time any grease that forms on the surface is spooned off. The stock is then strained through double muslin and left to refrigerate for 8–12 hours. The fat that forms is scraped off.

Calf's foot is a rich source of natural gelatine and makes the finest jellied stock. It has an excellent flavour and can be clarified and used for aspic.

Storing veal stock
Store the stock in an uncovered bowl in the

Scrag end Middle neck Best end of neck Loin Fillet Topside Hind knuckle Leg Shoulder Breast

refrigerator. It will need to be brought to the boil, left until cold and then returned to the refrigerator every day. It will keep for up to 4–5 days.

Stock in the freezer is best kept in small batches; spoon it into plastic bags as soon as it is completely cold then freeze.

Calf's head
Heads may not be very attractive to look at, but they can provide unusual and economical dishes with some added attractions: if you purchase a whole calf's head, you also get the tongue and brains, which cost more if bought separately.

A calf's head should be almost white in colour. Difficult to come by, they are usually sold skinned. A whole one weighs about 8 kg /17 lb, but you can sometimes buy a half. Ask for it split from back to front.

Buying and storing a head
If you are not buying a whole carcass you will probably have to order a head from your butcher about a week in advance.

Cook the calf's head the day you buy it. possible, store it, loosely wrapped, in t refrigerator until just before you are rea to cook it.

A whole head can be frozen, if you a sure it is very fresh and has not previous been frozen, for up two months.

Preparing a head
All heads should be washed thorough before cooking, and either parboiled salted water for 5 minutes (discard t water) or salted (pickled). Your butcher w usually salt the head for you. The meat usually boiled, and should always be ke covered with liquid to prevent discoloratio The tongue and brains can be cooked wi the head, or separately.

Using a head
Calf's head can be cooked in the same w as a pig's head, and served hot or col sliced, garnished with chopped onion capers and parsley and accompanied by vinaigrette.